**at a Glance**

JAMES A. BROWN
IBM Corporation

SANDRA PAKIN
Sandra Pakin & Associates, Inc.

RAYMOND P. POLIVKA
IBM Corporation

PRENTICE HALL, Englewood Cliffs, New Jersey 07632

Library of Congress Cataloging-in-Publication Data

Brown, James A.
    APL2 at a glance / James A. Brown, Sandra Pakin, Raymond P.
  Polivka.
        p.   cm.
    Bibliography: p.
    Includes index.
    ISBN 0-13-038670-7
    1. APL2 (Computer program language)   I. Pakin, Sandra.
  II. Polivka, Raymond P. (Raymond Peter).   III. Title.
  IV. Title: APL 2 at a glance. V. Title: APL two at a glance.
  QA76.73.A272B76 1988
  005.13'3--dc19   87-29795
                                                        CIP

Editorial/production supervision: *Jane Bonnell*
Cover design: *Photo Plus Art*
Cover art: *James A. Brown*
Manufacturing buyer: *Lorraine Fumoso*
Page layout: *Jon McGrew*

 © 1988 by Prentice-Hall, Inc.
A Division of Simon & Schuster
Englewood Cliffs, New Jersey 07632

Text set in 11-pt. Monotype® Century Schoolbook
and 11-pt. APL2 Light Italic
on an IBM 4250 Electroerosion Printer

Printed in the United States of America

10 9 8 7 6 5 4 3 2 1

ISBN 0-13-038670-7

Prentice-Hall International (UK) Limited, *London*
Prentice-Hall of Australia Pty. Limited, *Sydney*
Prentice-Hall Canada Inc., *Toronto*
Prentice-Hall Hispanoamericana, S.A., *Mexico*
Prentice-Hall of India Private Limited, *New Delhi*
Prentice-Hall of Japan, Inc., *Tokyo*
Simon & Schuster Asia Pte. Ltd., *Singapore*
Editora Prentice-Hall do Brasil, Ltda., *Rio de Janeiro*

To our families

for their patience and support

Contents

Preface . . . . **xiii**
Acknowledgments xvi

Foreword . . . . **xvii**

Chapter 1: Working with APL2 1

Section 1.1 – Doing Ordinary Arithmetic 2
   Simple Arithmetic 2
   Numbers 3
   Exercises for Section 1.1 5

Section 1.2 – Arithmetic on Arrays 6
   Thinking Arrays 7
   Adding up Numbers 8
   Exercises for Section 1.2 9

Section 1.3 – Remembering Data 10
   Assignment 10
   Names 11
   Exercises for Section 1.3 13

Section 1.4 – Evaluation of Expressions 14
   Order of Evaluation 14
   Use of Parentheses 16
   Use of Blanks 17
   Vector Notation 17
   DISPLAY Function 21
   Exercises for Section 1.4 22

Section 1.5 – Saving Your Work 25

Section 1.6 – Errors 26
   Types of Errors 26
   Clearing Errors 27
   Exercises for Section 1.6 29

Section 1.7 – Terminology 30
   Terms for Data 30
   Terms for Operations 31
      Functions 31
      Operators 32
   Commands 33

Chapter 2: Working with Vectors **34**

Section 2.1 – Functions that Produce Vectors 35
   Measuring the Size of a Vector: Shape 35
   Producing Consecutive Integers: Interval 36
   Joining Vectors: Catenate 37
      Catenate Versus Vector Notation 38
   Exercises for Section 2.1 39

Section 2.2 – Character Data 41
   Character Vectors 41
   Vectors with Both Numbers and Characters 43
   Functions that Work on Characters 44
   Exercises for Section 2.2 45

Section 2.3 – Empty Vectors 46
   Creating an Empty Vector 46
   Using Empty Vectors 47
   Exercises for Section 2.3 49

Section 2.4 – Functions that Manipulate Vectors 49
   Selecting Items from a Vector: Pick 50
   Selecting Items from a Vector: First 51
   Selecting Items from a Vector: Take 52
   Selecting Items from a Vector: Drop 54
   Selecting Items from a Vector: Indexing 55
   Replacing Items in a Vector: Selective Assignment 58
   Exercises for Section 2.4 59

Section 2.5 – Scalar Functions 61
  Scalar Conformability and Scalar Extension 62
  Scalar Functions and Nested Arrays 65
  Additional Scalar Functions 66
    Scalar Function: Power 66
    Scalar Functions: Maximum and Minimum 67
    Scalar Functions: Floor and Ceiling 68
    Scalar Functions: Magnitude and Direction 70
    Scalar Functions: Residue and Reciprocal 72
  Exercises for Section 2.5 74

Chapter 3: Working with Programs 78

Section 3.1 – Operators Apply to Functions 79
  Reduction on Vectors 79
    Naming Derived Functions 80
    Using Derived Functions 80
  Each 83
  Exercises for Section 3.1 85

Section 3.2 – Programs Remember Expressions 87
  Program Structure 88
    Defined Function Structure 89
    Defined Operator Structure 89
    Defined Sequence Structure 90
  Defining a Program 92
  Closer Look at the Header 93
    Header Syntax 93
    Local Names 94
    Comments 98
  Using Defined Functions, Operators and Sequences 98
  Errors during Program Execution 99
  Good APL2 Programming Practices 100
    Creating a Toolbox of Utility Programs 100
    Using Comments Liberally 101
    Using Local Names 101
  Exercises for Section 3.2 102

Chapter 4: Working in the APL2 Environment 106

Section 4.1 – Libraries 107
  Establishing a Workspace from Your Work 107
  Loading a Workspace from the Library:)*LOAD* 108
  Removing a Workspace from the Library:)*DROP* 108
  More about the Workspace *CONTINUE* 109
  Public Libraries 109

Section 4.2 – The Active Workspace 110
  Name of the Active Workspace 110
  Saving the Active Workspace:)*SAVE* 111
  Replacing the Contents of the Active Workspace 113
  Adding to the Contents of the Active Workspace:)*COPY* and
)*PCOPY* 113
  Moving APL2 Objects Between Computers:)*IN* and)*OUT* . . 114
  Removing Objects from the Active Workspace:)*ERASE* 115
  Listing the Contents of the Active Workspace:)*NMS*,)*FNS*,
)*OPS*,)*VARS* 115
  Seeing the State Indicator:)*SIS* 116
  Exercises for Section 4.2 117

Chapter 5: Working with Arrays **119**

Section 5.1 – Properties of Arrays 120
  Exercises for Section 5.1 122

Section 5.2 – Building and Displaying Arrays 123
  Reshape 123
  Default Display of Arrays 129
  Applying the *DISPLAY* Function to Arrays 132
  Exercises for Section 5.2 133

Section 5.3 – Measuring Arrays 134
  Shape 134
  Rank 135
  Count 135
  Depth 136
  Exercises for Section 5.3 138

Section 5.4 – Unshaping and Nested Shaping of Arrays 140
  Ravel 140
  Enlist 142
  Nested Reshaping of an Array: Enclose 143
  Nested Reshaping of an Array: Disclose 144
  Exercises for Section 5.4 146

Section 5.5 – Manipulating an Array along an Axis 147
  Take and Drop with Axis 149
  Catenate with Axis 152
  Ravel with Axis 155
  Reduction with Axis 157
  Enclose with Axis 158
  Disclose with Axis 160
  Scalar Functions with Axis 163
  Exercises for Section 5.5 164

Section 5.6 – Other Functions on Higher-Rank Arrays 170
  First 170
  Pick 171
  Scalar Functions 173
  Exercises for Section 5.6 174

Section 5.7 – Other Primitive Operators 176
  Scan 176
  N-wise Reduction 177
  Outer Product 180
  Inner Product 181
  Exercises for Section 5.7 184

Chapter 6: Working with Data **188**

Section 6.1 – Ways of Comparing 189
  Relational Functions 189
  Match 191
  Boolean Functions 193
  Exercises for Section 6.1 196

Section 6.2 – Selecting Subsets of Arrays 198
  Indexing 199
  Selecting Items with a Mask: Replication 205
  Selecting Items with a Mask: Expansion 209
  Without 212
  Selective Assignment 213
  Exercises for Section 6.2 217

Section 6.3 – Searching and Sorting 220
  Index Of 220
  Membership 222
  Find 224
  Grade Up and Grade Down 225
  Reverse 229
  Rotate 231
  Transpose 233
  Exercises for Section 6.3 236

Section 6.4 – Computation 241
  Power and Exponential 241
  Logarithm 245
  Decode 248
  Encode 251
  Factorial and Binomial 253
    Factorial 253
    Binomial 254
  Trigonometric Functions 256
    Pi-times 256

        Circular Functions 257
        Matrix Inverse 258
        Matrix Divide 261
        Exercises for Section 6.4 262

    Section 6.5 – Generating Random Numbers 266
        Deal 266
        Roll 266
        Exercises for Section 6.5 268

Chapter 7: Working with Program Control 270

    Section 7.1 – Control of Execution: Branching 271
        Branch in a Program 271
        Labels 273
        More about Conditional Branching 274
        More about Unconditional Branching 276
        Stopping Your Program 276
            Attention 277
            Interrupt 278
            Infinite Loops 279
        Good Programming Practices with Branching 281
            Placing the Test for More Data 282
            Style of Branch Expressions 283
        Exercises for Section 7.1 284

    Section 7.2 – Debugging Your Program 285
        Stopping Where You Choose 288
        Restarting Your Program 289
        Tracing Execution 291
        Exercises for Section 7.2 292

    Section 7.3 – Prompting for Input 292
        Evaluated Input 292
        Character Input 294
        Executing Character Input 297
        Exercises for Section 7.3 302

    Section 7.4 – Output with Quad and Quote-Quad 303
        Quad for Output 303
        Quote-Quad for Output 304
        Character Input Following Character Output 305
        Exercises for Section 7.4 305

    Section 7.5 – Controlling Output 306
        Format 306
        Format by Specification 307
        Format by Example 309
        Exercises for Section 7.5 312

Section 7.6 – Control of Execution: Iteration 313
    A Number Operator 314
    An Each Operator That Quits Early 316
    Exercises for Section 7.6 318

Section 7.7 – Control of Execution: Recursion 318
    Fibonacci Numbers 319
        Iteration or Recursion 320
        Closed Formula 321
    Tower of Hanoi 321
    Recursive Operators 323
    Inadvertent Recursion 326
    Exercises for Section 7.7 327

Chapter 8: Working with Applications **329**

Section 8.1 – A Magazine Collection 330
    Describing the Application 330
    Designing the Application 330
    Implementing the Application 335
        Building and Maintaining the Magazine Matrix 335
        Taking Subsets of the Magazine Matrix 339
        Rearranging the Magazine Matrix 340
        Computations on the Magazine Matrix 340
    Exercises for Section 8.1 341

Section 8.2 – Simulation of a Vector Computer 342
    Describing the Vector Architecture 343
    Designing the Vector Architecture 344
    Implementing the Vector Architecture 347
    Exercises for Section 8.2 359

Section 8.3 – A Puzzle-Solving Program 359
    Describing the Puzzle-Solving Program 360
    Designing the Puzzle-Solving Program 361
    Implementing the Puzzle-Solving Program 363
    A Puzzle-Solving Program Using Strategy 367
    Exercises for Section 8.3 370

Postscript: Expanding Your APL2 Knowledge **371**
    System Functions and System Variables 372
    Event Handling 372
    Complex Numbers 372
    Limiting Cases 372
    Shared Variables 373
    Auxiliary Processors 373
    External Names and Associated Processors 373

Appendix A: The *DISPLAY* Function 374

Appendix B: Editing with the Del Editor 376
Selecting an Editor 377
Displaying an Existing Definition 377
Entering Definition Mode Using the Current Editor 378
The APL2 Full-Screen Editor:)*EDITOR* 2 378
The APL2 Line Editor:)*EDITOR* 1 381

Appendix C: APL Blossom Time 383

Appendix D: The Great Empty-Array Joke Contest 386

Appendix E: APL2 Character Set 392

Appendix F: APL2 Release 3 Functions 394
Indexing 395
Partition 398

Glossary 400

Bibliography 404

Answers to Selected Problems 406

Index 431

Preface

Why learn APL2?

Computers do precisely what people program them to do. If you want to be in control, you need a way to tell the computer what *you* want it to do. Just as people invented languages so they could communicate with each other, people invented programming languages so they could communicate with computers and tell them what to do.

APL2 (A Programming Language-2) is a language designed to facilitate both kinds of communication. It is a precise and concise notation for the recording of ideas. It is perfectly suited for such diverse applications as commercial data processing, system design, mathematical and scientific computation, data base applications, Artificial Intelligence, and teaching. It does not suffer from the inaccuracies and vagueness of natural languages (like English). You can use it as a tool for working out the solution to a problem and then, unlike mathematics or other tools, you can use the computer directly to calculate the solution.

Of the many programming languages available, APL2 has these distinguishing features:

- **Few rules.** You will know most of the everyday rules for writing APL2 after you read Chapter 1. APL2's rules are simple, and you can learn to write correct expressions immediately.

- **Arrays.** APL2 deals with whole collections of data all at once. APL2 has arrays as the fundamental unit of computation.

- **Rich set of functions.** The APL2 language includes a wide variety of functions. These functions apply to whole arrays at one time.

- **Operations on functions.** APL2 has operators that modify functions, creating whole families of related functions in a uniform manner. You can pass functions as parameters to programs.

- **User operations.** When you write programs in APL2, you create your own functions and operators, which behave like the functions and operators defined as part of the language.

APL2 at a Glance introduces APL2 and demonstrates these distinguishing features. No prior APL experience is assumed; however, even a seasoned APL programmer will find the book valuable because of its emphasis on the APL2 data structures and the style of programming brought about by its new functions and operators.

Designed for private study or use in a classroom, *APL2 at a Glance* contains eight chapters that present the basic features of APL2:

- Chapter 1, *"Working with APL2,"* introduces APL2 and shows how APL2 handles data and performs operations. It defines important APL2 terms and explains how to respond to error messages.

- Chapter 2, *"Working with Vectors,"* explains the fundamental array structure of APL2 and describes several operations that manipulate vectors.

- Chapter 3, *"Working with Programs,"* describes the ways in which you can expand upon the set of operations APL2 provides. It discusses the use of operators and introduces APL2 programming.

● Chapter 4, *"Working in the APL2 Environment,"* presents system commands for saving, loading, copying, and listing variables and programs.

● Chapter 5, *"Working with Arrays,"* applies information from Chapter 2 to all arrays and provides operations for measuring, structuring, and manipulating arrays.

● Chapter 6, *"Working with Data,"* introduces operations for comparing, calculating, selecting, searching, and sorting of data.

● Chapter 7, *"Working with Program Control,"* describes branching, program debugging, prompting for input, controlling output, iteration, and recursion.

● Chapter 8, *"Working with Applications,"* demonstrates the development of APL2 applications by showing three applications: recordkeeping for a magazine collection, simulation of a vector computer, and Artificial Intelligence for solving puzzles.

Each chapter includes copious examples to demonstrate the ideas presented and exercises to give you practice in applying the information presented in the chapter.

If possible, you should try out examples on a computer as you read. To do this, you need to determine how to access APL2 on your system, how to use the terminal or keyboard to enter and display the APL2 character set, and how to use other features that may vary from one APL2 implementation to another.

Besides trying the examples, you can improve your understanding of APL2 by working the exercises. The exercises are of two types: practice in evaluating APL2 expressions and problems involving creation of APL2 expressions and programs. The answer key at the end of the book provides solutions to even-numbered problems.

APL2 at a Glance covers the basic APL2 features. The final section, *"Postscript: Expanding Your APL2 Knowledge,"* summarizes other APL2 features and capabilities.

The book concludes with several appendices, a glossary, bibliography, and an index.

Acknowledgments

Without the encouragement, thoughtful reviews, and critical comments of colleagues, family, and friends, *APL2 at a Glance* would have been a lesser book. We acknowledge with appreciation and respect the efforts of so many: Doug Aiton, Ev Allen, Luanne H. Amos, Anne Baldwin, Yonathan Bard, Phil Benkard, Norman Brenner, Karen Brown, Gary Burkland, Bill Buscher, Thomas W. Conrad, Dick Dunbar, Ed Eusebi, Sylvia Eusebi, Kenneth Fordyce, Bill Frank, Erik S. Friis, John Gerth, Julie Gerth, Jon Goodblatt, Sandra K. Gomez, Alan Graham, Brent Hawks, Björn Helgason, Bill Hillman, Evan Jennings, Howard Kier, M. J. Kingston, Joseph W. Lacenere, Jr., Stephen M. Mansour, Claudio Marescotti, Theodoro Marinucci, Blair R. Martin, Jonathan McCathy, Tom McCleskey, Jon McGrew, Yutaka Morita, Dan H. Norton, Jr., Richard Oates, Scott Pakin, William C. Rodgers, James P. Russell, Bob Sayles, David Selby, Cory Skutt, Darryl O. Smith, Richard C. Stitt, Norman Thomson, Beth Rush Tibbitts, Jean-Luc Verspieren, Russ Washburne, Nancy Wheeler, Ron Wilks, Sheryl Winton, Karen Youmans, and Marty Ziskind. Nevertheless, any errors or omissions in the text are our responsibility and not those of the people listed here.

We also thank International Business Machines Corporation (IBM) and Sandra Pakin & Associates, Inc. (SP&A) for their support and cooperation. Special thanks and much appreciation go to Jon McGrew for producing *The APL Gazette* and for his extraordinary help in the production of this book.

Foreword

Twenty years ago, in 1966, Kenneth E. Iverson and Adin Falkoff quietly introduced APL\360, the first interactive implementation of the programming language APL. Based on an earlier interpreter developed by Phil Abrams and Larry Breed while they were students at Stanford University, APL\360 was a time-shared implementation of the notation Iverson used in his book *A Programming Language* (Wiley, 1962). In fact, the name APL is derived from the initial letters of that book's three word title.

After many implementations of and variations on APL from IBM and other companies, IBM released the program product APL2. APL2 generalizes and expands APL in three important areas: types of data permitted in an array; provision for a data item in an array to itself be an array; and treatment of operators.

APL2 allows an array to contain both numeric and character data, thus removing an early implementation restriction of APL. By permitting an item of an array to hold any other array, APL2 introduces nested arrays, enriching the data structures of the language. Finally, APL2 allows any function, either primitive or defined, to be the operand of an operator and, moreover, permits defined operators.

The end result of this generalization and expansion is a highly usable programming language. APL2 permits rapid development of applications and models of application design. It opens up a wealth of new programming paradigms that did not exist in APL.

This book introduces APL2 as a language in its own right. It does not assume that you know APL, and so does not compare and contrast the programming techniques of the two languages. With this book, you learn APL2 by concentrating on the data structures and programming techniques needed to solve problems using APL2. If you are familiar with APL, you may want to look at this book to get a feel for how APL2 differs from the APL you have come to know. You will be surprised to find that problems difficult to solve in APL are often simple in APL2.

The authors of this book are well acquainted with using, teaching, writing about, and implementing APL and APL2. From the latter days of APL\360 to the present, Jim Brown has been associated with the implementation and development of APL and APL2. He worked summers for the APL Design Group while he pursued his doctorate in Computer and Information Science (then Systems and Information Science) at Syracuse University. His dissertation, *A Generalization of APL*, supported by Trenchard More's seminal work in array theory, forms the basis for APL2.

Sandra Pakin authored the *APL\360 Reference Manual*, and she co-authored with Ray Polivka the book *APL: The Language and Its Usage* and, with the staff of Computer Innovations, the book *APL: A Short Course*. Sandra Pakin was a major contributor to IBM's *APL2 Language Reference Manual*.

For many years, Ray Polivka has worked in IBM's Mid-Hudson Education Center in Poughkeepsie, New York, where he has been a prime mover in shaping and teaching the IBM internal education courses in APL and APL2.

The authors have combined their APL2 experience and knowledge into a book that deserves more than a glance.

Garth Foster
Syracuse, New York
November 27, 1986[1]

---

[1] Dr. Foster dated these introductory comments on the day that is now generally heralded as marking the twentieth birthday of APL.

Chapter 1

Working with APL2

"Working with APL2" introduces some of APL2's most important concepts. You start with simple computations. You learn how to represent data and how to perform computations on collections of data called *arrays*. Your APL2 work requires an APL or APL2 keyboard like the one shown. This keyboard provides the alphabetic characters and the special APL2 symbols.

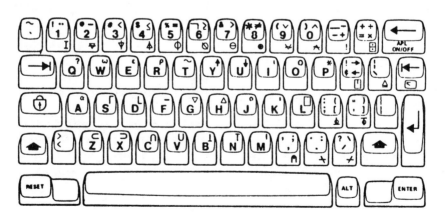

Keyboard for APL2

The arithmetic symbols you use in Section 1.1 are all on the keyboard's top row.

Section 1.1 – Doing Ordinary Arithmetic

In this section, you learn how to enter numbers and how APL2 displays numbers. You also learn some simple operations on numbers. With the information in this section, you will be able to use APL2 like a calculator.

If you are at a terminal, try out the examples as they arise.

Simple Arithmetic

One of the fundamental operations of APL2 is the *function*. A function applies to some data and produces some new data.

Here are examples of five basic arithmetic functions supplied with APL2:

        10+5   ←— **addition**
    15

        10−5   ←— **subtraction**
    5

        10×5   ←— **multiplication**
    50

        10÷5   ←— **division**
    2

        −2   ←— **negation**
    ‾2

APL2 prompts you for input by indenting six spaces. When you type something and press the enter key (or return key or send key or whatever key signals end of input on your terminal), APL2 executes the *expression* you entered and, starting at the left margin, displays the result of the computation. The values written next to the function symbols are the *arguments* of the function.

Addition and **subtraction** give the results you expect. Unlike many other computer languages, APL2 uses the traditional mathematical symbols × and ÷ for **multiplication** and **division**. (Some programming languages use * and / for these functions. In APL2, * and / have other meanings.)

Notice that the **subtraction** and **negation** functions share the same symbol. Most APL2 functions may be used with either one or two arguments.

Numbers

APL2 has some simple rules for entering and displaying numbers.

You represent *integers* by a string of decimal digits like this:

```
1
25
```

Numbers with fractional parts are represented with a decimal point separating the integer and fractional portions like this:

```
.1
2.3500
95.6372287356
```

How APL2 displays these numbers is not necessarily the way you enter them. If the number has no integer part, APL2 displays a leading zero. APL2 does not display trailing zeros on fractions.

Here are the above numbers displayed from APL2:

```
      .1
0.1
      2.3500
2.35
      95.6372287356
95.63722874
```

Notice that, for display, APL2 rounds the last result in the tenth digit.

Some numbers, when written in decimal notation, require an infinite number of digits (for example, the fraction one-third). If there are more than 10 significant digits in a number, APL2 displays only 10 digits.

You may enter very large or very small numbers in exponential or *E*-notation. The *E* stands for "times 10 to the." You might write the integer 123 followed by 45 zeros in *E*-notation as:

    123*E*45

APL2 displays such numbers with a single integer digit and an appropriate fractional part:

    123*E*45
  1.23*E*47

Negative numbers are represented by prefixing the number with an overbar (¯):

    ¯1
    ¯25
    ¯95.6372287356

Unlike arithmetic notation, APL2 does not use the same symbol for the property of negativeness and for the operations **negation** and **subtraction**. When you see an overbar (¯) on a number, it means that the number is negative. If you see a midbar (−) before a number, it means that something is being done to the number (**subtraction** if there is a number on the left, and **negation** if there is not).

    ¯25   ←——a negative 25
    −25   ←——negation of positive 25
    100−25   ←——difference of 100 and 25
    −¯25   ←——negation of a negative 25

APL2 does not recognize some conventions for writing numbers. For example, the following are incorrect ways to enter the number 123456789.123:

>   123,456,789.123
>   You cannot use commas to separate groups of digits.

>   123.456.789,123
>   You cannot use the European convention for separating groups of digits and showing fractional parts.

>   123 456 789.123
>   You cannot use blanks to separate groups of digits.

You can, however, make numbers display in these formats by using the APL2 format functions, discussed in Chapter 7.

Exercises for Section 1.1

1. Evaluate the following expressions:

    a. 100+20
    b. 1.3+2.7
    c. 100−90
    d. 45−145
    e. 100×1.3
    f. .01×314
    g. 100÷20
    h. 1÷3
    i. −30
    j. −⁻30

2. Write an equivalent number without using E notation for the following E-notation numbers:

    a. $1E2$
    b. $1E1$
    c. $1E0$
    d. $1E^{-}1$
    e. $1.4E3$
    f. $^{-}3.14159E5$

3. In 1987, a woman slept an average of seven hours per day. Write an expression to determine how many hours she slept last year.

Section 1.2 — Arithmetic on Arrays

The best way to learn how APL2 solves problems is to see its problem-solving capability in action. This book presents many features of APL2 as problems for you to solve. For example, here's a problem that involves doing the same calculation over and over again on a set of numbers.

> A music store sells recorded music in various formats: long-playing records at $6.95, cassette tapes at $7.95, and compact discs at $12.95. This week they have a special sale—10% discount on all items.

> How much do you have to pay for each kind of recording?

A 10% discount means you pay 90% of the price. You could compute the selling prices in three separate computations as follows:

```
        .9×6.95
  6.255
        .9×7.95
  7.155
        .9×12.95
  11.655
```

This piecemeal process works. But perhaps the most important feature of APL2 is that it can express computations on more than one piece of data at a time. You can do the preceding computations in one expression that produces all three answers at once:

```
        .9×6.95 7.95 12.95
  6.255 7.155 11.655
```

Notice that the single number .9 is multiplied by each of the numbers in the right argument.

Thinking Arrays

Applying a function like **multiplication** to whole arrays of data at one time is fundamental to the style of APL2. To be productive with APL2, you must learn to think in terms of arrays.

As another example of applying a function to a whole array of data, let's suppose that last week the store sold higher priced items at a higher discount: long-playing records at 90% (still), cassette tapes at 80% of retail, and compact discs at 70% of retail. How much would you have had to pay for one of each kind of recording if you bought them last week?

If you're not thinking arrays, you would do the calculations one at a time. Instead, think arrays and use the power of APL2 to compute the costs all at once:

```
      .9 .8 .7 × 6.95 7.95 12.95
6.255 6.36 9.065
```

You enter a list of three numbers on each side of the multiplication, and again this gives three answers. You can view this computation as taking place like this:

```
      (.9×6.95) (.8×7.95) (.7×12.95)
6.255 6.36 9.065
```

In fact, you can even enter the computation this way if you wish.

Continuing the music store example, suppose that, in addition to records at 10% off, the store also offers record cleaners (normally $2.50) at the same discount; and, in addition to pre-recorded cassette tapes at 20% off, it offers blank tapes (normally $3.55) and players (normally $295) at the same discount. Nothing other than the compact discs is offered at 30% off. You compute all the discounted prices at once as follows:

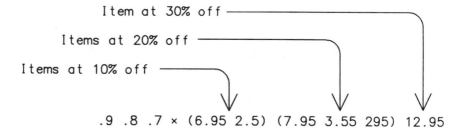

```
.9 .8 .7 × (6.95 2.5) (7.95 3.55 295) 12.95
```

Do you see how APL2 calculates this? There are three discounts on one side of the multiplication and three groups of prices on the other side and you get three groups of numbers as the answer. You can view this computation as taking place like this:

```
      (.9×6.95 2.5) (.8×7.95 3.55 295) (.7×12.95)
   6.255 2.25   6.36 2.84 236   9.065
```

Notice that APL2 does not use parentheses when displaying the answer. It does use spaces to suggest the grouping of the data. Two blanks separate the three groups of answers, whereas one blank separates the numbers within a particular group.

Adding up Numbers

Suppose that this week you decided to buy one record, three cassette tapes, and two compact discs.

You know the price you have to pay for one of each item—it's 90% of the list price:

```
      .9×6.95 7.95 12.95
   6.255 7.155 11.655
```

But you don't want just one of each item. How would you compute what you have to pay for the items you buy? Just multiply each price by the number you want to buy:

```
           1 3 2 × .9 × 6.95 7.95 12.95
   6.255 21.465 23.31
```

If you want to know only the bottom line— "How much money do I have to pay?"— you have to add up the three computed costs:

```
      6.255+21.465+23.31
   51.03
```

Instead of entering the numbers that the machine just gave you, you can use **reduction** (/) together with **addition** (+) to request the sum as follows:

```
      +/1 3 2 × .9 × 6.95 7.95 12.95
   51.03
```

The **summation** (+/) applies after the two multiplications.

Reduction (/) is an APL2 *operator*. **Reduction** takes a function like **addition** and applies it between the items of the right argument. For example, these two expressions produce the same result:

```
    +/10 15 20        ⟵ summation
45
```

```
    10+15+20          ⟵ addition
45
```

Exercises for Section 1.2

1. Evaluate the following expressions:

    a. `1 2 3 + 4 5 6`
    b. `10 × 1 2 3`
    c. `8 16 24 ÷ 8`
    d. `- 2 3 ¯4 5`
    e. `1+(2 3) (10 20 30)`
    f. `10 20 × (2 3) (10 20 30)`

2. Evaluate the following expressions:

    a. `+/ 1 2 3 + 4 5 6`
    b. `+/ 2 3 × (10 20)(30 40)`
    c. `×/1 2 3 + 4 5 6`

3. In 1987, one woman slept an average of 7 hours a day, another averaged 7.5 hours a day, and a third 8 hours a day. Write one expression to compute the total number of hours each woman slept in 1987.

4. Suppose one object is traveling at velocity X and another is traveling at velocity Y.

    a. Write an expression that computes the relative velocity of the objects (that is, how fast one is moving away from the other) if they are traveling in opposite directions.

    b. Suppose X is larger than Y. Write an expression that computes the relative velocity of the objects if they are traveling in the same direction.

5. Suppose you have a 10-volume set of the publication "*APL2 World*" on a shelf. Each volume is 4 centimeters thick, including .25 centimeters for each of the front and back covers.

a. Write an expression to compute how much linear space the
    10 volumes occupy on the shelf.

b. Between the front cover and page 1 of volume 1, there is a
    bookworm. It eats its way through the books until it reaches
    the last page of the last volume. How long is the hole it
    leaves in your collection? (Note: trick question.)

Section 1.3 – Remembering Data

The music store keeps changing its discounts from week to week.
You can save some time by remembering the original prices (which
apparently nobody pays). Then you need enter only the discounts
to determine the costs of the various items. This section explains
how APL2 uses names to remember data.

Assignment

Any collection of data can be remembered by giving it a name. For
example, the prices may be named *PRICE*:

```
PRICE←(6.95 2.5) (7.95 3.55 295) 12.95
```

A name that has been assigned values is a *variable*.

The association of a name with a set of values is an *assignment* of
the name, and the left arrow is an *assignment arrow*. Notice that
when you enter the expression, APL2 displays no numbers. When
you enter the name of the variable, APL2 displays the numbers
assigned to the name:

```
PRICE
6.95 2.5  7.95 3.55 295  12.95
```

Once you have assigned the name *PRICE*, you can compute last
week's consumer prices as follows:

```
.9 .8 .7 × PRICE
6.255 2.25  6.36 2.84 236  9.065
```

and this week's prices can also be computed:

```
.9×PRICE
6.255 2.25  7.155 3.195 265.5  11.655
```

These computations do not affect the value of the variable *PRICE*. Only an assignment can give a value to a variable or change it.

Any place where you use a set of values, you can instead use a name assigned those values. Using the name instead of the values reduces the chance that a typing error will introduce incorrect data.

You can associate different sets of data with different names and use them independently or in combinations. Here is an example:

```
DISCOUNT←.9 .8 .7
DISCOUNT × PRICE
6.255 2.25  6.36 2.84 236  9.065
```

A name like *DISCOUNT* or *PRICE* is called a variable not because its value is continually changing but because, at different times, it can have different constant values. At any time, you can give a new value to a variable:

```
DISCOUNT←.7 .5 .7
DISCOUNT × PRICE
4.865 1.75  3.975 1.775 147.5  9.065
```

Names

As you saw in the previous section, you can assign values to a name and use the name in a computation. This section contains the rules for forming names.

In ordinary usage, people's names are constructed as a list of characters chosen from the alphabet of their language. For example, "Caesar" is a name constructed from an alphabet consisting of uppercase and lowercase roman characters.

APL2 has rules that specify how to form valid names. In particular, no name may contain an imbedded blank. Blanks separate names. Thus, in APL2, the Roman leader's more complete name is viewed as two names separated by a blank:

```
Julius Caesar
```

Construction of names in APL2 follows these rules:

1. The first or only character is from this set:

    ABCDEFGHIJKLMNOPQRSTUVWXYZ
    abcdefghijklmnopqrstuvwxyz
    ∆∆̲

2. The remaining characters, if any, are from the above set together
    with these:

    0123456789¯_

3. APL2 distinguishes between uppercase and lowercase letters.
    The following are different names. Case is not ignored:

    Caesar
    CAESAR
    caesar

With some versions of APL2, underscored uppercase letters substitute
for the lowercase alphabet. In this book, except for this section,
neither the lowercase nor the underscored alphabetics are used for
names.

Here are some examples of valid names:

    A
    ABC
    Julius
    L1011
    This¯is¯a¯long¯name

Here are examples containing more than one name:

    A+B   ←——Two names separated by a function symbol
    GENGHIS KHAN   ←——Two names separated by a blank

Here is an example of an illegal name:

    3ABC   ←——Inappropriate first character

Names may be associated with different objects at different times or associated with no object at all.

To see the names that have values, enter the following command:

```
)NMS
PRICE.2 DISCOUNT.2
```

The .2 following each name indicates that the name represents a variable. Later, you'll see that the names of programs have the suffix .3 or .4.

Exercises for Section 1.3

1. Which of the following combinations of characters represent a single valid APL2 name? (For any combination that is not a single valid name, state why it is not.)

   a. *PART*3
   b. 3*RD*
   c. *ROW_*3
   d. *COLN* 4
   e. *_DEPT*
   f. *R2D2*
   g. *A_B*
   h. *A B*
   i. *A−B*
   j. *DEPT,NUMBER*
   k. *A⁻B*

2. In the following expressions, does the variable (or variables) change? If a variable changes, what is its new value?

   a. *X*←3
   b. *X*+3
   c. *Y*←4
   d. *X*+*Y*
   e. *Y*←*X*

Section 1.4 — Evaluation of Expressions

To understand the intent of an expression, you must know how APL2 evaluates that expression.

The following expression gives the same result no matter which **multiplication** is applied first.

```
      3×10×4
 120
```

3×10 multiplied by 4 is the same as 3 multiplied by 10×4.

But the value of the following expression depends on whether you apply **addition** or **multiplication** first:

```
      3+4×5
```

If 3 and 4 are added first, the result is 35. If 4 and 5 are multiplied first, the result is 23. The result in APL2 is 23. This section explains how APL2 evaluates this and other expressions.

Order of Evaluation

The order of evaluation does not matter if the functions in an expression are all **multiplication** or **addition** because these functions are associative. Most often, the order of evaluation does matter and affects the way you construct the expression. Look at the expression needed to solve this problem:

> You want to buy a shirt for $10.00 and a jacket for $20.00. There is a 5% sales tax on the purchase. How much do you have to pay?

The clothing costs $10 plus $20 (which is $30). Including the tax, that's 1.05 times $30. The following expression computes the cost of the shirt and jacket:

```
      1.05×10+20
 31.5
```

Do you see how APL2 computes this? In expressions with numbers and functions like the preceding one, APL2 evaluates the rightmost function first no matter what the function is.

This evaluation may be pictured as follows:

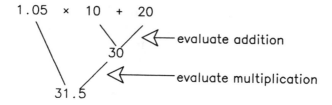

This evaluation is different from normal arithmetic where you multiply before you add regardless of the order of the functions in an expression. APL2 has over 80 functions and remembering which function is executed before another would be nearly impossible. Therefore, APL2 follows an easy rule: *Execute functions from right to left*. Thus, the right argument of × is the result of the entire computation to its right.

You will find the *right-to-left rule* useful and easy to apply because it does not depend on what functions you are using. To see how the right-to-left rule works, consider this variation of the previous example:

> Suppose that the $20 item you bought was not taxable. How would you prevent the multiplication by 1.05?

You can rearrange the computation as follows:

```
      20+1.05×10
30.5
```

This evaluation proceeds right to left as follows:

```
20  +  1.05  ×  10
        \    /  <─ evaluate multiplication
        10.5
  \     /      <─────── evaluate addition
   30.5
```

Use of Parentheses

APL2 uses a familiar way to control the order of execution: parentheses. You've already seen parentheses used to group data. You use parentheses to group a computation as follows:

        (2×5) + (3×6)
    28

The evaluation of this expression is illustrated here:

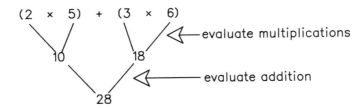

If you want to change the order of evaluation, use parentheses for grouping.

To make an expression clearer, you can use parentheses even when they are not necessary. Parentheses that can be removed from an expression without affecting evaluation are *redundant parentheses*. The rightmost pair of parentheses in the expression (2×5)+(3×6) is redundant since the right-to-left rule would have caused the rightmost multiplication to be done first in any case. The computation can be written more compactly by removing the redundant parentheses as follows:

        (2×5)+3×6
    28

Redundant parentheses have no effect on the order of execution or the result of the computation. If parentheses help you understand what you write, use them.

Use of Blanks

You have already seen blanks used to separate one number from another number. Blanks are not needed to separate a number from a symbol but may be used if you wish. Thus, the following expressions produce identical values:

```
        2-3
 ‾1
        2   -   3
 ‾1
```

Whenever you use one blank to separate one name, constant, or symbol from another, you can use multiple blanks as well. Thus, the following expressions produce identical values:

```
        2 3
  2 3
        2       3
  2 3
```

While you can use extra blanks on entry, APL2 discards them.

Vector Notation

A list of data is called a *vector*. You've already seen several examples of vectors.

You denote vectors of length two or longer by writing the values of the items next to each other. This is called *vector notation*. Here is a two-item vector:

```
        3 5
  3 5
```

To form this vector, you write the constant 3 next to the constant 5 separating them by a blank to avoid confusion with the number 35.

You can also compute 5 by placing in parentheses an expression that yields 5, such as:

```
        3 (1+4)
  3 5
```

These parentheses are not redundant. Removing them changes the meaning of the expression:

```
      3 1+4
7 5
```

At first glance, this expression might look as if it contains two things: 3 and 1+4. But APL2 is an array processing language and operates on whole collections of data in one gulp. Therefore, it is more important to form collections of data (like 3 1) than it is to apply functions. Thus, APL2 groups 3 and 1 before addition is evaluated. So APL2 evaluates this expression (using redundant parentheses) like this:

```
      (3 1)+4
7 5
```

The two-item vector resulting from 3 (1+4) has the same value as 3 5 and may be used in an expression anywhere 3 5 is used.

```
      3 5 × 10
30 50
      3 (1+4) × 10
30 50
```

You can also produce the same vector by using a name that has been assigned the value 5:

```
      AS←5
      3 AS
3 5
      3 (AS+2)
3 7
```

An assignment may be imbedded in an expression:

```
      3 AS←5
3 5
```

The assignment $AS←5$ produces its right argument 5 as its value.

When the assignment is leftmost in an expression, the resulting value does not print.

```
      AS←5
```

When the assignment is not leftmost in an expression, the value may be used for further computation:

        2+*AS*←5
    7

The assignment only applies to the name immediately on its left:

        AT←3
        AT AS←5
    3 5

More than one name may be assigned in one operation by using parentheses:

        (*AT AS*)←3 5
        AT
    3
        AS
    5

One value may be assigned to several names:

        (*AT AU*)←10
        AT
    10
        AU
    10

Again, the result of the assignment is the value to the right of the left arrow, and it does not print if the assignment is leftmost in the expression.

If the assignment is *not* leftmost in the expression, its value may be used for further computation as though the assignment were not present:

        3+(*AT AU*)←10
    13

You can write vectors containing vectors, surrounding each vector item by parentheses:

        (1 2 3) (4 5)
      1 2 3   4 5

This is a two-item vector each of whose items is also a vector. The parentheses group the items. Notice how the spacing of the displayed result gives you a hint that this result is something other than a five-item vector. Although APL2 uses spacing on output to suggest grouping, you cannot use spaces to indicate grouping on input. You must use parentheses.

Items of a vector of vectors may be assigned to different names:

```
      (AA BB)←(1 2 3) (4 5)
      AA
1 2 3
      10+BB
14 15
```

These are the important points about vector notation:

● You can write only a vector of length two or longer using vector notation.

● You represent each item in vector notation as a constant, a name, or an expression in parentheses.

● You use parentheses only for grouping. They do not indicate multiplication or have any other significance.

● Vectors are more important than functions. If, when looking at an expression, you have a choice between forming a vector or applying a function, form the vector.

DISPLAY Function

APL2 uses spaces to suggest the structure of a vector. If you are studying a result and want to know its structure for sure, you use the *DISPLAY* function.

The *DISPLAY* function is available with many APL2 systems. Appendix A shows the definition of the function and tells you how to locate it on your APL2 system.

To use *DISPLAY*, simply enter its name and, as its right argument, the expression whose value you want to examine:

```
      DISPLAY 2 4 6
 .→----.
 |2 4 6|
 '~----'
```

DISPLAY shows a numeric vector within a box with a right pointing arrow on the top edge, indicating data organized along one direction (a vector). The ~ on the bottom edge indicates numeric data.

If some of the items of a vector are vectors themselves, *DISPLAY* boxes these items as well:

```
         DISPLAY (3 4 6) 5 (9 7)
 .→------------------.
 | .→----.   .→--. |
 | |3 4 6| 5 |9 7| |
 | '~----'   '~--' |
 | ∈----------------'
```

The symbol ∈ appears on the bottom edge of any box that contains an item that is not a single number or character.

Chapter 5 tells you more about the *DISPLAY* function.

Exercises for Section 1.4

1. In the following expressions, indicate the order of execution of the functions by writing a number on the line below each function (1 under the first function evaluated, and so on):

    a. 54 − 17 × 10 − 12 + 3

        ___   ___   ___   ___

    b. (54 − 17 × 10) − 12 + 3

        ___   ___   ___   ___

    c. (54 − 17) × 10 − 12 + 3

        ___   ___   ___   ___

    d. (54 − 17) × (10 − 12) + 3

        ___   ___   ___   ___

2. Evaluate the following expressions. Indicate which, if any, parentheses are redundant:

    a. 5 × 3 × 2
    b. 5 × 3 − 2
    c. 5 − 3 × 2
    d. 5 × (3 − 2)
    e. (5 × 3) − 2
    f. 10 + 5 × 4 − 2
    g. (10 + 5) × 4 − 2
    h. (10 + 5) × (4 − 2)
    i. 10 + (5 × 4) − 2
    j. (10 + 5 × 4) − 2
    k. (((10 + 5) × 4) − 2)

3. Evaluate the following expressions:

    a. 10 20 30 + 5 8 4
    b. 10 20 30 + 5
    c. 30 + 5 8 4
    d. 2 + 3 4 + 5
    e. 2 + 3 − 4 + 5
    f. 2 + 3   4 + 5
    g. 2 + 3 4 − 5 6
    h. 2 + 3   4 − 5
    i. (2 + 3 ¯4)− 5
    j. 4 10 + 5   5 + 2 6
    k. 4 10 + 5 5 + 2
    l. 4 10 + 5 + 2 6
    m. 10 + 5 5 + 2
    n. 10 + 5 ¯5 + 2 6

4. Evaluate the following expressions. Write your answers with parentheses to show grouping:

   a.   .1 .2 .5 + 10
   b.   .1 .2 .5 + 10 20 30
   c.   .1 .2 .5 + (10 20) 30 (40 50 60)
   d.   (.1 .2) .5 + (10 20) 30
   e.   .1 (.2 .5) + 10 (20 30)
   f.   .1 (.2 .5) + (10 20) 30

5. State the value of the following expressions and indicate whether the value prints. Assume that assignments remain in effect through the end of the exercise:

   a. $X \leftarrow 3$
   b. $1 + X \leftarrow 3$
   c. $X + X$
   d. $X + X \leftarrow 4$
   e. $X - 1$
   f. $X + X$
   g. $(X \leftarrow 5) - 3$

6. Given five variables:

   $$A \leftarrow 2\ 3$$
   $$B \leftarrow 4$$
   $$C \leftarrow (1\ 5)(6\ 7)$$
   $$D \leftarrow A\ B\ C$$
   $$E \leftarrow A\ B$$

   Evaluate the following expressions:

   a. D
   b. $(A+1)\ A$
   c. $A\ 10$
   d. $A\ 10-1$
   e. $A(10-1)$
   f. $B+0\ 1\ 2$
   g. $B(B+1)(B+2)$
   h. $C\ 2\ C$
   i. $E+10$
   j. $E+E$

7. A polyhedron is a solid three-dimensional figure bounded by flat surfaces. Where two flat surfaces meet, a straight line is formed. Where three or more lines meet, a point called a *vertex* is formed. Write an expression that computes the sum of the vertices and surfaces, and then subtracts the number of edges, for the following figures:

    a. Tetrahedron (pyramid) with 4 vertices, 6 edges, and 4 surfaces.
    b. Octahedron with 6 vertices, 12 edges, and 8 surfaces.
    c. Icosahedron with 12 vertices, 30 edges, and 20 surfaces.

8. A light-year is the distance that light travels in a year.

    a. Write an expression to determine the number of miles light can travel in one, two, and three years if light travels 186,281 miles in one second.

    b. Write an expression to determine the number of kilometers light can travel in one, two, and three years if one mile is 1.6 kilometers.

9. Given that temperature in Fahrenheit is 32 plus nine-fifths of a degree in Celsius, write expressions to reflect the following computations:

    a. Convert Fahrenheit temperature *FEH* to Celsius.
    b. Convert Celsius temperature *CEL* to Fahrenheit.

10. In 1984, three women slept 7, 7.5, and 8.2 hours per day, respectively. Write an expression to determine the percentage of the year each woman slept.

11. Suppose you kept a weekly record of the length of time in minutes you slept each day. Here's an example:

    WEEK1←480 400 360 380 400 350 500

    Write an expression to determine the percentage of the week spent sleeping.

12. Write an expression to find the total cost *TCOST* of some items, given the following variables:

    ● *PRICES* — a vector of the individual item prices.
    ● *QTY* — the quantity of each item purchased.
    ● *STAX* — the sales tax as a percentage.

13. At a recent family visit to the dentist, your dentist provided the following services:

    ● Examined and X-rayed your two children's teeth.
    ● Filled two teeth for your spouse.
    ● X-rayed and checked your teeth and filled one tooth.

    An examination and X-ray cost $45 and each filling costs $15. Write an expression to determine your charges, assuming that your dental insurance pays 80% of the dental expense above $25 for each individual.

14. Write an expression to interchange the values of the two variables *A* and *B*.

Section 1.5 — Saving Your Work

When you begin an APL2 session, no name has a value. As you work, you may assign values to some names. You do not want to lose them when you have finished using APL2. Chapter 4 shows you the best way to save work when you have finished and get it restored when you want to use APL2 later. For now, it is sufficient to know that entering the following command stops APL2 and saves your work:

```
    )CONTINUE
1988-05-01 18.22.43 CONTINUE
```

This command saves your work and terminates the APL2 session. You may also see some termination messages depending on the particular APL2 implementation you are using. Next time you start up APL2, you should see the following message:

```
SAVED 1988-05-01  18.22.43
```

All the names you defined in your previous session are again available to you.

Using)*CONTINUE* is not the recommended way to save your work once you become familiar with the APL2 library system, but it will do the job until you reach Chapter 4.

Section 1.6 — Errors

Trying out the examples in this chapter may have led to any number of mistakes. Perhaps you spelled a name wrong, wrote an incorrect number, tried to add two numbers to three numbers, used a name before assigning it a value, and so forth.

Here's an example in which enter was pressed before the right argument was given for a function:

```
      2+
SYNTAX ERROR
      2+
      ^^
```

After each error, entering a → clears out APL2's memory of the error:

```
      →
```

Types of Errors

The following are some errors you may make. Each one contains a brief description of the type of error. Note that after each error occurs, the example shows a → being used to clear the error from APL2's memory:

● Entering a name that has no value:

```
      PRICF
VALUE ERROR
      PRICF
      ^
      →
```

● Entering a function with no right argument:

```
      2+
SYNTAX ERROR
      2+
      ^^
      →
```

● Trying to add vectors of different lengths:

```
      1  2  3 + 4  5
LENGTH ERROR
      1  2  3+4  5
      ∧       ∧
      →
```

● Using an argument not in the domain of a function:

```
      (X←5)÷0
DOMAIN ERROR
      (X←5)÷0
      ∧       ∧
      →
```

The error messages may seem rather terse at first, but you will quickly learn to spot the error they indicate. Whenever APL2 displays two carets (∧) in an error report, the rightmost one points to the function in which APL2 detected the error. The left caret shows how far to the left APL2 has looked at the expression in its application of the right-to-left rule. Thus, in the illustration of *DOMAIN ERROR*, the rightmost caret shows that the error occurred in **division**. The leftmost caret shows that the assignment to X has already been done.

When APL2 displays one caret in an error report, it is both leftmost and rightmost.

Clearing Errors

Suppose you make these errors and don't clear them with →:

```
      1  2  3 + 4  5
LENGTH ERROR
      1  2  3+4  5
      ∧       ∧

      2÷0
DOMAIN ERROR
      2÷0
      ∧∧
```

You can determine the errors that you have not cleared by entering
the following system command:

```
    )SIS
*   2÷0
    ^^

*   1 2 3+4 5
    ^     ^
```

This list of uncleared errors is a display of the *state indicator*. The
state indicator keeps track of expressions and programs that have
started execution but have not completed. *SIS* stands for State
Indicator with Statements.

In Chapter 7, you'll find that you can make use of the information
in the state indicator. For now, you should just clear it. To clear
the state indicator of uncompleted expressions, enter a right arrow
for each ⋆ that you see in the *SIS* display.

```
    →
    →
```

Then reenter)*SIS* to verify that you have cleared the state indicator
completely:

```
    )SIS
```

As an alternative to using → repeatedly to clear the errors, you can
enter the following command to clear them all:

```
    )RESET
```

Although)*RESET* is convenient, particularly if you neglected to
clear many errors, it is best to clear out each error immediately after
you make it.

If you ever want to clear out less than everything in the state
indicator, you can use)*RESET* with a number to remove that many
expressions from the top of the state indicator:

```
    )RESET 3
```

This command removes the top three expressions from the)*SIS*
display.

Exercises for Section 1.6

1. What error message (if any) would APL2 produce if the following
    expressions were entered in order? For each that results in an
    error message, explain what is wrong. Possible answers are:

    > no error — expression will execute
    > *SYNTAX ERROR* — expression doesn't make sense
    > *VALUE ERROR* — name has no value
    > *LENGTH ERROR* — lengths don't match
    > *DOMAIN ERROR* — cannot compute a function

    a. 2+3 4
    b. 1 2 3 + 3 4
    c. 2
    d. 10÷0
    e. 10÷0+2
    f. *ZZZZ*−2
    g. *A*←10
        B←20
        C←AB
    h. 123+(4 5)(6 7 8)
    i. 1 2 3+(4 5)(6 7 8)

2. Suppose the state indicator looks like this:

    ```
            )SIS
        *   2+
            ^^
        *   10÷0
             ^ ^
        *   2 3+4 5 6
             ^   ^
        *   PRICF
             ^
    ```

    What will the state indicator look like after each of the
    following (assume the same state indicator contents before each
    question):

    a. →
    b. →
        →
    c.)RESET 4
    d.)RESET

Section 1.7 – Terminology

This chapter has introduced many new ideas—some named, some shown only in examples. You learn faster if the key ideas all have names.   You probably already know the concepts; you've seen examples of them in use. In this section, the concepts get names.

The terms for describing data are the most important. Be sure you understand them. Terms used for describing functions and operators are important especially if you plan to read other APL or APL2 books or manuals.

Terms for Data

In APL2, any collection of data is an *array*. An array can be a single number or a single character or it can be a collection of thousands of numbers and characters. A single number or a single character is a *simple scalar*. Here are some simple scalars:

```
            5
  5
            37
  37
```

Note that 37 is a single number, and so it is a simple scalar, even though it contains more than one digit.

A list of data arranged in a line is a *vector* and the pieces of data in any arrangement are *items*.

If every item of a vector is a simple scalar, the vector is a *simple vector*. Here are some simple vectors:

```
      2 3 4
  2 3 4
        2 (2+1) 4
  2 3 4
```

If any item of a vector is not a simple scalar, the vector is a *nested vector*. Here is a nested vector:

```
    (6.95 2.5) (7.95 3.55 2.95) 12.95
  6.95 2.5   7.95 3.55 2.95   12.95
```

The first two items of this vector are simple vectors, and the third item is a simple scalar.

Terms for Operations

An *operation* takes inputs and produces an output. An operation can be a function or an operator.

Functions

A *function* is an operation that, when given data, produces new data. You've seen several functions in this chapter, and you'll see many more before you've finished with this book.

Functions supplied with your APL2 system are called *primitive functions*. Primitive functions are normally denoted by symbols. Appendix E lists the symbols and their names. They are always available for your use. Later when you begin to program in APL2, you will write *defined functions* which behave like the primitive functions except you provide their definition and you denote them by giving each a name.

The arrays to which a function applies are the *arguments* of the function (this word does not imply any difference of opinion). The array produced by the function is called the *explicit result* (or, loosely, the *result*).

Here is how these terms apply to the function **subtraction**:

```
      17-5
  12
```

Subtraction (–) is a primitive function.   17 and 5 are its arguments. The difference (12) is the explicit result. This explicit result can be used as an argument to another function:

```
      1+17-5
  13
```

Subtraction requires two arguments, one on the left and one on the right. A function that applies between two arrays is a *dyadic function*.

On the other hand, *negation* (−) is a function that applies to one array (its argument) and produces an array (its explicit result):

```
     − 2 3 ¯5
 ¯2 ¯3 5
```

A function that applies to one argument, written on the right, is a *monadic function.*

A dyadic function is one with both left and right arguments and a monadic function is one with only a right argument.

You have seen the mid-minus symbol (−) used as both the dyadic **subtraction** function and the monadic **negate** function. In general, any APL2 function symbol represents two functions—one monadic and one dyadic.

For a function in a given expression, if a left argument is present, the dyadic function is always the one applied.

Operators

An *operator* is an operation that produces a new function. You've only seen one operator so far: **reduction**. Operators supplied with the APL2 system are *primitive operators* and are denoted by symbols. Operators you write are *defined operators*. The functions or arrays to which an operator applies are the *operands* of the operator and the function which results is the *derived function.*

Operators may be *monadic* or *dyadic* according to whether they are defined to take one or two operands. The operand of a monadic operator is written to the left of the operation. An APL2 operator symbol always represents a single operator and is monadic or dyadic by definition, not by context.

Here is how these terms apply to the operator **reduction**:

```
    +/ 10 20 30
60
```

Reduction (/) is a monadic primitive operator that produces a monadic function. Its operand is the function **addition** (+). Applied to **addition**, **reduction** produces the derived function **summation** (+/). This derived function is then applied to its argument as with any other monadic function.

Commands

A line that begins with a right parenthesis is called a *system command*. So far you've seen four system commands: `)NMS`, `)CONTINUE`, `)SIS`, and `)RESET`. A system command is not an APL2 expression or an operation. You cannot execute a system command from within a program. It is a means of requesting some information or some action from the APL2 system. `)NMS` asks for a display of the names currently defined. `)CONTINUE` requests an end to the current APL2 session with retention of the definitions of any names for the next session.

Chapter 2

Working with Vectors

APL2 collects data in arrays. Every function in APL2 applies to arrays and produces an array as a result. The simplest arrays are simple scalars. They contain a single number or a single character. Other arrays contain numbers, characters, or mixtures of numbers and characters. This chapter presents the fundamentals of array manipulation by concentrating on vectors—linear arrangements of data. Chapter 5 applies the discussion to other arrays.

APL2 provides functions that measure and produce vectors, which may contain numbers or characters, or both, or which may be empty of data. APL2 broadens the arithmetic functions and extends them to vectors.

Section 2.1 – Functions that Produce Vectors

A vector is the simplest data structure that can contain more than one item. This section presents three functions for measuring and producing vectors:

- **shape**
- **interval**
- **catenate**

Measuring the Size of a Vector: Shape

The monadic function **shape** (ρ), when applied to a vector, tells you how many items are in the vector. The number of items is the *length* of the vector:

```
      ρ 10 20 30 40
4
      PRICE←(6.95 2.5) (7.95 3.55 295) 12.95
      ρPRICE
3
```

The shape of the shape of an array is the *rank* of the array:

```
      ρρ 10 20 30 40
1
      ρρPRICE
1
```

Thus, the shape of a vector is a one-item vector and a vector has rank 1.

Chapter 5 discusses the ranks of all arrays.

Producing Consecutive Integers: Interval

Here's an example of a function that produces a vector of numbers
from a single number:

```
      ι6
 1 2 3 4 5 6
```

This function, called **interval**, generates a vector whose items are
an increasing sequence of consecutive integers starting with 1 and
ending with the requested integer.   The shape of the result of
interval is the same value as the right argument:

```
      ρι6
 6
```

When the mathematician Gauss was a student, he was asked to add
up the first hundred integers as a punishment. He noted that $100+1$
is 101, $99+2$ is 101, and that there are 50 such pairings.   He
immediately wrote down the answer— 50×101 or 5050— to the
amazement of the teacher. Using APL2, you need not be so clever.
You merely enter this:

```
      +/ι100
 5050
```

You can generate any sequence of equally spaced numbers by a
simple expression using **interval**. The argument of **interval** is the
length of the sequence.   Multiply by the difference between two
numbers, and add a constant to make the first item right:

    constant + increment × ι length

Such a sequence of numbers is an *arithmetic progression*.

This expression yields the first six even integers:

```
      2×ι6
 2 4 6 8 10 12
```

To obtain six even integers starting with the number 10, you enter
this expression:

```
      8+2×ι6
 10 12 14 16 18 20
```

Multiplying by a negative number gives a decreasing progression:

```
      ¯1×ι6
¯1 ¯2 ¯3 ¯4 ¯5 ¯6
```

```
    7+¯1×ι6
6 5 4 3 2 1
```

Joining Vectors: Catenate

APL2 provides the function **catenate** to join two arrays. This example shows how **catenate** works to save time and reduce chances of errors.

RETAIL is the name previously assigned to represent the cost of long-playing records, cassette tapes, and compact discs at a record store:

```
RETAIL←6.95 7.95 12.95
```

Now the store begins to sell video disks and video tapes, so *RETAIL* should be a five-item vector rather than a three-item vector. You can redefine the value:

```
RETAIL←6.95 7.95 12.95 25.95 15.95
```

However, if *RETAIL* had hundreds of items, it would not be realistic to redefine the value of the variable every time you need to add items.   Redefining over and over again would be inefficient and error-prone.

The function **catenate** (,) takes two arrays and joins them end to end to form one array. Thus, instead of retyping the values in *RETAIL*, you can just join new numbers to the existing numbers. First, restore the original value of *RETAIL*. Then use **catenate** to append the new values:

```
RETAIL←6.95 7.95 12.95
RETAIL←RETAIL,25.95 15.95
```

Now *RETAIL* has the desired value:

```
RETAIL
6.95 7.95 12.95 25.95 15.95
```

Catenate Versus Vector Notation

You should carefully note the difference between using **catenate** to
append numbers to a list and using vector notation.

In simple cases, **catenate** and vector notation produce the same
result as in this example:

```
      5,7
 5 7
      5 7
 5 7
```

The results of these simple expressions might fool you into thinking
that vector notation implies catenation. A slightly more complicated example illustrates a difference:

```
      5,7+10
 5 17
      5 7+10
 15 17
```

These two expressions differ only by a comma. Remember that in
APL2 *comma* represents a function, not punctuation. The left
argument of **addition** is the scalar 7 in the first case and 5 7 in the
second case. APL2 always forms vectors with vector notation, if it
can, before applying functions.

As a further example, look at these expressions involving the
variable *RETAIL*, set back to its original value:

```
      RETAIL←6.95 7.95 12.95

      RETAIL,25.95 15.95
 6.95 7.95 12.95 25.95 15.95

      ρRETAIL,25.95 15.95
 5

      RETAIL  25.95 15.95
 6.95 7.95 12.95  25.95 15.95

      ρRETAIL  25.95 15.95
 3
```

The expression with **catenate** joins the three values in *RETAIL* to the two new values giving a five-item result. In the display of this result, single blanks separate the items.

The expression with vector notation forms a three-item list whose first item is the value of *RETAIL* and whose second and third items are the numbers given. In the display of this result, two blanks separate the group of three that comes from *RETAIL* from the others.

The use of *DISPLAY* shows the difference more explicitly:

```
      DISPLAY RETAIL,25.95 15.95
 ┌───────────────────────────────
 →
 │6.95 7.95 12.95 25.95 15.95│
 │~───────────────────────────┘
```

```
       DISPLAY RETAIL   25.95 15.95
 ┌──────────────────────────────────
 →                                 
 │ ┌─────────────────            │
 │ →                             
 │ │6.95 7.95 12.95│ 25.95 15.95 │
 │ │~───────────────┘            │
 │ ∈─────────────────────────────┘
```

Exercises for Section 2.1

1. Evaluate the following expressions:

    a.   ι5
    b.   ι5+2
    c.   2+ι5
    d.   ¯2+ι5
    e.   −2+ι5
    f.   2×ι5
    g.   .5×ι5
    h.   ¯2+.5×ι5
    i.   −2+.5×ι5

2. Evaluate the following expressions:

    a.   20 30 + 4 5
    b.   20 30 + 4,5
    c.   20,30 + 4 5
    d.   20,30 + 4,5
    e.   20,30 + (4,5)
    f.   (20,30) + 4 5
    g.   (20,30) + (4,5)
    h.   (10 20 + 30) + 4 5
    i.   (10,20 + 30) + 4 5

3. Write an expression using **interval** to generate each of the following vectors:

    a. 7 12 17 22 27 32
    b. ¯1.7 ¯1.4 ¯1.1 ¯.8 ¯.5 ¯.2
    c. ¯1.5 ¯.75 0 .75 1.5 2.25

4. Write an expression to generate the first ten odd numbers.

5. Write a progression to produce the following:

    a. A simple vector of the first five even numbers followed by the first five odd numbers.

    b. A two-item vector, whose first item is the first five odd numbers and whose second item is the first five even numbers.

6. Let *MONTHS* be a vector that contains the maximum monthly temperatures in Celsius for the first three months of the year.

    MONTHS← 9 13 18

    If the maximum monthly temperature for April is 65 degrees Fahrenheit, write a single expression to include in *MONTH* the maximum April temperature in Celsius.

7. Evaluate the following expressions:

    a. ρ(ι5),10 20
    b. ρ(ι5) 10 20
    c. ρ(ι5),(10 20)
    d. ρ(ι5) (10 20)

Section 2.2 – Character Data

You write a *character* as a symbol surrounded by single quotation marks. Unlike numbers, where one value may have many representations, there is only one way to write a given character as a constant: the graphic for the character surrounded by single quotation marks. For example, you write the character that begins this sentence as follows:

> 'F'
>
> F

The single quotation marks on input are punctuation and indicate the presence of a character. They are not part of the data and so are not displayed when APL2 displays the character data.

You write a *blank* character as a single space surrounded by single quotation marks:

> ' '

A single character is a simple scalar.

Character Vectors

To construct a character vector, you can write the individual characters in quotation marks separated by blanks. This expression is a three-item vector of characters:

> 'A' 'B' 'C'
>
> ABC

A simple vector containing only characters is a *character string*.

When every item of a vector is a simple character scalar, there is a more compact notation for writing the vector. The vector:

> 'A' 'B' 'C'

may be written as:

> 'ABC'

This compact notation is permissible as long as the three characters are not part of a longer vector. For example:

> `'A'  'B'  'C'  'D'`

is not

> `('A'  'B'  'C')  'D'`

or

> `'ABC'  'D'`

The first expression is not equivalent to the other two expressions. The first expression is a four-item simple character vector (which could be written as `'ABCD'`). The second and third expressions are equivalent.

The rewriting rule for simple character vectors extends to give a compact notation for writing a vector of character vectors:

> ```
>     ('J'  'I'  'M')  ('J'  'O'  'H'  'N')
> JIM JOHN
> ```

may be written

> ```
>     'JIM'  'JOHN'
> JIM JOHN
> ```

To construct a character string that itself contains the single quotation mark, you must write the single quotation mark twice. For example, this is the way you would assign the word *don't* to the variable *W*:

> ```
>     W←'DON''T'
>     W
> DON'T
> ```

W contains five characters:

> ```
>     ρW
> 5
> ```

In the expression that assigned *W*, the outermost quotation marks delimit the data and the paired inner quotation marks represent a single quote character.

How would you write the scalar constant consisting of a single quotation mark? You write any other scalar character by putting it in quotes:

        '*A*'
    A

If the character is a single quotation mark, you must double it and then put it within the pair of delimiting quotation marks. That is, to write a scalar character quote, you must enter four quotation marks—the character quotation mark doubled and the required surrounding quotation marks:

        ' ' ' '

    '

Vectors with Both Numbers and Characters

Characters and numbers may exist in the same array. Here are two examples with *DISPLAY* applied to the results so you can see the structure:

        DISPLAY '*LPS*',6.95
    ┌→────────┐
    │*LPS* 6.95│
    └+────────┘
        DISPLAY '*LPS*' 6.95
    ┌→──────────┐
    │┌→──┐   │
    ││*LPS*│ 6.95 │
    │└───┘   │
    └∈──────────┘

The first expression is a four-item vector with characters as the first three items and a number as the last item. The + along the bottom of the box indicates a mixture of characters and numbers. The second is a two-item vector with a character vector as its first item and a number as the second item. The box surrounding the character vector has no symbol along the bottom.

By using characters and numbers in an array, the record store can keep track of its products and prices in one array:

```
    PRD←('LPS' 6.95)('TAPES' 7.95)('CDS' 12.95)
    PRD
LPS 6.95     TAPES 7.95     CDS 12.95
```

```
    DISPLAY PRD
```

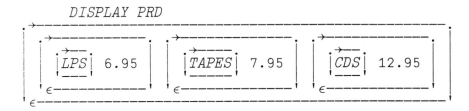

Functions that Work on Characters

You can apply functions that don't do some sort of calculation to characters. For example, **catenate** can join any two vectors. In the following example, **catenate** joins two character vectors:

```
    CV1←'BILLY'
    CV2←'JOE'
    CV1,CV2
BILLYJOE
```

This result is a character string containing eight characters.

Functions that do calculation don't work on characters:

```
    ι'A'
DOMAIN ERROR
    ι'A'
    ∧
    →
```

Exercises for Section 2.2

1. Let *A*, *B*, and *C* be defined as follows:

   $A \leftarrow {}'CAT'$
   $B \leftarrow {}'DOG'$
   $C \leftarrow {}'MOUSE'$

   Determine the shape of the vectors resulting from the following expressions. (Remember: form vectors before applying functions.)

   a. *A B C*
   b. *A,B,C*
   c. *A B,C*
   d. *A,B C*
   e. *(A B) C*
   f. *(A,B),C*
   g. *(A B),C*
   h. *(A,B) C*

2. Write an expression to create this simple character vector:

   I'VE GOT IT!

3. Create the four-item character vector containing the words "I'VE", "GOT", "IT", and the punctuation "!".

4. Evaluate the following expressions:

   a. $\rho{}'ABC' \; 'WXYZ'$
   b. $\rho{}'ABC','WXYZ'$
   c. $\rho{}'ABC' \; (\iota 4)$
   d. $\rho('ABC') \; 'WXYZ'$
   e. $\rho{}'ABC',(\iota 4)$
   f. $\rho('J' \; 'I' \; 'M')('J' \; 'O' \; 'H' \; 'N')$
   g. $\rho{}'JIM' \; 'JOHN'$
   h. $\rho{}'JIM''JOHN'$
   i. $\rho{}'JIM','JOHN'$

5. Suppose variables *J*, *S*, and *W* contain the deposit data for J. Jones, S. Smith, and W. White, respectively. Write an expression to collect together under one variable called *DEPOSITS* each name and its corresponding deposit data.

Section 2.3 — Empty Vectors

All of the vectors produced in examples so far have had one or more items. It is possible to have a vector containing no data and having length zero. Such a vector is an *empty vector*.

Creating an Empty Vector

You've seen the function **interval** used to generate a vector of consecutive integers starting with 1. The expression ιN produces a vector of length N.

This expression produces a vector of three consecutive integers:

       ι3
   1 2 3

This expression gives a vector of one consecutive integer of which there is only one:

       ι1
   1

Although it prints like a simple scalar, it is in fact a vector:

      DISPLAY ι1

   .→.
   │1│
   '~'

This expression produces a vector of zero consecutive integers:

       ι0

ι0 is an empty vector of numbers. The empty vector appears as a blank line on output.

You create an empty character vector by putting no character between quotation marks:

      ' '

Here is *DISPLAY* applied to empty numeric and character vectors:

```
      DISPLAY ι0
 .⊖.
 |0|
 |~|

      DISPLAY ''
 .⊖.
 | |
 |_|
```

The ⊖ at the top of the box indicates an empty array. The zero inside the box indicates a numeric empty vector, and the blank inside the box indicates a character empty vector.

The length of an empty vector is zero:

```
      ρι0
0
      ρ''
0
```

Using Empty Vectors

Empty vectors don't contain data, so you wouldn't expect to do a lot of useful computing with them. However, they allow you to establish variables that will have non-empty values later on.

You have been using the variable *RETAIL* to keep track of the prices of objects at the record store. When you want to add more prices, you catenate new values onto the existing list. In a real application, you may be keeping track of many lists of values.

A good scheme in designing such an application is to determine what quantities you want to keep track of and decide on names for each of them. Initialize each name by assigning an empty vector as its value:

```
      WHAT←''
      RETAIL←ι0
      DISCOUNT←ι0
```

Now when you get some data, you can use **catenate** to append it to each variable:

```
      WHAT←WHAT,'LPS' 'TAPES' 'CDS'
      RETAIL←RETAIL,6.95 7.95 12.95
      DISCOUNT←DISCOUNT,.9 .9 1
```

Scalars are arrays without shape. Thus, if you apply **shape** to a scalar, the result is a numeric empty vector:

          ρ5

          ρ'*A*'

          DISPLAY ρ5
```
 .θ.
 |0|
 '~'
```

          DISPLAY ρ'*A*'
```
 .θ.
 |0|
 '~'
```

The rank of a scalar is zero:

          ρρ'*A*'

     0

As you learn more APL2, it will become increasingly important for you to know whether a single item array is a scalar or a one-item vector. For example, the result of **shape** applied to a vector is a one-item vector. That is why applying **shape** again gives you 1 as the rank of the vector. If the result of **shape** were a scalar number, applying **shape** to that scalar would result in an empty vector.

The discussions of functions in this and the remaining chapters tell you the structure of arrays produced by the functions.

Exercises for Section 2.3

1. Evaluate the following expressions:

   a. ρι2
   b. ρι1
   c. ρι0
   d. ρ''
   e. ρ' '
   f. ρ'AB'
   g. ρ'A B'
   h. ρ'A''B'

2. Suppose function P is a monadic function which takes as right argument a list of data. Write an expression that will call P when the list is empty.

Section 2.4 — Functions that Manipulate Vectors

You have seen some ways to group data into vectors. APL2 functions, in general, operate on entire arrays all at once. Sometimes you may want to operate on only part of an array. This section presents five APL2 functions for extracting data from vectors and a way to replace items in vectors:

- **pick**
- **first**
- **take**
- **drop**
- **indexing**
- **selective assignment**

Selecting Items from a Vector: Pick

Given the *PRD* vector, suppose that only the item describing cassette tapes is of interest.

$$PRD \leftarrow (\text{'}LPS\text{'}\ 6.95)(\text{'}TAPES\text{'}\ 7.95)(\text{'}CDS\text{'}\ 12.95)$$

The following expression uses the function **pick** (⊃) to select the second item from *PRD*:

```
      2⊃PRD
TAPES 7.95
```

This result is the two-item vector that is the second item of *PRD*.

If you want only the name of the second product, you can apply **pick** twice:

```
      1⊃2⊃PRD
TAPES
```

By using a vector left argument, you can make this selection in a single operation:

```
      2 1⊃PRD
TAPES
```

The left argument means first select the second item ('*TAPES*' 7.95), then select the first item from that ('*TAPES*').

A three-item left argument further narrows the selection to one character from the product name:

```
      2 1 4⊃PRD
E
```

Do you see why the numbers 2 1 4 selected the *E* in *TAPES*? The vector of numbers means select the vector that is the second item of *PRD*. Then select the first item of that vector (giving '*TAPES*'). Finally, select the fourth item of that vector ('*E*').

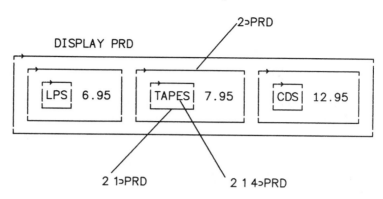

Selecting Items from a Vector: First

The monadic function **first** (↑) selects the leading item of its argument. You can think of **first** as a special case of **pick**. The following expression shows the relationship between **first** and **pick**. In this book the symbol ⟷ (not an APL2 symbol) means "equivalent to."

$$(↑V) \quad ⟷ \quad (1⊃V)$$

Compare the following two expressions, and you'll see that they produce the same result:

```
      ↑PRD
LPS 6.95

      ρ↑PRD
2

      1⊃PRD
LPS 6.95

      ρ1⊃PRD
2
```

There is another interesting property of **first**. When applied to empty vectors, it returns an array that identifies the type of data used to construct the empty vector. For example:

```
      ↑⍳0
0
      ↑''
←——(blank)
```

You may think that **first** is an unnecessary function, but, you'll see in Chapter 5 that it is useful with data structures more complicated than vectors.

Selecting Items from a Vector: Take

When the symbol ↑ has a left argument as well as a right argument, the function performed is **take**. To select adjacent items in a vector, you indicate in the left argument how many consecutive items to select from the right argument. For example:

```
      4↑'TAPES'
TAPE

      3↑5 7 9 11 13
5 7 9
```

A negative left argument selects consecutive items from the right end of the vector instead of from the beginning:

```
      ¯4↑'TAPES'
APES
      ¯3↑5 7 9 11 13
9 11 13
```

By successive applications of **take**, you can select items from the middle of a vector:

```
      3↑¯4↑'TAPES'
APE
      2↑¯3↑ 5 7 9 11 13
9 11
```

If you attempt to take more data than you have from a simple vector, APL2 pads the result with either blanks or zeros, according to whether the first item of the right argument is a character or a number:

```
      ¯8↑'TAPES'
   TAPES
        7↑5 7 9 11 13
 5 7 9 11 13 0 0
```

When you take more that you have from a nested array, the result is padded with items that look like the first item but with numbers replaced with zeros and characters replaced with blanks:

```
      3↑(2 'A' 3) (19 'B' 21)
  2 A 3   19 B 21   0     0
```

```
      DISPLAY 3↑(2 'A' 3) (19 'B' 21)
 .→────────────────────────────────.
 | .→────. .→──────. .→────.        |
 | |2 A 3| |19 B 21| |0    0|       |
 | '+────' '+──────' '+────'        |
 '∈────────────────────────────────'
```

Take applied to a vector always returns a vector result.

```
      1↑'APPLE'
 A
      ρ1↑'APPLE'
 1
```

Notice the important difference between **take** and **first**. **First** returns the contents of the first item of its argument, which can be any array at all. **Take** returns a number of items, as specified by its left argument; so a 1↑ produces a one-item vector that contains as its only item the first item of its argument:

```
      ↑'LPS' 'TAPES' 'CDS'
 LPS
      ρ↑'LPS' 'TAPES' 'CDS'
 3
      DISPLAY ↑'LPS' 'TAPES' 'CDS'
 .→──.
 |LPS|
 '───'
```

```
        1↑'LPS' 'TAPES' 'CDS'
LPS
        ρ1↑'LPS' 'TAPES' 'CDS'
1
        DISPLAY 1↑'LPS' 'TAPES' 'CDS'
```

```
.→──────.
| .→── . |
| |LPS| |
| |───| |
| ε──────' |
'ε────────'
```

Selecting Items from a Vector: Drop

With the function **drop**, you can discard consecutive leading or
trailing items:

```
        3↓'TAPES'
ES
        3↓5 7 9 11 13
11 13
```

A negative left argument indicates how many items to discard from
the right end of the right argument:

```
        ¯2↓'TAPES'
TAP
        ¯3↓5 7 9 11 13
5 7
```

Applying **drop** consecutively allows you to select items from the
middle of a vector:

```
        ¯1↓2↓'TAPES'
PE
```

If you attempt to drop more data than you have, the result is an
empty vector:

```
      10↓'TAPES'

      ρ10↓'TAPES'
0
      16↓ 5 7 9 11 13

      ρ16↓ 5 7 9 11 13
0
```

Drop applied to a scalar or a vector always returns a vector result.

Selecting Items from a Vector: Indexing

You may select items from a vector by specifying the position of the item in the vector. The operation that does this kind of selecting is **indexing**. You write, inside square brackets, the numbers that indicate the items selected:

```
      'TAPES'[2]
A

      (5 7 9 11 13)[4]
11
```

Whereas **take** and **drop** applied to vectors always return a vector, the array returned by **indexing** depends on the array used as the index. In the preceding examples, the index is a scalar so the result is a scalar.

The shape of the result is always the same as the shape of the index. This rule for the shape of the result applies even when the array being indexed is nested. For example, in this expression the result is a scalar because the index is a scalar. It is nested because the second item of the array indexed is not a simple scalar:

```
      ('SCOTT' 'STACY')[2]
STACY
      ρ('SCOTT' 'STACY')[2]


      DISPLAY ('SCOTT' 'STACY')[2]
  ┌─────────┐
  │ ┌─────→ │
  │ │STACY│ │
  │ └─────┘ │
  │ ∈───────┘
  └─────────┘
```

Here are some examples in which the index is a vector:

```
      'TAPES'[3 2 5 1 4]
PASTE
```

```
      'TAPES'[1 4 2]
TEA
```

```
      (5 7 9 11 13)[4 2 1]
11 7 5
```

If the index is a vector, the result is a vector of the same length.

Notice that parentheses are needed to index a numeric vector constant. This is because square brackets for indexing apply to the array immediately to the left of the brackets. Indexing is evaluated before vectors are formed. Application of this rule explains why the following expression works as you would expect:

```
      A1← 5 7 9 11 13
      A2← 10 20 30
      A1[2] A2[3] A1[4]
7 30 11
```

You can select the same item more than once by using its index number more than once:

```
      'TAPES'[5 4 4 3]
SEEP
```

You can do any computation inside the brackets as long as the result is integers that select items from the left argument. Suppose you had a vector of ones and zeros that represented a code. You can convert the vector to Morse code in either of these ways:

```
      CODE←0 0 1 0 1 1
      ('DOT' 'DASH')[1+CODE]
DOT DOT DASH DOT DASH DASH
```

```
      '.-'[1+CODE]
..-.--
```

Because the explicit result of **indexing** is an array, you can, of course, do further computations on it:

```
        RETAIL←6.95 7.95 12.95
        2 4 × RETAIL[1 3]
13.9 51.8
```

At first glance, **indexing** with a scalar and **pick** seem to make selections in the same way. However, they are distinct. **Pick** gives you the array at the indicated position. **Indexing** with a scalar, gives you a scalar containing the array at the indicated position. The following example shows the difference in the selection:

```
        ('DOT' 'DASH')[1]
    DOT
        ρ('DOT' 'DASH')[1]

        DISPLAY ('DOT' 'DASH')[1]
```

```
.┌───────┐.
| ┌→──┐ |
| |DOT| |
| └───┘ |
'∈───────'
```

```
        1⊃'DOT' 'DASH'
    DOT
        ρ1⊃'DOT' 'DASH'
3
        DISPLAY 1⊃'DOT' 'DASH'
┌→──┐
|DOT|
└───┘
```

Replacing Items in a Vector: Selective Assignment

Any expression that selects items from an array can be written on
the left of an assignment arrow to indicate replacement of the
selected items. Here are some examples using selection functions
you've just seen:

        PRD←('*LPS*' 6.95)('*TAPES*' 7.95)('*CDS*' 12.95)

        2 1⊃*PRD*
    TAPES

        (2 1⊃*PRD*)←'*SPOOLS*'

        PRD
    LPS 6.95   *SPOOLS* 7.95   *CDS* 12.95

        W←'*TAPES*'

        4↑*W*
    TAPE

        (4↑*W*)←'−'

        W
    −−−−*S*

        W[1 3]←'□▤'
        W
    □−▤−*S*

Selective assignment is discussed in more detail in Chapter 6.

Exercises for Section 2.4

1. Given the following:

    $$A← \ 'ABCD' \ (10 \ 20 \ 30) \ ((2 \ 4) \ (1 \ 3 \ 5))$$

    Evaluate:

    a. ρ*A*
    b. ↑*A*
    c. ρ↑*A*
    d. 1⊃*A*
    e. ρ1⊃*A*
    f. *A*[1]
    g. ρ*A*[1]
    h. ¯1↑*A*
    i. 1↓*A*
    j. ↑2↓*A*
    k. ↑↑2↓*A*
    l. ↑↑↑2↓*A*
    m. ↑↑↑↑2↓*A*

2. For *A* defined in exercise 1, fill in a left argument that selects the value shown as the result:

    a.   _____⊃*A*
         10 20 30

    b.   _____⊃*A*
          D

    c.   _____⊃*A*
          30

    d.   _____⊃*A*
          2 4

    e.   _____⊃*A*
          1

3. For a numeric vector *V*, write expressions for the following:

    a. Shift *V* left two places, replacing the emptied positions with zeros.
    b. Shift *V* right three places, replacing the emptied positions with zeros.

    Test your expressions on this vector:

$$V \leftarrow 10 \ 4.1 \ 7 \ ^{-}3.6 \ 5.2 \ ^{-}23.6$$

The answers should look like this:

    a. 7 ¯3.6 5.2 ¯23.6 0 0
    b. 0 0 0 10 4.1 7

4. Given the vector *DATA*:

$$DATA \leftarrow ('ABC' \ 25) \ ('DE' \ 463) \ ('FGHI' \ 87 \ 12)$$

Evaluate:

    a. 2⊃*DATA*
    b. 2 2⊃*DATA*
    c. 3 2⊃*DATA*
    d. 3 1⊃*DATA*
    e. 3 1 2⊃*DATA*
    f. ↑*DATA*
    g. ↑↑*DATA*
    h. (↑*DATA*)[2]
    i. *DATA*[3]

5. The vector *DIRECTORY* is a vector of two-item vectors. The first item is the last name of an individual. The second item is that person's telephone number, represented as a three-item vector (area code, exchange, and number). For example, the first two items of *DIRECTORY* are as follows:

DISPLAY 2↑*DIRECTORY*

Write expressions for the following:

   a. The name and telephone number for the second entry.
   b. The area code for the first entry.
   c. The name from the first entry.
   d. The name from the second entry.

6. Write an expression to select BUT from the word TRIBUTARY.

7. Given the following variables:

     CH←'*AAABCDEF*'
     DAT←'*ABC*' (ι4) '*DEFG*' (10 20 30) '*IJ*' (7 9)

Evaluate the following expressions:

   a. *CH*[3]
   b. *CH*[3 1 2]
   c. *CH*[¯1+2×ι3]
   d. *DAT*[3 4]
   e. *DAT*[2+ι4]

Section 2.5 – Scalar Functions

APL2 applies a *scalar function* to each simple scalar in its argument or arguments. You have already seen some scalar functions: **addition**, **subtraction**, **negation**, **multiplication**, and **division**. The other functions you have seen—**interval**, **catenate**, **pick**, **first**, **drop**, and **indexing**—are not scalar functions.

This section discusses scalar functions in general and introduces these additional scalar functions:

- **power**
- **maximum**
- **minimum**
- **floor**
- **ceiling**
- **magnitude**
- **direction**
- **residue**
- **reciprocal**

Scalar Conformability and Scalar Extension

APL2 defines the scalar functions first on simple scalar arguments. Here is **addition** applied between two simple scalars:

```
      2 + 5
7
```

When you apply a scalar function between arguments that are not simple scalars, APL2 decomposes the operation into simpler cases until finally it applies the function between simple scalars.

When arguments have the correct shape for a function (as opposed to the correct values), the arguments *conform*. For a dyadic scalar function, arguments of the same length conform. For example, the following expression shows **addition** applied between conforming vectors, giving a result whose shape matches the shape of the arguments:

```
      2 3 4 + 5 6 7
7 9 11
```

APL2 evaluates **addition** between conforming vectors by applying the function between corresponding items, one from each argument. The items are paired as follows:

```
      (2+5) (3+6) (4+7)
7 9 11
```

The preceding expression reduces the vector addition into three simple scalar additions.

If neither of the arguments is a scalar, the arguments must have the same length. Otherwise, a *LENGTH ERROR* results:

```
      3 5+2 1 7
LENGTH ERROR
      3 5+2 1 7
      ∧   ∧
```

Here is an example of **subtraction** that, when applied between conforming vectors, still results in an error:

```
        'ABC' - 1 2 3
DOMAIN ERROR
        'ABC' - 1 2 3
        ∧       ∧
```

A *DOMAIN ERROR* results because the values in the vectors are not all numbers even though the lengths of the vectors are correct.

Here is an example of **subtraction** between conforming vectors whose values are correct for the function:

```
        9 8 6 ¯5 - 4 ¯2 8 ¯3
     5 10 ¯2 ¯2
```

You can view the expression in terms of the **subtraction** of simple scalars:

```
        (9-4) (8-¯2) (6-8) (¯5-¯3)
     5 10 ¯2 ¯2
```

For monadic scalar functions, all arguments conform. The shape of the result is the same as the shape of the argument.

```
        -2 3 4
     ¯2 ¯3 ¯4
```

Negation is accomplished by applying the function to each item of the argument. The function is applied as follows:

```
        (-2) (-3) (-4)
     ¯2 ¯3 ¯4
```

The dyadic scalar functions permit one argument to be a scalar even when the other argument is not a scalar. In this case, the arguments always conform, because the scalar combines with each item of the non-scalar argument. Thus, the following expression adds 1 to each item of a vector:

```
        1 + 2 3 4
     3 4 5
```

The shape of the result always matches the shape of the non-scalar
argument. The scalar argument is paired with each item of the
non-scalar argument as follows:

          (1+2) (1+3) (1+4)
    3 4 5

This pairing of the scalar with the array argument is called *scalar
extension.*

Scalar extension applies as well when the non-scalar array is empty.
For example, the result of adding 2 to an empty vector has the shape
of the empty vector and this is empty:

         2+ι0

         ρ2+ι0
    0
         DISPLAY 2+ι0
     .θ.
    |0|
     '~'

For non-scalar functions, the result, if one of the arguments is
empty, depends on the definition of the function. For example,
catenate is not a scalar function. Catenating a scalar with an
empty vector results in a one-item vector:

         3,''
    3
         ρ3,''
    1

Scalar Functions and Nested Arrays

When you apply scalar functions to nested arrays, APL2 decomposes the operation so that the scalar function applies to simple arrays. For example, here is **multiplication** applied between two conforming nested arrays:

```
      1 (2 3) × 10 (20 30)
   10   40 90
```

You can view this application in terms of simple arrays as this:

```
      (1×10) (2 3×20 30)
   10   40 90
```

Then you can view the simple arrays in terms of simple scalars as this:

```
      (1×10) ((2×20)(3×30))
   10   40 90
```

Scalar extension works on nested arrays the same way as for simple arrays:

```
      1+(2 3) (4 5 6)
   3 4   5 6 7
```

The scalar argument pairs with each item in the nested argument as follows:

```
      (1+2 3) (1+4 5 6)
   3 4   5 6 7
```

In summary, APL2 defines the scalar functions on simple scalar arguments, then extends them to other arrays by decomposing them into operations on simple scalars.

Additional Scalar Functions

In demonstrating the definition of a scalar function, it is always
enough to show how the function works on simple scalar arguments,
because every scalar function ultimately applies to simple scalar
arguments.   Using vector arguments to illustrate the scalar
functions allows a single expression to demonstrate many cases at
one time.

Scalar Function: Power

You may have heard of King Shirham of India who wanted to honor
his grand vizier, Sissa Ben Dahir, for inventing the game of chess
(Gamow 1947).   Dahir requested one grain of wheat on the first
square of a chess board, two grains on the second square, four on the
third, eight on the fourth, and so on until square 64 had twice the
number of grains as square 63.

This seems like a reasonable request.   You could compute it as
follows (don't try it):

$$1+2+(2\times2)+(2\times2\times2)+(2\times2\times2\times2)+ \ldots$$

Operations like this produce really big numbers.   In this case, the
exact answer is 18,446,744,073,709,551,615 which represents the
world's wheat crop for two thousand years (assuming two billion
bushels a year and five million grains per bushel).   This number is
probably larger than your computer can represent exactly.

The **power** function, or **exponentiation**, expresses products of
repeated numbers.   The number to be multiplied by itself has a
superscript number that indicates the number of times the multiplication takes place.   In APL2, the mathematical expression 2^3 (or
$2\times2\times2$) has this form:

```
      2*3
8
```

The right argument of **power** is called the exponent. It is important
to remember that in APL2, * is the **power** function, and × is the
multiplication function.

If you use **power**, you would calculate the number of grains on the
last square as follows:

```
      2*63
9.223372037E18
```

Notice that APL2, by default, gives only the first 10 digits. The actual answer is 9223372036854775808.

Now with less typing, you could compute the number of grains on all the squares by entering the following expression (don't try it):

```
    1+(2*1)+(2*2)+(2*3)+(2*4)+ ... +(2*63)
1.844674407E19
```

You can write this computation more compactly using **reduction**:

```
    1++/2*ι63
1.844674407E19
```

You can write this computation even more compactly if you notice the following property of powers:

$$
\begin{array}{rcccl}
1+(2*1) & \longleftrightarrow & 3 & \longleftrightarrow & {}^{-}1+2*2 \\
1+(2*1)+(2*2) & \longleftrightarrow & 7 & \longleftrightarrow & {}^{-}1+2*3 \\
1+(2*1)+(2*2)+(2*3) & \longleftrightarrow & 15 & \longleftrightarrow & {}^{-}1+2*4 \\
1+(2*1)+(2*2)+(2*3)+(2*4) & \longleftrightarrow & 31 & \longleftrightarrow & {}^{-}1+2*5
\end{array}
$$

You can conclude that

```
1+(2*1)+(2*2)+(2*3)+(2*4)+ ... +(2*63)  ⟷  ⁻1+2*64
```

Thus, the same answer is computed as follows:

```
    ⁻1+2*64
1.844674407E19
```

Scalar Functions: *Maximum and Minimum*

Minimum (L) returns the smaller of its arguments, and **maximum** (Γ) returns the larger of its arguments:

```
    5L3
3
    5 8 3 ⁻6 ⁻2L6 2 3 ⁻7 4
5 2 3 ⁻7 ⁻2
```

```
      5⌈3
5
      5 8 3  ̄6  ̄2⌈6 2 3  ̄7 4
6 8 3  ̄6 4
```

Scalar Functions: Floor and Ceiling

Floor (⌊) applied to a number returns the biggest integer not bigger than the number. **Ceiling** (⌈) applied to a number returns the smallest integer not smaller than the number.

```
      ⌊7.3 7.9  ̄7.2 7
  7 7  ̄8 7
      ⌈7.3 7.9  ̄7.2 7
  8 8  ̄7 7
```

Notice that neither **floor** nor **ceiling** has any effect on a number that is already an integer.

Floor by itself does not round numbers to the nearest integer:

```
      ⌊6.35 6.45 6.55 6.65
  6 6 6 6
```

In order to round in this example, you need to adjust the numbers so that any number 6.5 or above becomes 7 or above. You can do this by adding .5. Then use **floor** to get rid of the fractional part:

```
      ⌊.5 + 6.35 6.45 6.55 6.65
  6 6 7 7
```

If you deal with amounts of money in a currency that uses fractional denominations, rounding requires more mechanism. For example, U.S. money has .01 dollar—a penny—as the smallest unit of money.

Suppose you have three bank accounts represented by the variable *AMOUNT*:

```
    AMOUNT←150.20 331.35 331.25
```

On a given day, the bank is going to credit 5% interest to each account. The amount of interest it credits is this:

```
    AMOUNT×.05
  7.51 16.5675 16.5625
```

Your new balance is this:

```
AMOUNT+AMOUNT×.05
157.71 347.9175 347.8125
```

You can factor out *AMOUNT* in the above expression and simplify it to:

```
AMOUNT×1.05
157.71 347.9175 347.8125
```

The bank is going to round these quantities to the nearest penny. How would you compute the round? You can add .005 to each amount but you can't use **floor** directly to discard the unwanted digits. One method for rounding decimal fractions is to adjust the numbers to integers, add .5, take the floor, and readjust. For U.S. money, the adjustment factor is 100. Here's an expression to round your new balance:

```
.01×⌊.5+100×AMOUNT×1.05
157.71 347.92 347.81
```

Notice that the first amount is exact, the second rounded up, and the third rounded down.

There are two cautions about this method of rounding that depend on the actual application. First, a bank would never round this way. If every account in the bank happened to round up, the sum of the amounts in the accounts would be more money than the bank had—an intolerable situation. Banks do not really round by adding half a penny. Instead, they round by adding a computed quantity such that the sum of the rounded amounts equals the round of the summed amounts. Here's an example where adding .5 would cause a problem for the bank:

```
AMTR← 136.557 121.406 380.816 149.777 721.566
```

Here is the rounded amount:

```
.01×⌊.5+100×AMTR
136.56 121.41 380.82 149.78 721.57
```

This is a correct round, but if you compare the sum of the original amounts to the sum of the rounded amounts, you see that the bank is out almost two cents:

```
      +/.01×⌊.5+100×AMTR
1510.14
      +/AMTR
1510.122
```

The second caution has to do with the precision of the computer you are using. On most computers, integer computations are exact and fractional computations are approximate. Even a machine whose internal hardware is decimal cannot do fractions exactly. (Can you compute 1÷3 exactly?) Therefore, in dealing with critical computations (and many people consider money critical), it is better to represent amounts as integer pennies rather than fractional dollars. If you do this, the rounding expression becomes simpler and computational errors caused by machine internal representations are reduced.

Here's the rounding expression for pennies:

```
      AMOUNT1←15020 33135 33125
      ⌊.5+AMOUNT1×1.05
15771 34792 34781
```

In this case, the amount of money in the rounded amounts is the same as when you rounded the fractional numbers. This is almost always the case, making the problem with fractional approximation, should one occur, all the more insidious.

Scalar Functions: Magnitude and Direction

The monadic **magnitude** function (|)—also called **absolute value**—always returns a nonnegative number. If you imagine the real numbers laid out on a line with zero at the center, the **magnitude** function measures the distance of a number from zero. This has the effect of mapping negative numbers into the corresponding positive number as pictured here:

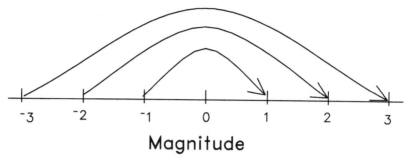

Magnitude

Maps negative number to corresponding positive number

$$|^-3 \ 3 \ 0$$
$$3 \ 3 \ 0$$

The **direction** function ($\times$) reports only the sign of a number, ignoring its magnitude. The result is 1 for a positive number, $^-1$ for a negative number, and 0 for zero.

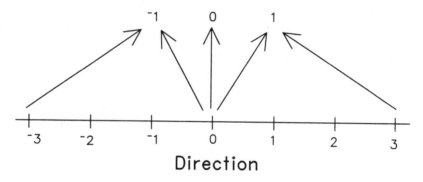

Direction

Maps negatives to $^-1$, zero to 0, Positives to 1

$$\times ^-3 \ 3 \ 0$$
$$^-1 \ 1 \ 0$$

Direction and **magnitude** are complementary in that the following identity holds:

$$A \ \longleftrightarrow \ (\times A) \times (|A)$$

Scalar Functions: Residue and Reciprocal

The function **residue** (|) gives the remainder after division:

```
      2|3 0 4 5
1 0 0 1
      10|35.4
5.4
      1.1|3.6
0.3
```

An interesting case of **residue** uses a left argument of 1. Remainder after division by 1 gives the fractional part of a number:

```
      1|13.5 29 3.45
0.5 0 0.45
```

In mathematics, **residue** is sometimes called *modulo*, and computing a residue is called *taking the modulus*.

Residue and **floor** are related in that for a given number N, $\lfloor N$ is the integer part of the number, and $1|N$ is the fractional part. This relationship gives rise to the following identity:

$$N \quad \longleftrightarrow \quad (\lfloor N)+1|N$$

Residue on negative numbers may not give the answer that you expect:

```
      10|23 ⁻17
3 3
```

Why is the remainder after division by 10 the same for these two numbers? A look at a number line divided into intervals of length 10 helps explain this. $10|N$ for any N maps to some number in the interval 0 to 10 (including zero, not including 10). Thus, $10|23$ is 3 because if you pick up the interval from 20 to 30 and lay it down on the interval from 0 to 10, the number 23 will fall on top of the number 3. Any number that is a multiple of 10 away from 23 will map to the number 3.

```
        23−10× ̄1+ι6
23  13  3   ̄7   ̄17   ̄27


        10|23−10× ̄1+ι6
 3  3  3  3  3  3
```

Here is a picture that shows this:

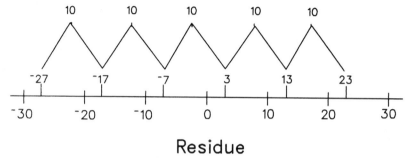

Residue

10 residue maps number to interval 0 to 10

If you have a number N, you would expect dividing N and $-N$ to give the same quotient and remainder except for sign. Here is a counterexample:

```
    V← ̄35.4  35.4
    10|V
 4.6  5.4
```

If you put ̄35.4 into the equation that relates **floor** and **residue**, you'll see that **residue** is giving the proper answer for negative numbers.

If you look at where ̄35.4 and 35.4 fall on a number line, you'll see that the **residue** function is doing the same thing to both numbers. In each case, the result subtracted from the original number gives a multiple of 10.

If you really want to get the same answer regardless of sign, always apply **residue** to a positive number:

```
    10||V
 5.4  5.4
```

If you want to preserve the sign, multiply by the **direction**:

$$(\times V) \times 10 \mid \mid V$$
¯5.4 5.4

Reciprocal (÷) is another function related to division. It returns 1 divided by its argument:

```
      ÷5 10
0.2 0.1
         ÷ι5
1 0.5 0.3333333333 0.25 0.2
```

Although **reciprocal** is scarcely less difficult than just writing 1÷..., it is useful enough to appear as a function key on many electronic calculators.

Exercises for Section 2.5

1. Evaluate the following expressions:

    a. 16*2
    b. 2*4
    c. 2 3 4 * 2
    d. 4 * 1 2 3
    e. 2 3 4 * 1 2 3
    f. (2 3) 4 * 2 (1 2 3)
    g. 25 ⌈ 6
    h. 25 ⌊ 6
    i. 25 5 ⌈ 6
    j. 25 ⌊ 35 ¯37
    k. 10 ¯12 5 ⌈ 4 ¯8 0
    l. ¯10 12 ¯5 ⌊ 4 ¯8 0
    m. 13 15 ⌈ (11 14) (16 10 14)
    n. 2 (3 5) ⌈ (1 4)(6 4)
    o. (2 3) 5 ⌈ (1 4)(6 4)
    p. (2 3) 4 * 2
    q. (2 3) 4 * 2 3
    r. (2 3) 4 * (2 3) 1
    s. (2 3) 4 * (2 3) (1 2 3)

2. Write an expression to guarantee that no numbers of a vector *V* will be positive.

3. Evaluate the following expressions:

    a. 5,''
    b. (ι0) 5
    c. 5 ''
    d. ι0+5
    e. 5+ι0
    f. ''+5
    g. 5+''

4. State the value and the shape of each of the following expressions:

    a. 2+ι 0
    b. 2+10
    c. 2+ι0
    d. 10×ι2
    e. 10×ι1
    f. 10×ι0
    g. 10×1

5. Write an expression to change negative numbers in array *A* to zero while leaving the non-negative numbers unchanged.

6. Most people over 15 years old give their age as an integer. This includes an 80-year-old woman who likes to report a smaller number for her age:

    a. How old is she if you don't count weekends?

    b. Some people only live for weekends. How old is she only counting weekends?

    c. If she is 80 years old Fahrenheit, how old is she Celsius?

7. A parcel shipper has the following charges: a basic charge of 15 cents per cubic foot with a minimum charge of 50 cents.

    Assuming the vector *DMEN* contains the three dimensions of a box, in inches, write an expression to determine its shipping cost.

8. A bank's service charge to exchange money from currency X to currency Y is 2% of the value of the new currency Y but with a minimum charge of 2.50 units of currency Y. Write an expression to determine the service charge levied on 100 units of currency X if the exchange rate for *Y* is 1.51×*X*.

9. Show at least three ways to make the scalar 5 into a one-item vector.

10. The total payment F owed on an amount of principal P on which interest R is compounded periodically is given by this equation:

$$F = P(1+R)^n$$

    where:

    ● P is the principal.
    ● R is the rate of interest per period stated decimally.
    ● N is the number of periods.

    a. Write an expression to determine the total amount to be repaid on a two-year loan of $1500 at a 9% annual interest compounded quarterly.

    b. Write an expression to determine the total interest charges paid on a three-year $5000 loan at a 12% annual interest rate compounded quarterly.

11. The following formula computes the total monthly payment *MP* made on a conventional mortgage loan:

$$MP = loan \times \frac{MIR \times (1+MIR)^{Y+12}}{(1+MIR)^{Y+12}-1}$$

    where:

    ● MIR is the monthly interest rate.
    ● Y   is the number of years.

    Write an expression to determine the total monthly payment of a 30-year loan of $600,000 at 12% annual rate of interest.

12. Write an expression that, given Jack Benny's chronological age, will compute his admitted age which is never greater than 39.

13. If f is a dyadic scalar function, indicate the results of the following:

    a. ρ 2 4 5 f 1 3 6
    b. ρρ 2 4 5 f 1 3 6
    c. 9 6 4 3 f 4 5

14. Circle the monadic functions in the following expressions:

    a.   `¯3+4`

    b.   `3--7`

    c.   `3||12 ¯1113 10`

    d.   `÷÷4`

    e.   `¯3 4 7 9⌈9 2 3,⌊6.7`

    f.   `−3 9 6××¯2 7 0`

15. Suppose you have seven people playing a card game using a deck with 52 cards. If all cards are dealt in turn to the players until all cards have been distributed, write the APL2 expression to compute the number of people who get an extra card.

16. Here is an electrical network consisting of a set of resistors connected in parallel:

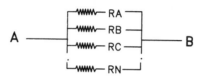

The effective resistance from A to B is computed by this mathematical formula:

$$\frac{R1 \times R2 \times R3 \times \ \ldots \ \times RN}{R1 + R2 + R3 + \ \ldots \ + RN}$$

    a. Write an expression to solve for the effective resistance if there are two resistors with values $R1$ and $R2$.

    b. Write an expression to solve for the effective resistance if there is a set of resistors whose values are represented in the vector R.

Chapter 3

Working with Programs

Chapter 1 introduced two important programming concepts:

- Functions apply to data.
- Variables remember data.

This chapter extends the concepts you need to program effectively by introducing two more programming concepts:

- Operators apply to functions.
- Programs remember expressions.

The last part of the chapter explains how to build a program.

Section 3.1 – Operators Apply to Functions

Each APL2 function applies to its arguments in some specified way. Operators control the way functions are applied to arguments. For example, in Chapter 2, you learned that the expression +/ι10 finds the sum of the first ten integers.   +/ applies the operator **reduction** (/) to the function **addition** (+) to *derive* the function **summation**. This derived function is then applied to the ten integers to produce the sum.   In effect, the operator causes **addition** to be applied nine times:

$$+/\iota 10 \quad \longleftrightarrow \quad 1+2+3+4+5+6+7+8+9+10 \quad \longleftrightarrow \quad 55$$

Operators are a powerful way to create whole families of new functions.   For instance, **addition** is just one function that **reduction** can operate on to derive a new function.   This section tells you more about operators by using **reduction** to illustrate the concepts involved in making and using derived functions, and then introduces you to the **each** operator.

Reduction on Vectors

You can use **reduction** with any dyadic function.   Some of the derived functions formed with **reduction** are very useful.   Others have limited use.   But they all apply to vectors in the same way.   In effect, *fn/ vector* puts the function *fn* between items of a vector and evaluates the resulting expression to reduce it to a scalar.

The derived function ×/ yields the product of a set of numbers. Suppose the variables *HEIGHT*, *DEPTH*, and *WIDTH* contain the height, depth, and width of a rectangular solid.   The following computation produces the volume of the solid:

```
HEIGHT←5
DEPTH←6
WIDTH←4
×/HEIGHT DEPTH WIDTH
```
```
120
```

As another illustration of this derived function, you can compute the number of seconds in five days as follows:

```
×/5 24 60 60
```
```
432000
```

Two more examples of **reduction** use the functions **minimum** (⌊) and **maximum** (⌈). **Maximum-reduction** (⌈/) produces the largest number in a list of numbers. **Minimum-reduction** (⌊/) produces the smallest number in a list. For example, suppose you have five test scores. You can compute the largest and smallest of the scores:

```
      SCORES←88 75 99 67 92
      ⌈/SCORES
99
      ⌊/SCORES
67
```

The difference between the high and low scores is:

```
      (⌈/SCORES) - (⌊/SCORES)
32
```

Naming Derived Functions

Because +/ has a counterpart in mathematics, namely, Σ, APL2 names this derived function **summation**. In general, derived functions have no special names and are simply named for the purpose of discussion by combining the function and operator names. For example, **multiplication-reduction** (×/), **division-reduction** (÷/), and **take-reduction** (↑/).

Using Derived Functions

For a monadic operator, the operand appears to the left of the operator (in contrast to a monadic function where the argument appears to the right of the function). Thus, +/⍳10 is a **summation** and ⍳ is a monadic function applying to the number 10.

An operator ends up applying its operand function to subsets of the data arguments. Thus, the permissible data for a derived function is related to the permissible data of the function operand. **Summation** and **multiplication-reduction,** for example, apply to all numbers, but not to characters. A **catenate-reduction** (,/) applies to both numbers and characters:

```
      ,/ 2 'A' 3 'B' 5
2 A 3 B 5
```

The argument to the derived function in the preceding example is a simple vector of numbers and characters, and the result is a nested scalar.

```
      DISPLAY ,/ 2 'A' 3 'B' 5
 .―――――――――――――.
 |  .→――――――――.  |
 | |2 A 3 B 5|  |
 | '+―――――――――'  |
 |∈――――――――――――|
 '――――――――――――'
```

You can extract the vector from the scalar using **first**:

```
      ↑,/ 2 'A' 3 'B' 5
2 A 3 B 5
```

```
      ρ↑,/ 2 'A' 3 'B' 5
5
```

Reduction applied to a vector always produces a scalar. The operator is called **reduction** because, in general, the result has rank one smaller than the argument. Thus, the result of the above **catenate-reduction** is not a five-item vector but a nested scalar containing a five-item vector.

Even with a nested argument, the function is still placed between each data item and the result is a scalar:

```
      +/(2 4 6)(1 3 5)(7 8 9)
   10 15 20
```

```
      DISPLAY +/(2 4 6)(1 3 5)(7 8 9)
 .――――――――――――――.
 |  .→―――――――――.  |
 | |10 15 20|  |
 | '~――――――――'  |
 |∈―――――――――――――|
 '―――――――――――――'
```

Reduction applies the function that is the operand of **reduction** between items of the argument. If the items are not appropriate for the function, APL2 generates an error. For example, in the following expression, the application of + between two vectors of different length causes a *LENGTH ERROR*:

```
      +/(2 4 6) (1 3 5 7) (8 9)
LENGTH ERROR
      +/(2 4 6) (1 3 5 7) (8 9)
      ∧∧
```

The **reduction** is correct. It is the implied **addition** of the four-item vector to the two-item vector that causes the *LENGTH ERROR*.

Here's an example of a correct summation with a nested argument:

```
      +/(2 5 3) 4 (6 8 1)
12 17 8
```

In this example, recall that the scalar 4 extends to be conformable with the three-item vectors in the argument.

You might be surprised at what happens when you apply **reduction** to an empty vector. The identity of the function operand determines the answer you get. For example:

```
      +/⍳0
0
```

The answer is 0 because 0 plus any number returns that number. That's what it means for 0 to be the identity of +. **Reduction** gives this answer because it makes programs work even on empty data. For example, if you have a vector of test scores *SCORES*, the expression +/*SCORES* adds up the sum of the scores even before you take any tests.

Here are two other examples of **reduction** on empty vectors:

```
      ×/⍳0
1
      ⌊/⍳0
7.237005577E75
```

Times-reduction gives 1 because multiplication by 1 does not alter a number. Thus, 1 is the identity for ×.

For **minimum-reduction,** the answer given is the largest number representable on the computer system and may be different for different machines. The actual identity element of **minimum** should be infinity. In a practical sense, the minimum between the largest number possible in the computer and any other number in the computer is that other number.

Each

Chapter 2 introduced the **interval** function (ι) as a way to generate a list of integers. If you want to obtain three lists of integers, you might enter this:

```
      (ι3)  (ι5)  (ι6)
   1 2 3   1 2 3 4 5   1 2 3 4 5 6
```

and get three answers, each of which is a sequence of integers. APL2 has a general way to do this kind of operation using the **each** operator (¨) to request that a function be applied to each item of data.

The **each** operator applies a function to each of the items of its argument. Here's a picture that shows how **each** works with an arbitrary monadic function *fn*:

fn ¨ *D E F*		
fn D	*fn* E	*fn* F

Here's the application of **each** to **interval**:

```
         ι¨3  5  6
   1 2 3   1 2 3 4 5   1 2 3 4 5 6
```

```
      DISPLAY ι¨3 5 6
.→-----------------------------------------.
| .→----.  .→--------.  .→------------.     |
| |1 2 3|  |1 2 3 4 5|  |1 2 3 4 5 6|       |
| |~----'  |~--------'  |~------------'     |
| ∊-----------------------------------------|
```

This expression literally means apply **interval** to each of the three numbers.

Like **reduction, each** modifies a function and applies it in a related but different way from its application without **each**.

When **each** is applied to a dyadic function, the function is applied between corresponding items from the two arguments. Here's a picture that shows how **each** works with an arbitrary dyadic function *fn*:

$$A \; B \; C \; \textbf{\textit{fn}}^{..} \; D \; E \; F$$

$A \; \textbf{\textit{fn}} \; D$	$B \; \textbf{\textit{fn}} \; E$	$C \; \textbf{\textit{fn}} \; F$

Suppose the nested vector *SC* contains the four test scores of a group of students. You can use the following expression to select the first two scores from the first student's grades, the first three scores from the second student's grades, and the first score from the third student's grades:

```
    SC←(95 83 71 85)(49 58 78 65)(75 90 81 72)
    2 3 1↑¨SC
95 83  49 58 78  75
```

If one argument is a scalar, the item of that scalar pairs with each item of the other argument. The following expression produces the first two test scores of each student as follows:

```
    2↑¨SC
95 83  49 58  75 90
```

```
    ρ2↑¨SC
3
```

A **pick-each** (⊃¨) extracts any score from each student's grade records. For example, the third score for each student is:

```
    3⊃¨SC
71 78 81
```

As you can see with **interval-each** (ι¨), **take-each** (↑¨), and **pick-each** (⊃¨), an **each**-derived function can be either monadic or dyadic, according to whether it is used with one or two arguments.

Each can be applied to a derived function. This expression applies **each** to a **reduction**-derived function to compute the largest score of each student:

```
    ⌈/¨SC
95 78 90
```

This result is a simple vector because the **reduction** of each item produced a simple scalar.

Because scalar functions already apply to their arguments item-by-item, **each** has no effect when applied to them. The following two expressions produce the same result:

```
      2 4 6 +¨ 1 3 5
3 7 11
```

```
      2 4 6 + 1 3 5
3 7 11
```

This is a simple vector of three numbers.

Later when you write your own programs, you can apply **each** to them also.

Exercises for Section 3.1

1. Given the variable *A*:

    $$A \leftarrow 'ABC' \ (10 \ 20 \ 30 \ 40)$$

    Evaluate:

    a. ρ*A*
    b. ρ¨*A*
    c. ↑*A*
    d. ↑¨*A*
    e. 2↑¨*A*
    f. 2⊃*A*
    g. 2⊃¨*A*
    h. 2 3⊃¨*A*

2. Evaluate:

    a. +/ 1 2 3 4
    b. +/(1 2) (3 4)
    c. +/¨(1 2) (3 4)
    d. +/¨1 2 3 4
    e. +/¨(1 2) 3 4
    f. +/(1 2) 3 4

3. Given the following variables:

   ```
   A← 'CHARLES'  'BROWN'
   B← 'LUCY' 'SMITH'
   C← 'WALTER' 'MUDD'
   NAMES← A B C
   ```

   Write an expression to select the following:

   a. The first name in the *NAMES* vector.
   b. The third name in the *NAMES* vector.
   c. The first name of each individual in the *NAMES* vector.
   d. The last name of each individual in the *NAMES* vector.
   e. The lengths of the last names.

4. A light-year is the distance that light travels in one year. Using **reduction**, write an expression to compute the number of meters in a light-year given that a year is 365 days and that light travels at 300,000 meters per second.

5. Suppose three people kept a weekly record of the length of time in minutes they slept each day:

   ```
   WK1A←480 400 360 380 400 350 500
   WK1B←395 350 350 400 415 450 515
   WK1C←345 490 355 500 430 300 480
   WEEK1←WK1A WK1B WK1C
   ```

   a. Write an expression to determine the maximum amount of time each person slept during the course of *WEEK*1.

   b. Write an expression to determine the percentage of the week that each person spent sleeping.

Section 3.2 — Programs Remember Expressions

You saw how you could save time and typing by using variables to remember data. Not every computation you want to express can be written as a single APL2 expression. Even if you can write a single expression, you don't want to reenter the entire computation each time you need it. APL2 provides a way to remember a set of expressions by giving the set a name. A set of remembered expressions is a *program*. You can write three kinds of programs in APL2. They are distinguished by the way they are used:

- Defined functions— Programs used just like APL2 primitive functions.
- Defined operators— Programs used just like APL2 primitive operators.
- Defined sequences— Programs used like APL2 constants except that APL2 computes the explicit result each time the program is used. (Note: These programs are often called *niladic functions*, but the term is a misnomer. These programs do not take arguments, cannot be applied with operators, and cannot be used like functions.)

When you want to compute on data, you write a defined function. When you want to compute on functions and data, you write a defined operator. When you just want to gather expressions, you write a defined sequence.

Programs are used in expressions in the same way as primitive operations. For instance, if a program is a monadic defined function, its argument is placed to the right of the program name.

Just as you do not have to know how a primitive operation like **shape** or **pick** is coded to use it, you need not know how a program is coded to use it. To use a primitive operation or a program, you must know the following information:

- Its name
- Its purpose
- The number of arguments for a function and their characteristics
- The number of operands for an operator and their characteristics
- The characteristics of the result

For example, ○ is a monadic primitive function. It returns a result of pi (3.14159...) times its argument. With this explanation, you should be able to write an expression to find the area of a circle whose radius is 3:

```
      O3*2
28.27433388
```

AVG is a monadic defined function that calculates the average of its vector right argument. It returns an explicit result. Without knowing how *AVG* is coded, you can use it in expressions. For example, compute the average of a set of numbers:

```
      V←6  4  7  11
      AVG  V
7
```

As another example, calculate the difference between the largest value in *V* and the average of *V*:

```
      (⌈/V)−AVG  V
4
```

In your APL2 work, you will be using programs created by other people as well as programs you create yourself. This chapter explains the basics of program creation. Chapter 7 presents further techniques for program creation.

Program Structure

Each program has this structure:

```
┌─────────────────────┐
│                     │
│       header        │
│                     │
├─────────────────────┤
│                     │
│                     │
│        body         │
│                     │
│                     │
│                     │
└─────────────────────┘
```

There are two distinct parts of the definition: the header and the body. The body is just the set of APL2 expressions that APL2 remembers and evaluates every time the program is used. The header is not an APL2 expression. Rather, the header describes the program's use. It is often called line zero of the function because it comes before line 1 and some editors number it zero.

Defined Function Structure

The following listing shows the definition of the *AVG* defined function used in the previous section. The definition begins and ends with a **del** (∇). The top line is the header; the numbered lines are the body. Line [1] is a *comment* line. The symbol ⍝ indicates that everything to its right is a comment and thus is not to be executed:

```
     ∇Z←AVG N
[1]  ⍝ computes average of a vector
[2]  Z←(+/N)÷⍴N
[3]  ∇
```

The header contains the name of the function *AVG*. The name *N* to the right of the function name indicates that the program requires a right argument. Notice in the body of the program (at line [2]) the use of *N* in the expression that calculates the average. The value given as the right argument to *AVG* is the value used for *N*.

The left arrow in the header means that this function produces an explicit result. The name *Z* to the left of the arrow indicates that in the program body name *Z* represents the result. The value *Z* is computed during execution of the function.

Appendix B shows how to use the APL2 editors to enter *AVG* and other programs.

Defined Operator Structure

The listing below shows the definition of the *WORDWISE* defined operator. It is similar in structure to the defined function *AVG*. The top line is the header; the numbered lines are the body. The header of an operator differs from that of a defined function in that parentheses surround the name of the operator and the names of the operands. Whenever you look at a program definition, if the header contains parentheses, the program is a defined operator.

```
     ∇ Z←A(FN WORDWISE)B;DIGITS
[1]   ⍝ Apply function FN to one digit numbers
[2]   ⍝   written in English
[3]   ⍝ Result is English, expressed as digits
[4]    DIGITS←'ZERO' 'ONE' 'TWO' 'THREE' 'FOUR' 'FIVE'
[5]    DIGITS←DIGITS,'SIX' 'SEVEN' 'EIGHT' 'NINE'
[6]    A←10⊥¯1+DIGITS⍳⊂A
[7]    B←10⊥¯1+DIGITS⍳⊂B
[8]    Z←A FN B
[9]    Z←(DIGITS,'POINT' 'MINUS')['0123456789.¯'⍳⍕Z]
[10]∇
```

This program uses a lot of interesting primitive functions that are not introduced until later chapters. Nonetheless, you can use the operator because you know its name, its purpose, the required arguments and operands, and the result. Here are some sample uses of *WORDWISE*:

```
      'TWO' +WORDWISE 'THREE'
FIVE

      'FIVE' ×WORDWISE 'FOUR'
TWO ZERO

      'TWO' ÷WORDWISE 'FIVE'
ZERO POINT FOUR

      'TWO' —WORDWISE 'FIVE'
MINUS THREE
```

Defined Sequence Structure

The defined sequence header is the simplest form of the three types of programs. It has no operands or arguments. Often it does not have an explicit result.

A defined sequence is usually the main program of an application. A user of the application enters only one name to get the program running. The program often prompts for some required data and calls some subprograms. The user of the application does not need to know anything about the syntax of APL2. For example, *PAVG* is a defined sequence that prompts for a student's grades, calculates the average, and displays a message indicating the average:

```
     PAVG
ENTER GRADES SEPARATED BY SPACES:
□:
     89 81 75 93
YOUR GRADE AVERAGE IS 84.5
```

Here is the definition of *PAVG*. The prompt for input at line 3 uses APL2 notation that is discussed in Chapter 7.

```
     ∇PAVG;X
[1]   ⍝ asks for grades and computes average
[2]   'ENTER GRADES SEPARATED BY SPACES:'
[3]   X←□
[4]   'YOUR GRADE AVERAGE IS',AVG X
[5]   ∇
```

PAVG is the program name. It has no arguments and no explicit result. The *X* after the semicolon identifies a *local* name—a name that has meaning only during execution of the program. All programs can have local names. Local names are discussed later in this chapter.

Because this program does not produce an explicit result, you cannot use it in an expression which does further processing:

```
     100-PAVG
ENTER GRADES SEPARATED BY SPACES:
□:
     90 85 92 99 88
YOUR GRADE AVERAGE IS 90.8
VALUE ERROR
     100-PAVG
         ∧
```

Notice that the *VALUE ERROR* occurs after APL2 executes the sequence. If a defined sequence is to have an explicit result, the header must contain a left arrow and the name of the explicit result.

Here is a different average program that returns an explicit result that can be used in further calculations:

```
      ∇A←PAVGR;X
[1]   ⍝ asks for of grades and computes average
[2]   'ENTER GRADES SEPARATED BY SPACES:'
[3]   X←⎕
[4]   A←AVG X
[5]   ∇

      100-PAVGR
ENTER GRADES SEPARATED BY SPACES:
⎕:
      90 85 92 99 88
9.2
```

Defining a Program

There are two parts to defining a program: the creative and the mechanical. In the creative part, you decide what you want the program to do and what header and APL2 expressions are necessary for that purpose. In the mechanical part, you must enter the program in the proper form for APL2. For this, you use an *editor*. Every APL2 system provides one or more editors. Appendix B describes two of these editors—the full-screen editor and the line editor.

The *del* (∇) that you see at the beginning of the programs shown in the preceding sections switches you to an APL2 editor and enters *definition mode*. What you type while in definition mode becomes part of the program. The *del* at the end of the program ends definition mode and returns you to *immediate execution* mode. In immediate execution mode, APL2 executes the expressions you enter immediately.

To enter any of the programs shown in this chapter so that you can try them out, type them exactly as they are shown. However, before you work the exercises, you should read Appendix A to learn how to use an editor.

The command)*NMS*, which you have been using to display variable names, also displays defined function, operator, and sequence names. Defined functions and sequences have the suffix .3 and defined operators have the suffix .4:

```
      )NMS
CV1.2    CV2.2    D.2      H.2      PAVG.3   PAVGR.3
RETAIL.2          SCORES.2          WORDWISE.4
```

The actual response you get to the command)*NMS* depends on the names you have defined.

The rest of this chapter concentrates on the creative part of defining a program.

Closer Look at the Header

Headers contain three parts; only the first part is essential:

1. Syntax to show the use of the program. The syntax identifies the program as a defined function, a defined operator, or a defined sequence and names the operands, arguments, and explicit result, if any.

2. List of local names to identify those variables whose values will be assigned within the program for use only in the program.

3. Comments to provide a description of the program.

Header Syntax

The syntax of the *AVG* program identifies it as a monadic defined function with an explicit result. There are four function headers that identify defined functions. These are shown in Table 3.1.

	Monadic	**Dyadic**
With Explicit Result	Z←FNAME R	Z←L FNAME R
Without Explicit Result	FNAME R	L FNAME R

Table 3.1 Defined Function Headers

FNAME is the name of the defined function.   *Z* is a name for the explicit result; *L* and *R* are names for the left and right arguments. You can use any names you want. It is their position in the header that is important.

The forms without explicit results limit the use of the defined functions in expressions and therefore are not frequently used. This book concentrates on the two forms with explicit results.

The syntax of a defined operator identifies first whether the operator is monadic or dyadic and then whether the derived function is monadic or dyadic and with or without an explicit result. Table 3.2

shows the syntactic forms for defined operators whose derived functions have explicit results. The syntactic forms for defined operators whose derived functions have no explicit results are the same except that $Z \leftarrow$ does not appear in the header:

	Monadic Derived Function	Dyadic Derived Function
Monadic Operator	$Z \leftarrow (F \ ONAME) \ R$	$Z \leftarrow L \ (F \ ONAME) \ R$
Dyadic Operator	$Z \leftarrow (F \ ONAME \ G) \ R$	$Z \leftarrow L \ (F \ ONAME \ G) \ R$

Table 3.2 Defined Operator Headers

ONAME is the user name of the defined operator. *Z* is a name for the explicit result; *F* and *G* are names for the left and right operands; and *L* and *R* are names for the left and right arguments, respectively. You can use any names you want. It is their position that is important. The parentheses delimit the derived function name and are essential. Note that for monadic operators the operand is to the left of the operator name just as it is for a primitive operator.

Defined sequences have two syntactic forms:

	Defined Sequence
With Explicit Result	$Z \leftarrow SNAME$
Without Explicit Result	$SNAME$

Table 3.3 Defined Sequence Headers

SNAME is the name of the defined sequence.

Local Names

The best way to understand operands, arguments, and other local names is to see some in action. The function *PVALUE*, shown next, calculates the amount of money you must invest in order to generate a given balance in a given amount of time at a given yearly interest rate:

```
      12000 PVALUE 5 10
8000
```

Here is the definition of the function:

```
     ∇Z←AMT PVALUE NI;RATE    ⍝ present value
[1]  ⍝ AMT is the given balance
[2]  ⍝ NI[1] is years, NI[2] is interest rate
[3]  ⍝ Z is the amount to be invested
[4]    RATE←NI[2]×.01       ⍝ rate into fraction
[5]    Z←AMT÷1+NI[1]×RATE   ⍝ get present value
[6]  ∇
```

The header includes names for the explicit result (Z) and the left (AMT) and right arguments (NI). It also includes a local variable—$RATE$—following the semicolon.

When you call the defined function $PVALUE$, you give it values as the left and right arguments:

```
12000 PVALUE 5 10
```

After you request execution of the program, and just before the expressions in the program start to execute, APL2 implicitly evaluates these expressions:

```
AMT←12000
NI←5 10
```

Then the program begins the computation you requested.

The program computes a value that becomes the program's *explicit result*. The header defines which of perhaps several internally computed values is to become the explicit result; the explicit result is the name to the left of the left arrow. Thus, in $PVALUE$, Z is the explicit result and $RATE$ is not an explicit result even though APL2 computes both each time the function is called.

There is something special about the names Z, AMT, NI, and $RATE$ in $PVALUE$ (that is, every name in the header except the name of the program). They have values only while the function is being evaluated.

```
12000 PVALUE 5 10
```
```
8000
```

Even though $RATE$ gets a value inside the program, it does not have a value outside the program:

```
        RATE
VALUE ERROR
        RATE
        ∧
```

If the name *RATE* does have a value outside the program, the use of
RATE inside the program does not affect the outside value:

```
        RATE←'A CHARACTER STRING'
        12000 PVALUE 5 10
 8000
        RATE
 A CHARACTER STRING
```

Names that have values only while a program is executing are *local
names*. All of the names mentioned in the header (except for the
name of the program itself) are local names and never conflict with
values the same names have outside the program. The names that
have values outside any program are *global names*. Names that are
local to one program may be global to a called subprogram. During
program execution, the local value of the name *shadows* the global
value, meaning that the global value can't be seen.

Here is a summary of what the system does when a defined function
is called:

1. Gets names of all locals.

2. Remembers current global values of names to be localized.

3. Defines local names as having no values.

4. Associates any arguments and operands to the operation by
    means of the local name of the argument or operand.

5. Executes the function.

6. If a result is specified in the header, remembers its local value.

7. Deletes all local values.

8. Restores values remembered in step 2.

9. Sets the value remembered in step 6 as the explicit result.

This summary covers all local names. Up to now, you know only
about local names mentioned in the header. Chapter 7 describes
another set of local names called *labels*.

The following analysis of a call of *PVALUE* applies the previous discussion to a real example:

```
RATE←'A CHARACTER STRING'
12000 PVALUE 5 10
```

1. Names of locals are *Z*, *AMT*, *NI*, and *RATE*.

2. *RATE* has `'A CHARACTER STRING'` as value; *Z*, *NI*, and *AMT* have no global values.

3. *Z*, *RATE*, *NI*, and *AMT* now have no value.

The system then performs these steps:

4. Does the following assignments:

```
AMT←12000
NI←5 10
```

5. Executes *PVALUE*, causing *RATE* to get the value .1 and *Z* to get value the 8000.

6. Remembers value of the result local name *Z*.

7. Deletes values given to *AMT*, *NI*, *Z*, and *RATE*.

8. Restores values remembered in step 2:

```
RATE←'A CHARACTER STRING'
```

9. The value remembered in step 6 becomes the result of the function and (in this case) prints.

A defined operator undergoes the same execution steps as a defined function except that there are local names for the operands as well as for the arguments.

Comments

The header may include a comment to describe something about the program. A comment may also appear within the body of the program at the end of a line or on a line by itself. The symbol *lamp* (ⴰ) indicates that everything following on the line is a comment and not to be executed.

It is a good idea to include comments in your programs for these reasons:

● To remind yourself how the program works.
● To assist others who may want to learn or modify your program.

Using Defined Functions, Operators and Sequences

You use a defined function with an explicit result like any primitive function. You can use *AVG*, for instance, like any other APL2 monadic function:

● You can display its result immediately:

```
        SCORE←95 83 75 62 99 78 81
        AVG SCORE
81.85714286
```

● You can assign its result to a variable name:

```
        ASCORE←AVG SCORE
        ASCORE
81.85714286
```

● You can use it in an expression with other functions and operators defined or primitive. For example, the difference between the high score and the average score is:

```
        (⌈/SCORE) - AVG SCORE
17.14285714
```

● You can make it the operand of an operator. If student scores reside in separate vectors *STDNT*1, *STDNT*2, *STDNT*3, the following expression determines the average of each student:

```
STDNT1 ← 95 83 75 62 99 78 81
STDNT2 ← 93 73 78 60 95 75 80
STDNT3 ← 88 89 90 67 94 79 83
```

```
AVG¨ STDNT1 STDNT2 STDNT3
81.85714286   79.14285714   84.28571429
```

You use a defined operator like any primitive operator.

- Its operands can be primitive, defined, or derived functions. Operators can form a limitless number of derived functions because you can apply them to defined as well as primitive functions.

- You can use a defined operator in an expression with other functions and operators.

A defined sequence acts like a named constant. It looks like a variable except that you may not assign a new value to it using an assignment arrow (←).

Errors during Program Execution

When you are in definition mode, APL2 does no error-checking except to validate headers. If a line has a syntax error, if a variable has no value, or if arguments are not conformable, you will not know it until you try to execute the program.

When APL2 detects an error during program execution, it interrupts execution and displays an error message along with the program line in which the error occurred and carets to indicate where the error occurred.

Suppose, for instance, that the *AVG* program contained a typing error. You would see this message:

```
VALUE ERROR
AVG[2]   Z←(+/MUN)÷ρNUM
              ∧
```

Whenever you encounter an error, you should clear it out—by using → or)*RESET*—or fix it and restart execution of the program. If you don't clear the errors, you can fill the space available to you with partially evaluated expressions. Chapter 7 discusses restarting execution of a program and Appendix A tells you how to use an editor to change an existing program.

Good APL2 Programming Practices

Good programming practices make programming easier—and program maintenance much easier. This section covers three important aspects of good APL2 programming:

- Creating a toolbox of utility programs.
- Using comments liberally.
- Using local names.

Creating a Toolbox of Utility Programs

Once you have written a defined function, there is little reason ever again to enter the expressions that comprise it. You can always use the defined function. For example, *MN_DEV* is a function that calculates the mean deviation of a set of numbers *N*. It uses the function *AVG*:

```
       ∇MD←MN_DEV N
[1]      ⍝ finds the mean deviation of N
[2]      MD←(+/|N-AVG N)÷N
```

A good tool is a program that accepts arguments and produces results (like *AVG*). It can be used in expressions as though it were primitive. Functions that do not take arguments or produce results do not make good tools. For example, *PAVG*, the program that prompts for input and prints an answer, can only be used by itself. *PAVGR* is a little better because at least its result can be used. It could not, however, be applied by an operator because it is a defined sequence not a defined function.

With some notable exceptions, programs which prompt for input do not make good tools even if they are not defined sequences. If you ever applied the **each** operator to one of them with a 100-item argument, you would have to respond to 100 prompts. An exception is a program whose purpose is to prompt. Chapter 7 shows some examples of such a program.

Good programmers build toolboxes of useful programs they use over and over. As time goes by, they write less and less code to do a given job, relying on their toolboxes to save them repetitive efforts.

Using Comments Liberally

You can place comments in APL2 in the header of a program, on a separate line in the program body, or at the end of a line of code. When APL2 encounters the comment symbol (⍝) during execution of a program, it ignores all characters to the right of the symbol.

Comments should include the purpose of the program; description and source of data used, including rank, type, and shape; meaning of local names; processing logic; and any other information that will make the program more understandable. You should describe any global names used in the program. Internal comments in the program should describe the results produced by that part of the program.

Using Local Names

As discussed earlier, local names are names that are assigned values and used only within the program and may hold intermediate results.

Because you assign values to local names within the program, there is never any doubt what their values will be at any time during the program execution. If possible, you should always use values in a program that are local. Pass needed values as arguments to a program. Make an argument a nested vector if many values must be passed. If variables are specified outside the program and then used in the function, there is always the possibility that someone will assign a different value to the variable name and your program will have no control over this re-assignment. Also, by localizing variables, you ensure that your programs do not interfere with any variables that the user of your program may have assigned.

If you want to have a global value available to several programs but want to protect it from being accidentally assigned a different value, you may define the value as a defined sequence instead of a variable. A defined sequence with an explicit result is used exactly like a variable except that you cannot replace its value using an assignment arrow:

```
        ∇Z←VALUE
[1]     Z←45
[2]     ∇


        10+VALUE
55


        VALUE←20
SYNTAX ERROR
        VALUE←20
        ∧     ∧
```

Exercises for Section 3.2

1. For the following function headers, state whether the header is a header for a function, an operator, or a sequence, or is an invalid header. If the header is valid, give the name of the program. If the header is invalid, say why. State whether an operator is monadic or dyadic. State whether the function (or derived function) is monadic or dyadic, and state whether an explicit result is produced.

   a. ∇Z←F X;Y Z
   b. ∇Z←(B C) D;E;F
   c. ∇F←A B
   d. ∇F A B C
   e. ∇F A B
   f. ∇(A B C);Z
   g. ∇Z←(A B C);Z
   h. ∇Z←L (A B C);Z
   i. ∇(A B C) LEFT;Z

2. Define a dyadic function *DENTAL* that returns a two-item vector containing:

   • The amount of the dental bill you have to pay.
   • The amount of the dental bill your insurance company will pay.

   The function should have the following inputs:

   • Percentage of the bill that the insurance company will cover after the deductible is subtracted.
   • Deductible amount (amount that insurance does not cover).
   • Total dental cost.

Sample execution:

```
      .75 25 DENTAL 65
   35 30
```

3. Create the following functions and expression:

    a. Define a function to compute the total cost of several items, given the cost per item and the quantity of each to be purchased.

    b. Define a function to compute the total cost of an item, given as arguments the sales price of the item and the sales tax stated as a percent.

    c. Using the functions created in parts a and b, write an expression to determine the cost of purchasing three pairs of jeans retailing at $19.50 each, and two sweaters retailing at $15.50 each, where the sales tax is 6.25%.

    Do not define a new function or change the functions created in the previous two parts.

4. Define a function to determine the shipping charge for a parcel, given:

    - Cubic foot charge
    - Minimum charge
    - Dimensions of the parcel in inches (One foot is 12 inches.)

5. Define a function to determine the amount you would get in currency Y when you exchange currency X for it. Assume the function is given the following data:

    - Service charge (in currency Y)
    - Minimum service charge (in currency Y)
    - Exchange rate in terms of currency X
    - Amount to be exchanged

6. A survey containing multiple choice questions was answered by 85 different people. Question 1 had 4 parts. 10 people gave the first answer, 15 the second answer, 57 the third answer, and 3 the fourth answer. This data is represented in the variable $A1$:

    ```
    A1←10 15 57 3
    ```

    The second question had five answers with this distribution:

    ```
    A2← 10 14 30 14 6
    ```

(One person did not answer.)

Write a function to determine the percentage distribution of choices made for each question.

Test case:

    DIST A1 A2
11 17 67 3   13 18 40 18 8

    DISPLAY A1 A2

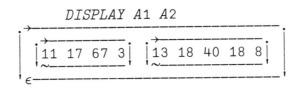

7. In several areas, the sales tax varies according to the nature of the item purchased. For example, in New York State there is no sales tax on most food.

Write a dyadic function *TOTALCOST* to determine the total cost of sets of items each with its own sales tax.

Test case:

            FOOD← 1.49 7.85 1.99
            NONFOOD← 8.48 4.54
            0 5.5 TOTALCOST FOOD NONFOOD
    25.07

8. Write a set of functions to allow a person to enter this expression and get the correct answer:

    WHAT IS 7 PLUS 9

9. Given the following nested vectors:

            W← 'ABCD' 'EFGHI' 'JKLMNOP'
            I← (2 4) (1 3 5) (2 3 5 6)

Write an expression to use each item of *I* to index the corresponding item of *W*, giving:

    BD EGI KLNO

Hint: Write a defined function that processes one index and then apply it with the **each** operator.

This problem illustrates good APL2 programming style. Solve the simple case first; then use operators to apply the simple solution to more complicated data.

10. Write a one-line expression to compute the present value as an alternative to the function *PVALUE* shown in the section "Local Names."

11. The derivative of a function in mathematics is approximated by computing the function at two very close points and dividing by the distance between the points. The derivative of f is $(f(\mathsf{x}+\mathsf{h}) - f(\mathsf{x})) \div \mathsf{h}$ for a small value of h (near zero).

   a. Write a defined operator *PRIME* to approximate the derivative of an arbitrary function F at points X. F is the operand and X is the right argument of *PRIME*. Let H be $1E^{-}10$.

   b. This book introduces the functions **exponential** and **logarithm** in Chapter 6. Without knowing how those functions are defined, you should be able to make conclusions about their derivatives. Guess the derivative of **exponential** and **logarithm** by experimentation. Here are some good samples to try:

   ```
   *ι4
   *PRIME ι4
   ⊛ι3
   ⊛PRIME ι4
   ⊛PRIME ÷ι3
   ```

12. Examine the following two expressions. What situation could cause the *SYNTAX ERROR?*

   ```
         XX+10
   19
         XX←XX+1
   SYNTAX ERROR
         XX←XX+1
         ∧ ∧
   ```

Chapter 4

Working in the APL2 Environment

When you start an APL2 session, you're working within an APL2 environment called the *active workspace*. All APL2 primitive functions and operators as well as the APL2 editors are available to you. You receive error reports if APL2 cannot evaluate something you type. And you can enter system commands like)RESET and)NMS.

As you worked through the previous chapters, each time you quit APL2 by entering)CONTINUE, APL2 saved the variables and programs you created. When you started another APL2 session, these variables and programs were again available to you. The system command)CONTINUE stored the contents of the active workspace in a storage workspace named CONTINUE. Whenever you enter APL2, APL2 automatically brings the contents of the CONTINUE workspace into the active workspace.

Using)*CONTINUE* to save and recall your work was sufficient for the early exercises. However, it doesn't give you the ability to group variables and programs in any way. To control the saving and recalling of your variables and programs, you use the APL2 library system and system commands for saving, loading, and copying workspaces, and you use the command)*OFF* to exit from APL2.

Section 4.1 – Libraries

Every APL2 user has a private library in which to store workspaces. You can list the names of the workspaces in your private library by typing the system command)*LIB*:

```
     )LIB
CONTINUE
```

If you have saved any other workspaces, their names are listed as well.

Establishing a Workspace from Your Work

Exiting APL2 with)*CONTINUE* is one way to put a workspace into your library. A better way to do this is with the)*SAVE* system command.)*SAVE* **wsname** puts a copy of the current active workspace into your user library under the name **wsname**.

```
     )SAVE LEARN
SAVED 1988-03-20  5.53.54
```

The response tells you the time and date of the save. Now your library contains at least these two workspaces:

```
     )LIB
CONTINUE LEARN
```

A later section discusses the)*SAVE* command in more detail.

Loading a Workspace from the Library:)*LOAD*

Your library's only use is the storage of workspaces. To use a workspace, you must bring its contents into the active workspace. The)*LOAD* command brings the contents of a library workspace into the active workspace:

```
)LOAD LEARN
SAVED 1988-03-20 5.53.54
```

This response tells you the time and date the workspace was last saved. Specifying)*LOAD* causes APL2 to replace the contents of your active workspace with the contents of the library workspace. Be careful not to load a workspace if the active workspace has something you want to keep. To keep the contents of the active workspace, save it before loading a workspace.

Loading a workspace does not change the contents of the library workspace, nor does any work you do in the active workspace change the contents of the library workspace. If you update the active workspace and want the changes to be recorded in the library, you must save the updated workspace into your library.

Removing a Workspace from the Library:)*DROP*

The system command)*DROP* removes a workspace from the library:

```
)DROP CONTINUE
1988-03-27 10.21.42

    )LIB
LEARN
```

Caution: Once you drop a workspace, you cannot retrieve its contents, so, before you drop it, be sure it contains nothing you want.

More about the Workspace *CONTINUE*

The workspace *CONTINUE* gets the contents of the active workspace in three situations:

● If you exit APL2 using)*CONTINUE*.

● If you use the command)*SAVE CONTINUE*.

● If there is a system failure or line drop (if you are attached to a timesharing system that supports this facility).

APL2 automatically loads the workspace *CONTINUE* into your active workspace the next time you enter APL2.

Now that you know how to save and load workspaces, you should not use)*CONTINUE* for permanent storage because you cannot control its contents. Before you exit APL2, save your work in library workspace, using the)*SAVE* command as described in the section "Saving the Active Workspace."

Public Libraries

Only you have access to your private library unless you permit access to other users following the rules established by your installation.

Every APL2 system has one or more public libraries which anyone can use. Public libraries are identified by integers from 1 to 999. You can list the names of workspaces in a public library with the)*LIB* command. For example, to see the contents of library 1:

```
)LIB 1
DISPLAY  EXAMPLES MATHFNS  MEDIT    UTILITY  WSINFO
```

The actual list you see may be different from that shown here.

To access a public library workspace, you must include the library number as part of the command:

```
)LOAD 1 DISPLAY
SAVED 1985-10-05  9.40.21
```

After loading someone else's workspace, you can use)*NMS* to see the names defined in it and you can use an editor to look at the programs. A well-documented workspace contains documentation (typically called *DESCRIBE*) that tells what the workspace does.

Looking at the techniques used in other people's APL2 programs can be a good way to learn more about the language. Looking at these programs also points out the value of good documentation.

Historical note: The very first workspace that was ever saved was 1 *CLEANSPACE*. Some APL2 systems still have this workspace. You can try to load it if you are curious about the date when it was saved.

Section 4.2 – The Active Workspace

Assuming you are no longer using)*CONTINUE*, starting an APL2 session gets you an empty workspace indicated by the message *CLEAR WS*. *CLEAR WS* means that the active workspace has no library name associated with it and contains no variables or programs. You can also clear the contents of the active workspace by using the)*CLEAR* command:

```
     )CLEAR
CLEAR WS
```

Name of the Active Workspace

The system command)*WSID* gives you the name currently associated with the active workspace:

```
     )WSID
CLEAR WS
```

You change the name of the active workspace by using one of these three commands:

- Executing a)*LOAD* command. The active workspace is replaced by the loaded workspace and takes the name of the loaded workspace.

```
     )LOAD LEARN
SAVED 1988-12-05 16.42.27
     )WSID
IS LEARN
```

- Executing a)*SAVE* command with a new workspace name. The active workspace takes the name of the saved workspace. This method works only if the named workspace does not already exist (except for *CONTINUE* which can be saved at any time).

```
      )SAVE TEMP
SAVED 1988-12-05 17.42.27
```

● Executing a *)WSID* command to specify a new workspace name. The active workspace takes the name you enter following the command.

```
      )WSID NEWNAME
WAS TEMP
```

Saving the Active Workspace: *)SAVE*

You've already used the *)SAVE* command to make a permanent library workspace for your work. Now that you know about the name of the active workspace, you are ready for a fuller discussion of the *)SAVE* command.

The *)SAVE* command has two forms, with and without a workspace name:

```
      )SAVE
      )SAVE wsname
```

The first form, *)SAVE*, saves the active workspace in the library space using the same name as the active workspace name. You use this form most often to save a workspace that you previously loaded.

```
      )WSID
IS LEARN
      )SAVE
SAVED 1988-12-05 16.42.27 LEARN
```

Notice that the *SAVED* timestamp includes the active workspace name.

Because *CLEAR WS* means that the active workspace has no name, you can't use *)SAVE* if this is reported as the name of the workspace.

```
      )CLEAR
CLEAR WS
      )SAVE
NOT SAVED, THIS WS IS CLEAR WS
```

The second form,)*SAVE* **wsname**, saves the active workspace under these circumstances:

● If **wsname** is *CONTINUE*.

● If no workspace in the library has the name **wsname**. This form of)*SAVE* establishes a new workspace in the library.

● If **wsname** names a workspace in the library and the active workspace has the same name.

The third item restricts your use of)*SAVE* **wsname**.   This restriction prevents you from inadvertently overriding a workspace library with totally unrelated contents from the active workspace. Using)*WSID* to name a workspace, usually from)*CLEAR WS*, and then using)*SAVE* does not give you this protection.

Suppose you have a workspace *TEACH* in your library.   These examples illustrate the difference between the two commands. This is the first form of)*SAVE*:

```
      )WSID TEACH
WAS CLEAR WS
      )SAVE
SAVED 1988-13-05 12.42.27 TEACH
```

Because the active workspace's name matches one in the library, the)*SAVE* command saves the contents of the active workspace on top of the library workspace.   This means you now have the active workspace's contents saved in the library but you have lost the previous library workspace's contents. In contrast,)*SAVE* **wsname** only executes if the active workspace's name is not the same as any in the library or if the active workspace name matches the name given in the command:

```
      )WSID
CLEAR WS
      )SAVE TEACH
NOT SAVED, THIS WS IS CLEAR WS
```

Replacing the Contents of the Active Workspace

You replace the contents of the active workspace in the following ways:

- Use the)*LOAD* command to bring in a different workspace from the library.

  A duplicate of the library workspace replaces the entire contents of the active workspace. The active workspace takes the name of the loaded workspace.

- Use the)*CLEAR* command to start over again.

Adding to the Contents of the Active Workspace:)*COPY* and)*PCOPY*

When you create variables and write programs, you add these variables and programs to the active workspace. You can also copy variables and programs from library workspaces with the)*COPY* command. Here is the general form of the)*COPY* command:

>)*COPY* **libnumber wsname objname**

In the command, **libnumber** is the number of the library (leave it out if you mean your private library). The workspace name shown here as **wsname**, and **objname** is one or more variable or program names. If an object with the name **objname** already exists in the active workspace, the copied object replaces it. If no objects are listed after the workspace name, all objects from the library workspace are added to the active workspace.

Here is an example of)*COPY*:

```
    )COPY 1 DISPLAY DISPLAY
SAVED 1985-10-05  9.40.21
```

The first *DISPLAY* in the example is the workspace name, and the second is the name of a function in that workspace. If your system has the workspace 1 *DISPLAY*, and it contains an object named *DISPLAY*, the object is copied from it and added to the contents of your active workspace, replacing anything else having the same name. If the named workspace or the objects you want copied do not exist, an error message is displayed.

To protect current objects during copying, you can use the)*PCOPY* command, which copies objects only if the name does not already exist in the active workspace:

```
)PCOPY 1 DISPLAY DISPLAY DISPLAYG
SAVED 1985-10-05  9.40.21
```

If an object name is written in parentheses, then it must be the name of a character matrix in the library workspace that contains one name per row. The group of objects so named are copied into the active workspace. Matrices are discussed in Chapter 5.

Copying does not change the contents of the library workspace—only the active workspace.

Moving APL2 Objects Between Computers:)*IN* and)*OUT*

Workspaces are stored in the APL2 library using some encoding that is efficient for the computer you are using. If you have a second computer that also has an APL2 system, it is unlikely that the second computer can access the library system on the first computer. Therefore, APL2 supports a transfer form for APL2 objects that is independent of the representation used for objects in the workspace. The command)*OUT* takes objects from the active workspace and puts their transfer forms in a host operating system file called a *transfer file*. This file can be transmitted to another computer using standard file transfer facilities supplied with your computer. The receiving computer uses the command)*IN* to add the objects from the transfer file to the active workspace.

There are two forms for both of these commands: without a list of objects and with a list of objects:

●)*OUT filename*— Create a transfer file containing all of the objects from the active workspace.

●)*OUT filename obj1 obj2* ...— Create a transfer file containing only the requested objects from the active workspace.

●)*IN filename*— Add all objects in the transfer file to the active workspace

●)*IN filename obj1 obj2* ...— Add the requested objects in the transfer file to the active workspace.

)*OUT* does not alter the contents of the active workspace.

Removing Objects from the Active Workspace:)ERASE

The)*ERASE* command removes the listed global objects from the active workspace. You can try this system command by doing the following:

```
        )CLEAR
CLEAR WS
        A←B←C←D←E←1
        )NMS
  A.2       B.2       C.2    D.2    E.2
        )ERASE C E

        )NMS
  A.2    B.2    D.2
```

If an object name is written in parentheses, then it must be the name of a character matrix which has one name per row. Each object so named is erased. Matrices are discussed in Chapter 5.

Erasing doesn't change the contents of a library workspace, it changes only the active workspace.

Listing the Contents of the Active Workspace:)NMS,)FNS,)OPS,)VARS

You've been using the system command)*NMS* to list the variables and programs in the active workspace. You can also list just the variables with the command)*VARS*, just the defined functions and sequences with the command)*FNS*, and just the defined operators with the command)*OPS*.

Seeing the State Indicator:)*SIS*

The state indicator keeps track of the execution of expressions and defined functions. Whenever the execution of an expression or a defined function is incomplete (perhaps because of an error), the expression or function statement goes into the state indicator. You can see the state indicator by issuing the system command)*SIS*:

```
        3+
SYNTAX ERROR
        3+
        ^^


        )SIS
 *    3+
      ^^
```

The asterisk indicates that the expression was entered in immediate execution mode.

You clear the last error from the state indicator by entering one right arrow:

```
        →
```

Using → removes all entries up to and including the entry with the * from the state indicator. In this example, the line with the * is the only line in the state indicator. The single right arrow has emptied the state indicator:

```
        )SIS
```

To see the way the state indicator handles a function whose execution is not completed, do this exercise: First save anything that you want to keep. Then clear the active workspace and enter the following definition exactly as shown (assuming that you are using *EDITOR* 1):

```
        )CLEAR
CLEAR WS


      ∇ Z←AMT PVALUE NI;RATE
 [1]    RATE←NI[2]×.01
 [2]    Z←AMT÷1+NI[1]×RAT
 [3] ∇
```

Execution of the function stops on line 2 because the name *RAT* on line 2 doesn't have a value and you get this message:

```
      12000 PVALUE 5 10
VALUE ERROR
PVALUE[2]    Z←AMT÷1+NI[1]×RAT
                               ∧
```

The state indicator shows the line that contains the error as well as the immediate execution line that called the function:

```
      )SIS
PVALUE[2]    Z←AMT÷1+NI[1]×RAT
                               ∧
*   12000 PVALUE 5 10
      ∧       ∧
```

A single right arrow clears the state indicator down to and including the entry with the *, again leaving the state indicator clear.

```
      →
      )SIS
```

If you neglect to clear the state indicator after each error, you must enter a → for each immediate execution line. Alternatively, you can use the system command *)RESET* to clear the entire state indicator. (Chapter 7 discusses the use of the state indicator in debugging programs.)

Exercises for Section 4.2

1. As you gain experience in writing programs in APL2, you will write utility functions in one workspace and then use them in others. As you identify these programs, it is a good idea to gather them together into a *TOOLBOX* workspace. You can then treat these functions as extensions to the APL2 language. When you sit down to write a new application, you don't need to start from scratch each time. Rather, you use parts of programs you've written before.

   a. Write the commands you need to create a *TOOLBOX* workspace.

   b. Write the commands to put the program *AVG* from your *LEARN* workspace into the *TOOLBOX* workspace.

2. Match the system commands shown the first column with the corresponding statements in the second column:

___ 1.   ) *OFF*

___ 2.   ) *LIB*

___ 3.   ) *WSID*

___ 4.   ) *ERASE*

___ 5.   ) *SAVE*

___ 6.   ) *COPY*

___ 7.   ) *VARS*

___ 8.   ) *NMS*

___ 9.   ) *PCOPY*

___ 10.) *DROP*

___ 11.) *FNS*

___ 12.) *RESET*

___ 13.) *LOAD*

___ 14.) *CONTINUE*

___ 15.) *CLEAR*

___ 16.) *OPS*

a. List all the named objects in an active workspace.

b. Initiate an APL2 session.

c. Automatically save the active workspace and terminate the session.

d. Delete named objects from the active workspace.

e. Delete all objects from the active workspace.

f. List all workspace names in a library.

g. List all function names in the active workspace.

h. List all the variable names in the active workspace.

i. Terminate the APL2 session without saving objects in the active workspace.

j. Fetch named workspace and replace the active workspace.

k. List all operator names in the active workspace

l. Fetch a named workspace or selected named objects overlaying similarly named ones in the active workspace.

m. Fetch a named workspace or selected named objects without overlaying similarly named ones in the active workspace.

n. Put a copy of the active workspace into your library.

o. Put a copy of a named object into the library.

p. Query or change the name of an active workspace.

q. Clear all or the first part of the state indicator.

r. Delete a workspace from your library.

Chapter 5

Working with Arrays

In the previous chapters, you worked only with scalar and vector data. APL2 allows you to represent data organized in other ways. This chapter shows different ways of arranging data in arrays and discusses functions that create, measure, and manipulate arrays.

Before continuing with this chapter, remember to)*LOAD* your *LEARN* workspace so you'll have access to the work you've done in the first four chapters. When you are finished, be sure to)*SAVE LEARN* before exiting APL2.

Section 5.1 – Properties of Arrays

APL2 has two types of data: numbers and characters. A collection of data is an *array*. An array is a rectangular arrangement of data called the *items* of the array. Each item is a number, a character, or another array. The number of items in an array is the *count* of the array.

An array that has rows and columns is sometimes called a *matrix* or a *table*. A matrix can be pictured as a rectangle:

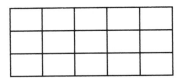

Notice that in this rectangle, all the rows have the same length, and all the columns have the same length.

It is not the geometry that is important but rather the fact that every row of an array has the same number of items and every column in an array contains the same number of items. That is, the length of a row (or column) is the same for all rows (or columns). The term *rectangular* is, then, extended to collections of data organized along any number of independent directions.

The directions along which data in an array is arranged are the *axes* of the array. The number of directions is the *rank* of the array. Thus a table having rows and columns has two axes and a rank of 2. A vector (such as 1 2 3) has one axis and a rank of 1. A single number (such as 3) is not arranged along any axes and so has rank 0. Ranks higher than 2 are allowed up to some implementation limit (typically 64).

APL2 has special names for arrays that have rank 0, 1, or 2:

● Rank 0 – Scalar

● Rank 1 – Vector

● Rank 2 – Matrix

You should attach no other significance to these words. Scalar means only rank 0. A single number or character must be called a simple scalar because it is possible to have a scalar whose item is a non-scalar array. Vector means only rank 1. You don't need to know vector algebra to understand APL2 vectors (although a vector in algebra is closely related to an APL2 simple numeric vector).

Because arrays are rectangular, a simple vector of integers gives the lengths of each axis. This vector is the *shape* of the array. It is this vector that is returned as the result of the **shape** (ρ) function introduced in Chapter 2.

Arrays also have a property called *depth*. Depth is best understood by looking at a few examples.

Simple scalars are depth-zero arrays. Here are two depth-zero arrays:

```
2.345
'A'
```

Any other array that contains only items of depth 0 has a depth of 1. These two arrays have depth 1:

```
2  3  4
'ABC'
```

An array that contains an item of depth 1 and no item of greater depth has depth 2. Here are two depth-2 arrays:

```
(2  3)  (4  5)  (6  7)
'AB'  'CD'  'XYZ'
```

In general, an array that contains an item of depth n and no item of greater depth, has depth $n + 1$ (for n not less than 0). Here's a vector of depth 4:

```
(((2  3  4)  (5  6  7))  (2  3  4))  5
```

Arrays have two classifications according to depth that this book uses in later discussions:

- Simple array — Array of depth 0 or 1
- Nested array — Array of depth 2 or more

Exercises for Section 5.1

1. Classify the following arrays as scalar or vector:

   a. `'ABC'`
   b. `'A' 'B' 'C'`
   c. `'A' 'B'`
   d. `'A'`
   e. `2.3`
   f. `2 3`

2. Classify the following arrays as simple or nested. State the shape and the depth of each:

   a. `'A' 'B' 'C'`
   b. `'A' 'B'`
   c. `'A'`
   d. `'A' 'B' 'C' 2.3`
   e. `'ABC' 2.3`
   f. `('ABC' 2.3) 'D'`
   g. `((ι3)(2.3 'ABC'))4`

3. Can a scalar be an empty array?

4. Is there such a thing as a scalar that contains no data?

Section 5.2 — Building and Displaying Arrays

Using vector notation, you can construct any vector of length two or longer as long as its items are scalars or vectors of length two or longer. You cannot use vector notation to construct a one-item vector, a zero-item vector, or a matrix.

The function **reshape** (ρ), together with vector notation, can form any array. This section introduces that function and discusses the rules governing the display of arrays.

Reshape

The function **reshape** (ρ) takes the items from its right argument and forms them in the shape specified by the left argument. For example, the following expression arranges the numbers from 1 through 24 in a matrix (rank 2):

```
      A← 4 6ρι24
      A
  1  2  3  4  5  6
  7  8  9 10 11 12
 13 14 15 16 17 18
 19 20 21 22 23 24

      DISPLAY A
.→──────────────────.
↓ 1  2  3  4  5  6│
│ 7  8  9 10 11 12│
│13 14 15 16 17 18│
│19 20 21 22 23 24│
'~──────────────────'
```

This array has four rows and six columns. When given a matrix, *DISPLAY* puts arrows on the left edge and the top edge.

The examples use **interval** (ι) as a convenient means of generating data, but the right argument could be any array containing any data and the discussion of **reshape** would remain the same. Just remember that the left argument of **reshape** is the shape of the desired array and the right argument is the set of values that become the items of the desired array.

The rank of the result of **reshape** is the length of the left argument. In the preceding example, the left argument has two integers, and so the resulting array has rank 2.

You can use **reshape** to form the same data into other structures as well. In the following example, **reshape** produces a rank-3 structure:

```
      B←2 3 4ρ⍳24
      B
 1  2  3  4
 5  6  7  8
 9 10 11 12

13 14 15 16
17 18 19 20
21 22 23 24
```

The array *B* has two planes, three rows, and four columns. Notice that the rank-3 display is composed of two rank-2 displays which are separated by a blank row. The arrangement and spacing gives you a visual hint that the array is a rank-3 array. The result of applying *DISPLAY* to a rank-3 array has two left edges each marked with an arrow:

```
      DISPLAY B
 . .→──────────.
↓↓↓ 1  2  3  4│
 ││ 5  6  7  8│
 ││ 9 10 11 12│
 ││           │
 ││13 14 15 16│
 ││17 18 19 20│
 ││21 22 23 24│
 ' '~──────────'
```

The right argument of **reshape** need not be a vector. APL2 ignores the structure of the right argument and uses its items in *row-major order* (that is, all items from row 1 are used before any items from row 2, and so on). Thus, *B* could have been defined from *A* as follows:

```
      B←2 3 4ρA
```

You form higher-rank arrays in exactly the same way. Here is the construction of a rank-4 array:

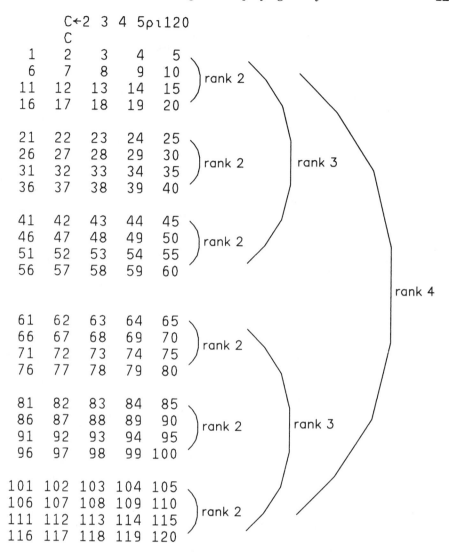

```
C←2 3 4 5ρι120
C
 1   2   3   4   5
 6   7   8   9  10
11  12  13  14  15
16  17  18  19  20

21  22  23  24  25
26  27  28  29  30
31  32  33  34  35
36  37  38  39  40

41  42  43  44  45
46  47  48  49  50
51  52  53  54  55
56  57  58  59  60


61  62  63  64  65
66  67  68  69  70
71  72  73  74  75
76  77  78  79  80

81  82  83  84  85
86  87  88  89  90
91  92  93  94  95
96  97  98  99 100

101 102 103 104 105
106 107 108 109 110
111 112 113 114 115
116 117 118 119 120
```

Notice that the rank-4 array appears as two rank-3 arrays separated by two blank lines. Each rank-3 array appears as three rank-2 arrays separated by a blank line.

In general, in a rank-*n* array, its rank *n*-1 parts are displayed separated by *n*-2 blank lines (for *n* greater than 1).

In higher-rank arrays, like *C* above, the rightmost axis is called *columns*, the second from the rightmost axis is called *rows*, and the third from the right is usually called *planes*. The other axes are not normally given names but are sometimes collectively called *hyperplanes*.

It is not necessary to use all the items from the right argument in producing the result of **reshape**. The following expression uses only the first six items from the right argument:

```
      D←2 3ρA
      D
 1 2 3
 4 5 6
```

If the right argument does not have enough items to define every item in the result, the items are used over and over again as necessary as in this example:

```
      E←3 3ρ 1 0 0 0
      E
 1 0 0
 0 1 0
 0 0 1
```

The 1 is used three times, and each zero is used twice.

If the right argument has only one item, it is used to define every item of the result:

```
      F←3 3ρ0
      F
 0 0 0
 0 0 0
 0 0 0
```

Since **reshape** can use items repeatedly, you can use it to easily produce vectors of repeating values:

```
      9ρ 1 2 3
 1 2 3 1 2 3 1 2 3
```

All the examples of **reshape** so far have used numbers in the right argument. In fact, the right argument could contain anything and the result would be a rearrangement of those things. Here's a hypothetical example (don't try to enter this):

```
      G←2 2ρ (item 1) (item 2) (item 3) (item 4)
```

G will have two rows and two columns with the four items arranged like this:

item 1	item 2
item 3	item 4

Each item in the matrix is any array at all.

Here's an example that is suitable for entry:

```
        G←2 2ρ A 'TWO' F (3 4)
        G
  1   2   3   4   5   6    TWO
  7   8   9  10  11  12
 13  14  15  16  17  18
 19  20  21  22  23  24

 0 0 0                      3 4
 0 0 0
 0 0 0
```

```
        DISPLAY G
  .→------------------------------------.
  ↓ .→--------------------.  .→--. 
  | ↓  1   2   3   4   5   6| |TWO|
  |    7   8   9  10  11  12| '---'
  | 13  14  15  16  17  18|
  | 19  20  21  22  23  24|
  | '~--------------------'
  | .→----.               .→--.
  | ↓0 0 0|               |3 4|
  | |0 0 0|               '~--'
  | |0 0 0|
  | '~----'
  '∊------------------------------------'
```

The right argument is a four-item vector. The first and third items come from the variables *A* and *F* defined in earlier examples. The second and fourth items are the vectors shown. Remember that writing four arrays next to each other produces a four-item vector.

The same result could have been computed without using the variables *A* and *F* as follows:

```
        G←2 2ρ (4 6ρι24) 'TWO' (3 3ρ0) (3 4)
```

Because you can use **reshape** itself to form any item in the right argument of another **reshape**, you can construct every possible APL2 array using the function **reshape** together with vector notation.

Reshape produces arrays of any rank, while vector notation can produce only arrays of rank 1. **Reshape** can also produce rank-1 arrays including those that vector notation cannot express—namely, vectors of length less than 2.

```
      1ρ5
5
```

This is not the scalar 5 even though it is printed the same way. It is a one-item vector containing 5 as its only item:

```
      DISPLAY 1ρ5
.→.
│5│
'~'
```

Reshape can produce a vector with no items at all:

```
      0ρ5
```

This result is an empty vector. It is displayed on one line with no data.

An empty array may be an item of a non-empty array:

```
      H← 2 3ρ(2 3)(ι0)(0 5ρ0)(4 5) '' 'ABC'
      H
 2 3


 4 5     ABC
```

Notice that the empty arrays yield spaces in the result.

DISPLAY puts φ on the left edge if a matrix has zero rows, and ⊖ on the top edge if the matrix has zero columns:

```
     DISPLAY H
 .→─────────────────────────
↓→─────────────────────────┐
│ ┌→──┐  ┌⊖┐  ┌→────────┐ │
│ │2 3│  │0│  ǀ0 0 0 0 0│ │
│ └~──┘  └~┘  └~────────┘ │
│                          │
│ ┌→──┐  ┌⊖┐  ┌→──┐        │
│ │4 5│  │ │  │ABC│        │
│ └~──┘  └_┘  └───┘        │
│ ∊────────────────────────
```

Default Display of Arrays

You've seen several examples of the presentation of arrays on an output device. Basically, these presentations are rectangular arrangements of the items. Knowing the rules that govern these displays can help you interpret what you see. The rules may vary somewhat on different implementations, so check the documentation for your implementation to be sure. Here is the set of rules for the IBM APL2 implementation and some examples.

1. The width of a column depends only on the data in the column. Each column is only as wide as necessary. Here's a simple array of numbers:

```
1  1  1   1    1    1     1     1
2  4  8  16   32   64   128   256
3  9 27  81  243  729  2187  6561
4 16 64 256 1024 4096 16384 65536
```

2. At least one blank separates any column containing a number from adjacent columns. Numbers are right-justified in a column on the decimal point. There is no separation between adjacent columns that contain only scalar characters. Here's a simple 3 by 5 array where columns 1, 2, and 3 are numbers, columns 4, 5, and 6 are characters, and column 7 is a mixture of numbers and characters:

```
1  2  3 DOG 5
8 19 10 CAT 7
8  7  6 MAN D
```

3. If a column contains only character vectors or scalars, the characters are left-justified. Here's a two-column array where column 1 has character vectors and column 2 has single numbers:

```
YEAR    1988
MONTH      2
DAY       23
```

4. If a column contains character vectors and numbers, the
   character vectors are right-justified. Here's an array where each
   item in row 1 is a four-item character vector and every other
   item is a number:

```
COL1 COL2 COL3 COL4 COL5 COL6  COL7   COL8
   1    1    1    1    1    1     1      1
   2    4    8   16   32   64   128    256
   3    9   27   81  243  729  2187   6561
   4   16   64  256 1024 4096 16384 65536
```

5. Other nested items are displayed with a leading and trailing
   blank for each level of nesting (depth). Here's an example
   you've seen before:

```
1  2  3  4    TWO
5  6  7  8
9 10 11 12

0 0 0        3 4
0 0 0
```

   Three blanks separate the columns: one is the trailing blank for
   the nested items in column 1; one is the blank separating
   non-character columns; and one is the leading blank for the
   nested items in column 2.

6. Arrays that are wider than the output device are truncated near
   the right margin, then continued on subsequent lines indented
   six spaces. Here is a five-by-eleven numeric matrix presented on
   an output device 40 characters wide:

```
1  1   1   1    1     1      1        1
2  4   8  16   32    64    128      256
3  9  27  81  243   729   2187     6561
4 16  64 256 1024  4096  16384    65536
5 25 125 625 3125 15625  78125   390625
```

```
        1        1         1
      512     1024      2048
    19683    59049    177147
   262144  1048576   4194304
  1953125  9765625  48828125
```

Does knowing the rules for output allow you to always unambiguously deduce the properties of an array, given its display? Here's an output. Can you determine what array it represents?

```
  1 2 3
```

Did you guess a three-item vector of the integers 1, 2, and 3? It does look like that and it's a good guess, but here are some expressions that produce the same output:

```
    1 '2' 3
    1 3ρ 1 2 3
    '1 2 3'
```

In general, you cannot be sure what you're looking at. APL2 displays data without explicit indication of its type or structure. APL2 output is designed to display data in a pleasing form. If you need to know exactly what the value, type, and structure of an array are, you must apply functions to the data. Section 5.3 discusses the functions you use to determine this information about an array.

Applying the *DISPLAY* Function to Arrays

You have seen examples of *DISPLAY* applied to all types of arrays. The following table summarizes the symbols the *DISPLAY* function uses:

	Placement	Meaning
_	beneath a character	scalar character
→	top edge of box	vector or higher-rank array
~	lower edge of box	numeric data
+	lower edge of box	mixed data
⊖	top edge of box	empty vector or higher-rank array
↓	left edge of box	matrix or higher-rank array
φ	left edge of box	empty matrix or higher-rank array
∈	lower edge of box	nested array

Table 5.1 Summary of *DISPLAY* Symbols

Exercises for Section 5.2

1. State the shape and result of the following expressions:

    a. 4ρ'*ABCD*'
    b. 6ρ'*ABCD*'
    c. 3ρ'*ABCD*'
    d. 3ρ'*AB*' '*CD*'
    e. 4 1ρ '*ABCD*'
    f. 2 3ρ '*AB*' 5
    g. 2 2ρ '*BUILT*' 25 '*SHIPPED*' 20

2. Write an expression whose value displays as five blank lines.

3. Create a defined function to produce *N* blank lines.

4. Given the following variables:

    $$D \leftarrow 5\ 10\ 15\ 20\ 1\ 3\ 6\ 12$$
    $$A \leftarrow 3\ 2$$
    $$R \leftarrow 4$$
    $$C \leftarrow 3$$

    Write a general expression to build an array from *D* to reflect each of the following specifications:

    a. An array with as many rows as the value of *R* and as many columns as the value of *C*.

    b. An array with as many rows as *D* has items and three columns.

    c. An array with as many rows as 3 times the number of items in *D* and as many columns as the product of *R* and *C*.

5. An identity matrix is a matrix in which every item is zero except those along the main diagonal, which are 1's. Here is a 3-by-3 identity matrix:

    ```
    1 0 0
    0 1 0
    0 0 1
    ```

    Given *N*, a nonnegative scalar integer, write an expression using **reshape** and **catenate** to produce an *N*-by-*N* identity matrix.

6. Write an expression to produce a 2-by-3 array that contains no data.

7. Given non-empty array *AR*, write an expression using only
    reshape and vector notation to produce the following arrays:

    a. A five-item vector with each item being *AR*.
    b. A vector whose items are the items of *AR*.
    c. A scalar whose only item is *AR*.

Section 5.3 – Measuring Arrays

This section discusses the main functions used to compute the
properties of arrays: **shape**, **rank**, **count**, and **depth**.

Shape

You have seen **shape** applied to vectors and scalars. It applies to
any array and returns as its result an integer vector representing the
shape of the array. Here are the shapes of some of the arrays used
in the examples of **reshape**:

```
        A←4 6ρι24
        ρA
    4 6
        B←2 3 4ρι24
        ρB
    2 3 4
        C←2 3 4 5ρι120
        ρC
    2 3 4 5
```

Shape applied to an empty array produces a vector containing at
least one zero:

```
        ρι0
    0
        ρ 0 5ρ0
    0 5
```

The functions **shape** and **reshape** are related by the following
identity:

$$A \longleftrightarrow (\rho A)\rho A \qquad \text{for any array } A$$

This identity says that if you reshape *A* to the shape it already has, you get the same *A* as the result.

Rank

Shape also measures the rank of an array. Because **shape** measures any array, it can measure the result of the application of **shape** itself. Thus, in the expression ρρ*A*, the rightmost ρ produces a vector containing the length of each axis. The second ρ counts the number of items in the length vector, and so computes the rank of an array:

```
        ρρA
2
        ρρB
3
        ρρC
4
```

Remember that **shape** always returns a vector. Therefore, the numbers produced are one-item vectors, not simple scalars:

```
        DISPLAY ρρA
  .→.
 |2|
  '~'
```

Count

You can compute the number of items in an array from its shape. Clearly an array of shape 2 3 5 has 2×3×5 items. A **multiplication-reduction** (×/) computes the count of an array:

```
        ×/ρA
24
        ×/ρB
24
        ×/ρC
120
```

In a nested array, the items of the items do not contribute to the count. Thus, the count of a two-item vector is 2 no matter how much data is in each item:

```
      ×/ρ(1 2)(2 5ρι10)
2
```

You use **each** to measure the count of each item in an array:

```
      ×/¨ρ¨(1 2)(2 5ρι10)
2 10
```

A scalar has one item:

```
      ×/ρ2.345
1
```

Depth

The monadic function **depth** (≡) measures the depth of an array. Applied to a simple scalar, **depth** returns a zero:

```
      ≡5
0
      ≡'X'
0
```

Unlike **shape** (ρ), **depth** (≡) returns a simple scalar:

```
      DISPLAY  ≡5

0
```

The depth of other arrays containing only simple scalars is 1:

```
      ≡A
1
      ≡C
1
```

The depth of an array that contains at least one depth-1 array and no array of greater depth has depth 2:

```
      ≡G
2
```

The depth of an array is easy to determine from the *DISPLAY*
function output. If you draw a line from outside the display to some
simple scalar, just count 1 for every box you enter and ¯1 for every
box you exit. The resulting number is the depth of that scalar. The
largest number you get by doing this to every simple scalar in the
array is the depth of the array.

Here is the *DISPLAY* of a depth-4 array:

$$T \leftarrow (2\ 2\rho\,'ABC'\ 'DE'\ ((1\uparrow 5)(\iota 2))\ 10)\ 'ABC'$$
$$DISPLAY\ T$$

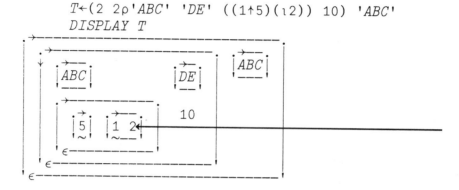

You can see that drawing a line to the number 1 or 2 from the right
(or to the number 5 from the left) will cross the most lines (four) so
the array is a depth-4 array.

Note that **depth** ($\equiv$) tells you nothing about the shape or contents
of an array—only the maximum depth of nesting.

Exercises for Section 5.3

1. Give the shape, rank, count, and depth of the following arrays. Write a one-item vector N as $1\rho N$ to distinguish it in your response from a scalar.

   a. 2
   b. 3 4
   c. 'ABC'
   d. 'AB'
   e. 'A'
   f. 'A' 'B' 'C'
   g. 'A' 'B' 'C' 2.3
   h. (1 2 3)(4 5)
   i. 'ABC' 2.3
   j. ('ABC' 2.3) 'D'
   k. ((ι3)('ABC' 2.3)) 4

2. Write an expression that describes the result of **shape-each** ($\rho\ddot{\ }$) applied to each expression in exercise 1. For example, for the array (1 2 3) (4 5) 6 write (1ρ3) (1ρ2) (ι0).

3. Create for your toolbox a monadic function $DISP$ that produces the following output:

```
          DISP ι¨ι3
     SHAPE:  3  DEPTH:  2  COUNT:  3
   .→─────────────────────────.
   ↓ .→. .→──. .→────.        │
   │ │1│ │1 2│ │1 2 3│        │
   │ '~' '~──' '~────'        │
   '∈─────────────────────────'
```

4. Apply $DISP$ of the previous problem to the output of the $DISPLAY$ function applied to a nested array as in this example:

   $DISP\ DISPLAY\ ι¨ι4$

5. Given the following variables:

$$A \leftarrow 2\ 3\rho\iota 6$$
$$B \leftarrow 5$$
$$C \leftarrow 'APL2'$$
$$D \leftarrow A\ B\ C$$
$$E \leftarrow A\ B$$

State the value, shape, and depth of the result of each of these expressions:

a. *D*
b. *A* 8
c. *A* 8−2
d. *A* (8−2)
e. *A* *A*+100
f. *A* (*A*+100)
g. *C*
h. '*A*' '*P*' '*L*'
i. '*APL*'
j. '*A*' '*P*''*L*'
k. '*AP*' '*L*'
l. *A* *B* × 10 *A*
m. 1 (2 3)+(1 2 3) 4
n. (*D*)(≡*D*)
o. *A*(10 (20 30))
p. *B*+0 1 2
q. *B* (*B*+1)(*B*+2)
r. *B*(*B*+1)*B*+2
s. *B* *B*+1 (*B*+2)
t. *B* *B*+1 *B*+2

Section 5.4 — Unshaping and Nested Shaping of Arrays

Ravel and **enlist** are functions that ignore structure and rearrange their arguments into vectors. **Enclose** and **disclose** are functions that change the depth of arrays.

Ravel

The monadic function **ravel** might be compared to unraveling a ball of string. The items of its argument are simply arranged in a vector. Because all the items of the arguments are kept intact, the result of **ravel** preserves the count of the argument. Except when applied to a scalar, **ravel** also preserves depth. The rank of the result is always 1. Here is an example:

```
      B←2 3 4ρι24
      ,B
 1 2 3 4 5 6 7 8 9 10 11 12 13 14 15 16 17 18 19
      20 21 22 23 24
      ρ,B
24
```

```
      G←2 2ρ (4 6ρι24) 'TWO' (3 3ρ0) (3 4)
      ,G
   1  2  3  4  5  6    TWO     0 0 0    3 4
   7  8  9 10 11 12            0 0 0
  13 14 15 16 17 18            0 0 0
  19 20 21 22 23 24
      ρ,G
4
      ρρ,G
1
```

Ravel does not drop or add items to an array—it merely rearranges items into a vector. If an item of the argument is empty, it appears empty in the result:

```
H← 2 3ρ(2 3)(ι0)(0 5ρ0)(4 5) '' 'ABC'
 ,H
```
2 3   4 5   ABC

        DISPLAY ,H

```
.→─────────────────────────────────────────────.
| .→─.  .⊖.  .→─────────.  .→─.  .⊖.  .→──.     |
| |2 3| |0| ⌽|0 0 0 0 0|  |4 5| | | |ABC|      |
| '~──'  '~'  '~─────────'  '~──'  '_'  '───'    |
'∈─────────────────────────────────────────────'
```

Ravel is related to **reshape** by the following identity:

$$,A \quad \longleftrightarrow \quad (\times/\rho A)\rho A \qquad \text{for any array } A$$

Recall that $\times/\rho A$ computes the count of items in an array. A single number as the left argument of **reshape** specifies the creation of a vector of that length. **Ravel**, like **reshape**, is often used to overcome a limitation of vector notation. Vector notation cannot express a vector of length less than 2. Whereas 2 3 is a two-item vector, 2 is not a one-item vector. It is a simple scalar. To produce a one-item vector from a simple scalar, you can enter either of the following equivalent expressions:

```
        ,2
2
        1ρ2
2
```

Enlist

The monadic function **enlist** (ϵ) produces a vector but does not preserve any of the array's properties—rank, rank, shape, depth, or count. **Enlist** always returns a simple vector that contains every simple scalar contained anywhere in the array. Here's an example:

```
        G←2 2ρ (4 6ρι24) 'TWO' (3 3ρ0) (3 4)
        εG
  1 2 3 4 5 6 7 8 9 10 11 12 13 14 15 16 17 18 19
        20 21 22 23 24 TWO 0 0 0 0 0 0 0 0 0 3 4
        ρεG
38
```

Notice that items in the result are selected in row-major order. Every simple scalar in the first item is listed before any scalar in the following items.

If the argument to **enlist** contains empty items, they do not contribute to the result:

```
        H← 2 3ρ(2 3)(ι0)(0 5ρ0)(4 5) '' 'ABC'
        εH
  2 3 4 5 ABC
        ρεH
7
```

```
        DISPLAY εH
  .→----------.
  |2 3 4 5 ABC|
  '+----------'
```

If the argument to **enlist** is a simple array, the result is the same as **ravel**:

$$,S \quad \longleftrightarrow \quad \epsilon S \qquad \text{for simple array } S$$

Nested Reshaping of an Array: Enclose

Reshape (ρ) merely rearranges the items of its argument, possibly repeating some of them. Depth is only increased when a scalar is reshaped into a non-scalar. If not all the items from the right argument are used in the result, the depth of the result might be less than the depth of the argument:

```
      ≡ 1 2 'ABC'
2
      ≡ 2ρ1 2 'ABC'
1
```

The monadic function **enclose** ($\subset$), like **reshape**, only rearranges data in an array; but, except for simple scalars, it does produce a result whose depth is one greater than the depth of its argument. The **enclose** of a simple scalar is the simple scalar. Its depth does not change.

Enclose has only one purpose: the production of scalars. Given an array, **enclose** produces the scalar that contains that array as its only item. Whenever you see the **enclose** function, think of scalars.

The rank of the result of **enclose** is always zero—that is, **enclose** always produces a scalar. The following identity expresses this fact:

$$,0 \longleftrightarrow \rho\rho\subset A \qquad \text{for all } A$$

Whenever you are not interested in the array's structure, you can use **enclose** to turn that array into a scalar. For example, if you are writing an application that deals with people's names, the fact that the name *Shakespeare* contains 11 characters may be of no interest.

```
      ρ'SHAKESPEARE'
11
```

By enclosing the 11-character vector, you may treat the resulting scalar as a unit of data within the application.

```
      ρ⊂'SHAKESPEARE'
←——(empty vector)
```

In Chapter 2, you saw that the following expression catenates three new names onto a vector of names:

```
      WHAT←⍳0
      WHAT←WHAT,'LPS' 'TAPES' 'CDS'
```

This expression added three items onto *WHAT* because the right argument of **catenate** is a three-item vector. Suppose you want to append one more item to the vector: the character string '*VIDEOTAPE*'. You might be tempted to write the following (don't do it):

```
      WHAT←WHAT,'VIDEOTAPES'
```

If you wrote that expression, the right argument to **catenate** would be a ten-item vector and you would append ten letters—not what you want to do. You really want to append one name. Use **enclose** to make the nine-item vector into a scalar with one item:

```
      WHAT←WHAT,⊂'VIDEOTAPES'
```

Now you've appended one name to the list *WHAT*:

```
      WHAT
LPS TAPES CDS VIDEOTAPES
```

Note: IBM's APL2 Release 3 adds a dyadic function **partition**, which is related to **enclose**. For information on this new function, see Appendix F.

Nested Reshaping of an Array: Disclose

The monadic function **disclose** in its simplest form undoes what **enclose** does. Given a scalar argument, **disclose** produces the array that is the only item of the scalar:

```
      SX←⊂2 3⍴⍳6
      ⊃SX
1 2 3
4 5 6
```

The following relationship is always true between **enclose** and **disclose**:

$$A \quad \longleftrightarrow \quad \supset \subset A$$

But **disclose** does more than undo the result of **enclose**. For example, **disclose** can turn a nested vector into a matrix, with one row per product and one column per type of information.

Earlier you worked with this vector:

```
PRD←('LPS' 6.95)('TAPES' 7.95)('CDS' 12.95)
PRD
```
```
LPS 6.95     TAPES 7.95     CDS 12.95
```

This structure is a depth-3 array that contains one item per product. Each product item contains two fields: one for the product name and one for product cost. **Disclose** turns this vector into a matrix with each item providing data for one row:

```
PRDTBL←⊃PRD
PRDTBL
LPS       6.95
TAPES     7.95
CDS      12.95
```

This result is a depth-2 array with one row per product:

```
ρPRDTBL
3 2
```

Exercises for Section 5.4

1. State the shape and depth of the results of following expressions:

    a. ,2 3ρι6
    b. ε2 3ρι6
    c. ,2 2ρ 'ABC:' 5 'XY:' 6
    d. ε2 2ρ 'ABC:' 5 'XY:' 6

2. Given the variables:

    $$A\leftarrow 3\ 4\rho\iota 12$$
    $$B\leftarrow 3$$
    $$C\leftarrow \text{'}APL\text{'}$$
    $$D\leftarrow A\ B\ C$$

    State the shape and depth of the result of each of the following expressions:

    a. B C
    b. D
    c. ⊂D
    d. ⊂⊂D
    e. ⊂B C
    f. ⊃B C
    g. ⊃⊂A
    h. ⊃ B (B×5) (B×10)
    i. ⊃ A (A×10)

3. Write a three-item vector whose enlist is empty.

4. Write an expression to construct a 2-by-3 matrix. Each item should be the name 'RAY'.

5. Given a simple vector of non-negative integers, write an expression to produce a horizontal bar chart. For example, from V←4 1 3 0 2, the expression should produce the following simple character matrix:

6. Write an expression that replaces the second item of the vector V with the matrix M.

7.　Let *VV* be a vector of words like the following:

$$VV \leftarrow 'DISTRIBUTION' \ 'OF' \ 'SCORES'$$

Write an expression that returns a simple character vector containing the words separated by a single blank. For the example *VV*, this result is

$$'DISTRIBUTION \ OF \ SCORES \ '$$

Section 5.5 — Manipulating an Array along an Axis

One source of APL2's power is the fact that the primitive operations apply to whole arrays at one time. Sometimes it is useful to think of arrays as split apart in some organized way so you can apply a function to each of the pieces. For example, a matrix can be split up in the following two ways. You can split the matrix into vectors along axis 1:

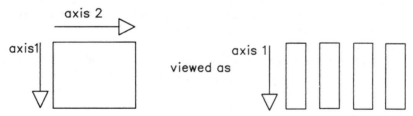

Splitting along axis 1

You can split the matrix into vectors along axis 2:

Splitting along axis 2

Similarly, a rank-3 array can be split into vectors three ways: along each of its three axes.

Many APL2 primitives allow specification of an axis to indicate the type of split. The axis is specified in square brackets on the right of the function. For example, ↑[1] indicates a **take** along the first axis.

Some dyadic functions with axis split both of their arguments, while others split only one of their arguments.

Here is a general outline of how functions with axis form their result:

1. Split the appropriate arguments along the axis specified.
2. Apply the function (as defined without an axis) to each piece.
3. Put the resulting pieces back together again in some appropriate way.

The description of the function will tell you which arguments are split and how the pieces are put back together.

The best way to understand how functions with axis operate is to understand the relationship between the shape of the arguments and the shape of the result. The shape of the result is the same as the shape of an argument, with the exception of the axes specified. Those axes may be longer or shorter than the corresponding axes in the argument. The specified axes may not appear in the result at all or new axes may appear.

If you don't specify an axis for a primitive, one of three defaults applies:

● Function applies along the rightmost axis.
● Function applies along the leftmost axis.
● Function applies to all axes.

The default taken is also part of the description of each function.

The following sections discuss seven operations that allow an axis specification:

- **take**
- **drop**
- **catenate**
- **ravel**
- **reduction**
- **enclose**
- **disclose**

You have worked with these operations before, so the discussions concentrate on their use with axis specification.

Take and Drop with Axis

You apply **take** and **drop** to arrays of rank 2 or greater by specifying the axis along which the vector definition is to apply. Here is an example:

```
      A← 4 6ρι24
      A
 1  2  3  4  5  6
 7  8  9 10 11 12
13 14 15 16 17 18
19 20 21 22 23 24

      3↑[1] A
 1  2  3  4  5  6
 7  8  9 10 11 12
13 14 15 16 17 18
```

Here is the analysis of this example using the general outline for functions with axis specification. Given the original four-by-six array:

```
 1  2  3  4  5  6
 7  8  9 10 11 12
13 14 15 16 17 18
19 20 21 22 23 24
```

- Split the appropriate arguments along the axis specified.

  Take splits the right argument as shown here:

1	2	3	4	5	6
7	8	9	10	11	12
13	14	15	16	17	18
19	20	21	22	23	24

(Note that these pictures are not using the *DISPLAY* function.) The four-by-six matrix is split into six four-item vectors. The vectors are drawn vertically to show the orientation of the axis that was split.

● Apply the function without an axis to each piece:

1	2	3	4	5	6
7	8	9	10	11	12
13	14	15	16	17	18

The vector definition of **take** is applied to each of the four-item vectors, producing a set of three-item vectors.

● Put the resulting pieces back together again in some appropriate way:

```
 1  2  3  4  5  6
 7  8  9 10 11 12
13 14 15 16 17 18
```

The six three-item vectors are reassembled into a three-by-six matrix.

Notice that axis 2 (the one not specified in square brackets) has the same length as before. Axis 1 (the one specified in square brackets) is shorter.

You should be able to apply the same analysis to the following example:

```
      3↓[2] A
 4  5  6
10 11 12
16 17 18
22 23 24
```

Notice again, the axis specified in brackets changes length and the axis not specified stays the same length.

If more than one axis is specified, APL2 applies the function independently along each axis:

```
      W←3 4 2ρι24
      2 3↑[1 2] W
1   2
3   4
5   6

 9 10
11 12
13 14
```

Because APL2 applies the function independently along each axis, the following is an equivalent expression:

```
      2↑[1] 3↑[2] W
1   2
3   4
5   6

 9 10
11 12
13 14
```

If no axis is specified, all axes are implied and the left argument must have as many items as there are axes in the right argument:

```
      A←4 6ρι24
      2 3↑A
1 2 3
7 8 9
```

Take and **drop** allow no scalar extension on the left argument.

Catenate with Axis

Catenate can be used to join data to an array much as it attaches
data to a vector. With **catenate**, the axis mentioned is one that will
get longer as a result of the operation. For example, here's a
catenate with axis that joins two matrices along the first axis.

```
        A← 2 3ρι6
        B←4 3ρ⁻ι12

        A,[1]B
   1    2    3
   4    5    6
  ⁻1   ⁻2   ⁻3
  ⁻4   ⁻5   ⁻6
  ⁻7   ⁻8   ⁻9
 ⁻10  ⁻11  ⁻12

        ρA,[1]B
 6 3
```

Notice that axis 2 (the one not specified in square brackets) has the
same length as before. Axis 1 (the one specified in square brackets)
is longer.

When both arguments have the same rank, **catenate** splits both
arguments along the specified axis, joins corresponding vectors
together, and reassembles the result. Even when the arguments are
higher-rank arrays, the splitting of the arguments ends up with
vectors which are joined by **catenate**.

You may also join an array with another array whose rank is one
less. When the ranks of the arguments differ by one, **catenate** splits
the argument of higher-rank and each vector so formed is joined
with the corresponding scalar from the lower-rank argument. For
example, here's a **catenate** that adds a new row to the top of the
PRDTBL matrix:

```
      PRDTBL
LPS      6.95
TAPES  7.95
CDS    12.95
      PRDTBL←'PRODUCT' 'COST',[1] PRDTBL
      PRDTBL
PRODUCT   COST
LPS       6.95
TAPES     7.95
CDS      12.95
```

In this case, the axis specified is one longer in the result.

If the music store decides that it should keep track of a third piece of information, it can add another column to the matrix. Suppose that, in addition to product name and cost, the store wants to keep track of the number of each item in its stock. The following expression adds this third column to the matrix:

```
      PRDTBL←PRDTBL,[2] 'STOCK' 1250 1375 495
      PRDTBL
PRODUCT   COST STOCK
LPS       6.95  1250
TAPES     7.95  1375
CDS      12.95   495
```

If no axis is specified, **catenate** applies along the rightmost axis and, in the case of a matrix, adds new columns. If an axis is specified, it can contain only one number.

If one argument to catenate is a scalar, the non-scalar array is split along the specified axis, and the scalar is joined to each vector so formed:

```
      (3 4ρι12),1000
1  2  3  4 1000
5  6  7  8 1000
9 10 11 12 1000
```

Unlike most other functions with axis, **catenate** allows a fractional axis to indicate creation of a new axis of length 2. **Catenate**, when written with a fractional axis, is called **laminate**. For example, two vectors may be catenated as follows to form the rows or columns of a matrix:

```
        'ABCD',[.5] 1 2 3 4
A B C D
1 2 3 4

        'ABCD',[1.5] 1 2 3 4
A 1
B 2
C 3
D 4
```

In the first case, a new axis of length 2 is inserted before axis 1 of the vector, giving a 2 4 array. In the second case, the new axis is added after axis 1, giving a 4 2 array.

Laminate can build a matrix from a set of equal length vectors. For example, suppose you have the following three vectors:

```
        WHAT←'LPS' 'TAPES' 'CDS'
        DISCOUNT←.9 .9 1
        RETAIL←6.95 7.95 12.95
```

They describe the names of various possible purchases, applicable discounts, and retail prices. To keep this data under one name, use **laminate**:

```
        PURCHASES← WHAT,DISCOUNT,[1.5]RETAIL
        PURCHASES
LPS     .9  6.95
TAPES   .9  7.95
CDS     1   12.95
```

The rightmost axis is fractional, causing the two vectors *DISCOUNT* and *RETAIL* to be joined into a two-column matrix. Then *WHAT* is attached as a new column, giving a three-column matrix.

Keeping the data as a matrix is, in fact, a better representation than keeping three separate variables. By using a matrix, you have only one name to keep track of instead of three, and there is no chance that the values can get out of sync (some longer than others). For instance, if you ever discovered that *WHAT* had five items but *RETAIL* had six items, you wouldn't know how to line up the corresponding items. In a matrix, it is impossible for one column to be shorter than the others.

Instead of catenating new values to each of three variables, you can catenate a new row to the matrix:

```
      PURCHASES←PURCHASES,[1] 'VIDEODISCS' 1 19
      PURCHASES
LPS            .9   6.95
TAPES          .9   7.95
CDS          1     12.95
VIDEODISCS 1     19
```

In writing an application to maintain the matrix, you would initialize the matrix to have zero rows but three columns:

```
      PURCHASES←0 3ρ0
```

This makes *PURCHASES* a 0-by-3 matrix of numbers. Because there is no data, it doesn't matter if you make the empty matrix numeric or character. Each time a new product comes along, you catenate the data for it onto the matrix. This **catenate** works even for the first product.

Ravel with Axis

As seen earlier, **ravel** without an axis turns any array into a vector of its items. It combines all the axes from an array to produce one long vector. **Ravel with axis** selects a set of adjacent axes that are combined:

```
      B← 2 3 4ρι24

      ,[2 3]B
 1  2  3  4  5  6  7  8  9 10 11 12
13 14 15 16 17 18 19 20 21 22 23 24

      ρ,[2 3]B
2 12
```

Ravel splits its argument along all the axes specified. In the preceding example, two axes are specified, so **ravel** splits the rank-3 array into matrices. Each matrix is raveled and the resulting vector shape appears in the result shape in place of the whole set of axes.

The following picture shows how the shape of the result for the example is formed:

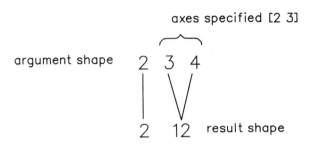

Thus, the result is a vector if all axes are specified; a matrix if one axis is not specified; a rank-3 array if two axes are not specified; and so forth for higher-rank arrays.

There is a useful special case of **ravel with axis**. If the axis is empty, a new axis of length 1 is appended on the right.

If you have a long vector that is too wide to fit on your display device, you can use `,[ι0]` to turn it into a one-column matrix. A one-column matrix displays vertically instead of horizontally:

```
        NAMES←'JANE' 'JIM' 'EV' 'MIKE'
        ,[ι0] NAMES
JANE
JIM
EV
MIKE
        ρ,[ι0] NAMES
4 1
```

Like **laminate**, **ravel with axis** can take a fractional axis specification to create a new axis of length 1. For example, a vector can become a matrix with either one row or one column:

```
      ,[.5] 'RAY' 'SANDY' 'JIM'
 RAY SANDY JIM
      ρ,[.5] 'RAY' 'SANDY' 'JIM'
1 3


      ,[1.5] 'RAY' 'SANDY' 'JIM'
 RAY
 SANDY
 JIM
      ρ,[1.5] 'RAY' 'SANDY' 'JIM'
3 1
```

Reduction with Axis

You've seen many applications of **reduction**: adding up a vector of numbers (+/V), computing the number of items in an array (×/ρA), and so forth. In each of these applications, **reduction** applied to vectors and produced scalars. **Reduction** applies to other arrays as well—with axis specification. Axis specification, when used with **reduction**-derived functions, determines how to split an array into vectors. Given a matrix, the vectors could come from splitting the rows or the columns.

```
      +/[1] 3 4ρι12
15 18 21 24
      ρ+/[1] 3 4ρι12
4


      +/[2] 3 4 ρι12
10 26 42
      ρ+/[2] 3 4 ρι12
3
```

Reduction splits the array along the specified axis and reduces each vector. Since **reduction** of a vector always returns a scalar, each result is a scalar. Reassembling the pieces into the result produces an array with rank one less than the argument. The axes not specified in square brackets appear in the result unchanged; the axis specified does not appear in the result at all.

Reduction without an axis, by default, applies to the rightmost axis.

```
      +/3 4ρι12
10 26 42
```

If an axis is specified, it can contain only one number.

Instead of specifying **reduction** on the first axis as /[1], APL2 permits the alternative symbol ⌿:

```
      +⌿3 4⍴⍳12
15 18 21 24
```

Enclose with Axis

Given a matrix, **enclose with axis** produces a vector whose items come from either the rows or the columns of its argument:

```
      D←2 3⍴⍳6
      D
1 2 3
4 5 6
      ⊂[2] D
 1 2 3  4 5 6
```

```
      DISPLAY ⊂[2] D
┌→─────────────────┐
│ ┌→────┐ ┌→────┐  │
│ │1 2 3│ │4 5 6│  │
│ └~────┘ └~────┘  │
│∈─────────────────┘
      ⍴⊂[2] D
2
```

In the preceding example, each row of the matrix becomes a vector in the result. The 2 which is the row length of *D* becomes the shape of the items of the result:

```
      ⍴¨⊂[2] D
3   3
```

Enclose with axis splits its argument along the axes specified just like **ravel with axis** does. Each piece is enclosed, giving a scalar. Just as in **reduction with axis**, reassembling the scalars into the result array gives a result that does not contain the axis specified in the square brackets.

Enclose with axis applied along axis 1 of a matrix produces a vector whose items come from the columns of the argument array:

```
        ⊂[1]D
 1 4   2 5   3 6
        DISPLAY ⊂[1]D
```

```
.→─────────────────.
| .→──. .→──. .→──. |
| |1 4| |2 5| |3 6| |
| '~──' '~──' '~──' |
'∈─────────────────'
```

```
        ρ⊂[1]D
3
```

You can **enclose** along more than one axis at a time:

```
        H←2 4 3ρι24
        ⊂[1 3]H
 1  2  3    4  5  6    7  8  9   10 11 12
13 14 15   16 17 18   19 20 21   22 23 24
```

```
        ρ⊂[1 3]H
4
```

```
        ρ¨⊂[1 3]H
 2 3   2 3   2 3   2 3
```

Enclose along all axes of an array is the same as **enclose** with no axis:

```
        ⊂[1 2 3]H
 1  2  3
 4  5  6
 7  8  9
10 11 12

13 14 15
16 17 18
19 20 21
22 23 24
```

```
        ρ⊂[1 2 3]H
```

In most cases, **enclose with axis** produces a result with smaller rank and greater depth that its argument. Only an empty axis specification produces a result with the same rank as the argument:

```
      ⊂[ι0] (1 2) (3 4 5)
  1 2   3 4 5

      ρ⊂[ι0] (1 2) (3 4 5)
2

      ≡⊂[ι0] (1 2) (3 4 5)
3
```

DISPLAY ⊂[ι0] (1 2) (3 4 5)

Enclose with an empty axis is the same as **enclose-each**.

Disclose with Axis

Given a vector of vectors, **disclose with axis** (⊃[]) produces a matrix whose rows or columns come from the items of the vector. Unlike other functions with axis, the numbers in brackets refer to the result axes, not the argument axes. **Disclose with axis** does not split its argument. It only does the rearranging with the axis specification saying where in the result new axes are inserted. Here is an example:

```
      ⊃[1] 'FRED' 'JOHN' 'PAUL'
FJP
ROA
EHU
DNL
      ρ⊃[1] 'FRED' 'JOHN' 'PAUL'
4 3
      ⊃[2] 'FRED' 'JOHN' 'PAUL'
FRED
JOHN
PAUL
      ρ⊃[2] 'FRED' 'JOHN' 'PAUL'
3 4
```

Notice that **disclose** reduces the depth of its argument if the depth is at least 2 to start with:

```
        ≡ 'FRED' 'JOHN' 'PAUL'
2
        ≡ ⊃[2]'FRED' 'JOHN' 'PAUL'
1
```

The default axis for **disclose** is the rightmost axis, so the second example gives the same result if the [2] is left off:

```
        ⊃ 'FRED' 'JOHN' 'PAUL'
FRED
JOHN
PAUL
```

Unlike **enclose with axis**, **disclose with axis** can cause data to be added to an array. If the items of the argument are not the same length, they are padded on the right to the length of the longest:

```
        ⊃[2]'FRED' 'RALPH' 'EV'
FRED
RALPH
EV
        ρ⊃[2]'FRED' 'RALPH' 'EV'
3 5
```

You can't see the padding blanks but they are there. Here's an example, using numbers, where the padding with zeros is obvious:

```
        ⊃[2] (10 20 30 40)(ι5)(8 7)
10 20 30 40 0
 1  2  3  4 5
 8  7  0  0 0
```

If some items are numeric and others are character, APL2 pads the numeric arrays with zeros and the character arrays with blanks:

```
        ⊃[2] (10 20 30 40)(ι5) 'AB'
10 20 30 40 0
 1  2  3  4 5
 A  B
```

If the rank of each item is 2, then two numbers must be given as axes because two of the result axes come from the shapes of the argument items:

```
      ⊃[1 3](2 2ρι4) (3 4ρι12)
1   2   0   0
1   2   3   4

3   4   0   0
5   6   7   8

0   0   0   0
9  10  11  12
```

The axes numbers determine where in the result shape the shapes from the items are placed:

```
      ρ⊃[1 3](2 2ρι4) (3 4ρι12)
3 2 4
```

The following picture shows how the shape of the result is constructed:

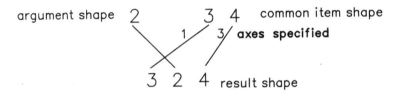

A scalar item is treated as a one-item array of the proper rank:

```
       ⊃[2] (10 20 30 40)(5) 'AB'
10 20 30 40
 5  0  0  0
 A  B
```

If the wrong number of axes is specified, an *AXIS ERROR* is generated:

```
       ⊃[2 3](10 20 30 40)(ι5)
AXIS ERROR
       ⊃[2 3](10 20 30 40)(ι5)
       ∧
```

If the items do not have the same rank, a *RANK ERROR* is generated:

```
      ⊃[1] (10 20 30 40)(2 3⍴⍳6)
RANK ERROR
      ⊃[1] (10 20 30 40)(2 3⍴⍳6)
      ∧
```

Recall that the function **disclose** (⊃) is closely related to **enclose**. Whatever **enclose** does, **disclose** undoes it:

$$A \longleftrightarrow \supset\subset A$$

The same is true for **enclose with axis** and **disclose with axis**.

$$A \longleftrightarrow \supset[I]\subset[I]A$$

Here's an example:

```
      A←4 6⍴⍳24

      ⊃[1]⊂[1] A
 1  2  3  4  5  6
 7  8  9 10 11 12
13 14 15 16 17 18
19 20 21 22 23 24
```

Scalar Functions with Axis

When used with an axis specification, the scalar functions split the array of higher-rank along the specified axes, then apply the whole array of lower rank to each of the pieces. For example, you can add a three-item vector to each row of a four-by-three array as follows:

```
      10 20 30 +[2] 4 3⍴⍳6
11 22 33
14 25 36
11 22 33
14 25 36
```

The matrix is split along the second axis, giving four three-item vectors which are then added to the three-item vector which is the other argument.

In the same manner, you can add a vector to each column of a matrix:

```
      10 20 30 40  +[1] 4 3ρι6
11 12 13
24 25 26
31 32 33
44 45 46
```

The number of axes specified matches the difference in their ranks of the arguments. A scalar may be applied to each item of a matrix by specifying both axes:

```
      10+[1 2] 4 3ρι6
11 12 13
14 15 16
11 12 13
14 15 16
```

Thus in the limiting case of scalars, a scalar function with axis reduces to ordinary scalar extension.

Exercises for Section 5.5

In problems 1 through 5, assume that I, J, K, L, M, and N are non-negative scalar integers and A is a simple array.

1. State the shape, rank, and depth of the results of the following expressions. Also give the shape of the items of the result. Indicate an error if one would occur:

   a. ⊂[1] *M N*ρ*A*
   b. ⊂[2] *M N*ρ*A*
   c. ⊂[1 2] *M N*ρ*A*
   d. ⊂[ι0] *M N*ρ*A*
   e. ⊂[1] *M*ρ*A*
   f. ⊂[1 3 5] *I J K L M N*ρ*A*
   g. ⊂[5 3 1] *I J K L M N*ρ*A*
   h. ⊂[ι6] *I J K L M N*ρ*A*
   i. ⊂[ι0] *I J K L M N*ρ*A*

2. State the shape, rank, and depth of the results of the following
    expressions. Indicate an error if one would occur:

    a. ⊃[1] *M*ρ⊂*N*ρ*A*
    b. ⊃[2] *M*ρ⊂*N*ρ*A*
    c. ⊃[1 2] *M*ρ⊂*N*ρ*A*
    d. ⊃[2 1] *M*ρ⊂*N*ρ*A*
    e. ⊃[ι0] *M*ρ⊂*N*ρ*A*
    f. ⊃[1 3 5] *I J K*ρ⊂ *L M N*ρ*A*
    g. ⊃[3 1 5] *I J K*ρ⊂ *L M N*ρ*A*

3. State the shape, rank, and depth of the results of the following
    expressions. Indicate an error if one would occur:

    a. (*I J*ρ*A*),[1] (*I J*ρ*A*)
    b. (*I J*ρ*A*),[2] (*I J*ρ*A*)
    c. (*I J*ρ*A*),[1 2] (*I J*ρ*A*)
    d. (*I J*ρ*A*),[ι0] (*I J*ρ*A*)
    e. (*I K*ρ*A*),[1] (*J K*ρ*A*)
    f. (*I K*ρ*A*),[2] (*J K*ρ*A*)
    g. (*I J*ρ*A*),[1] (*I K*ρ*A*)
    h. (*I J*ρ*A*),[2] (*I K*ρ*A*)
    i. (*I J*ρ*A*),(*I J*ρ*A*)

4. State the shape of the result of the following expressions, where
    F is any dyadic function and *A* is any array:

    a. *F*/*I J K*ρ*A*
    b. *F*/[1]*I J K*ρ*A*
    c. *F*/[3]*I J K*ρ*A*
    d. *F*/[1 2]*I J K*ρ*A*
    e. *F*/[ι0]*I J K*ρ*A*

5. State the shape of the result of the following expressions:

    a. ,[1 2 3]*I J K*ρ*A*
    b. ,[3 2 1]*I J K*ρ*A*
    c. ,[2 3]*I J K*ρ*A*
    d. ,[3]*I J K*ρ*A*
    e. ,[ι0]*I J K*ρ*A*

6. You saw that the following identity is true:

    $$A \quad \longleftrightarrow \quad ⊃[I] \ ⊂[I] \ A$$

    Give an example that shows that the following identity is *not*
    true:

    $$A \quad \longleftrightarrow \quad ⊂[I] \ ⊃[I] \ A$$

7. Suppose you have the following two arrays:

$$M \leftarrow 3\ 4\rho\iota 12$$
$$A \leftarrow 3\ 4\ 2\rho^-\iota 24$$

Determine the value and shape of the following expressions:

   a. 2 3↑M
   b. 2↑[1]M
   c. 3↑[2]M
   d. 2↑[1]3↑[2]M
   e. 4↑[2]2↑[1]M
   f. 2 3↓M
   g. 2↓[2]M
   h. 2↓[1]M
   i. 4 4↑M
   j. 3 ‾6↑M
   k. 4 5↑M
   l. 4 4↓M
   m. 1 1 1↑A
   n. 1 1 1↓A
   o. 1 ‾2 1↑M
   p. 1 ‾2 1↓A
   q. ‾1 2↑[1 2]A
   r. ‾1 2↓[1 2]A
   s. ‾1 2↑[2 3]A
   t. ‾1 2↓[2 3]A
   u. ‾1 2↑[2 1]A
   v. ‾1 2↓[2 1]A

8. Write an expression to extract the following:

   a. The last row of a rank-2 array *M*.
   b. The first column of a rank-2 array *M*.
   c. The last plane of a rank-3 array *M*.
   d. The last row of the last plane of a rank-3 array *M*.
   e. The first two items in the last row of the last plane of a rank-3 array *M*.

9. Let *A* be defined as follows:

$$A \leftarrow 3\ 4\rho 'ABCDEFGHIJKL'$$

State the result, shape, and depth of the following expressions:

   a. ⊂A
   b. ⊂[1]A
   c. ⊂[2]A

d. ⊂[ι0]A
e. ⊃[2]⊂[2]A
f. ⊃⊂A
g. ⊃[1]⊂[2]A
h. ⊃⊂[1]A
i. ⊂[1 2]A

10. Given the following arrays:

    > V←10 20 30
    > M←4 3ρι12
    > N←3 3ρι9
    > A←2 4 3 ρ100×ι24

    Determine the value and shape of the following expressions:

    a. N+[1]V
    b. N+[2]V
    c. N+V
    d. A+[3]V
    e. A+[2 3]M
    f. M+[2 3]A

11. Given variable M, which is either a character matrix or a vector of character vectors, write an expression to produce a vector of character vectors.

12. Given a vector of vectors where each of the items is a vector of the same length:

    > D←(2 4 6 8)(10 20 30 40)

    Write an expression to create another vector of vectors where the first item contains the first items of the original vector; the second item contains the second items of the original vector; and so on. With D as just defined, your expression should produce the following:

    > (2 10)(4 20)(6 30)(8 40)

13. Given the following variables:

    ```
    TITLE←'NAME' 'PRICE' 'QUANTITY'
    DATA←3 3ρ'OX' 3.95 35 'ANT' 10 100 'PIG' 45.5 13
    ```

    The following expression displays a small report:

    ```
          TITLE,[1]DATA
    NAME PRICE QUANTITY
    OX      3.95        35
    ANT    10          100
    PIG    45.5         13
    ```

    How would you modify the preceding expression if you wanted each column to be at least 10 positions wide?

14. Write a function *APPEND* which, given a matrix, a scalar, and an integer, catenates the scalar onto the matrix on the front of and on the back of the axis indicated by the integer. Here is an example:

    ```
          M←2 3 ρι6

          M
    1 2 3
    4 5 6

          APPEND M '|' 2
    | 1 2 3 |
    | 4 5 6 |
    ```

15. Suppose you have a numeric matrix *GRADES* that reflects the grades a set of students earned on a series of quizzes and examinations:

    ```
          GRADES
     90  93  89
     81  89  90
     88  90  89
    145 160 150
    120 121 125
    ```

    You really want to see the data displayed with row and column titles as follows:

	J. SMITH	D. BROWN	R. WHITE
QUIZ 1	90	93	89
QUIZ 2	81	89	90
MIDTERM	88	90	89
PROJECT	145	160	150
FINAL	120	121	125

Define a function *REPORT* that takes as right argument the numeric matrix and as left argument the row and column titles and returns the report (like the one shown) as an explicit result.

16. Write an expression to multiply each row of matrix M by the corresponding item in vector V.

17. Define a dyadic function *CALENDAR* to return a matrix that displays like a traditional calendar. Inputs to the function should be as follows:

   ● A left argument indicating the starting day of the week (0 = Sunday, 1 = Monday, ... 6 = Saturday).

   ● An integer right argument indicating the number of days in the month.

Sample execution:

```
     3 CALENDAR 31

 S  M  T  W  T  F  S
             1  2  3  4
 5  6  7  8  9 10 11
12 13 14 15 16 17 18
19 20 21 22 23 24 25
26 27 28 29 30 31
```

18. Given numeric matrix M and numeric vector V, where $(\rho V) = ^-1\uparrow\rho M$, write an expression that gives the value of M with no value in any column greater than the corresponding item in V.

Section 5.6 – Other Functions on Higher-Rank Arrays

Other functions that you've seen applied to vectors also apply to higher-rank arrays:

- **first**
- **pick**
- **scalar functions**

First

The **first** (↑) function ignores the structure of its argument and selects the leading item. For any array:

$$↑A \quad \longleftrightarrow \quad ↑,A$$

Therefore, if you know how **first** works on a vector, you know how it works on any array. Here is an example:

```
      G←2 2ρ(4 6ρι24) 'TWO' (3 3ρ0) (3 4)
      ↑G
 1  2  3  4  5  6
 7  8  9 10 11 12
13 14 15 16 17 18
19 20 21 22 23 24

      ρ↑G
4 6

      ↑↑G
1
```

First applied to an empty array returns an array that identifies the kind of data used in constructing the empty array. Here is an example:

```
      ↑ι0
0

      NA1←(1 2 3)(4 5 6)(7 8 9)(10 11 12)
      ↑0ρNA1
0 0 0
```

This result may be a surprise. *NA*1 is a four-item vector of three-item vectors.   0ρ*NA*1 is an empty vector. The result of ↑0ρ*NA*1 indicates that the empty vector 0ρ*NA*1 was constructed from an array whose first item was a three-item numeric vector. If you experiment with various empty arrays, you'll see that the first item of the non-empty array determines the nature of the result you get from using **first** on the empty array. This structure of an empty array is called the *prototype* of the array.

Empty arrays with structure gave rise to the Great Empty Array Joke contest described in Appendix D.

Pick

In Chapter 2, you saw **pick** applied to vectors. Recall this example from Chapter 2:

        PRD←('*LPS*' 6.95)('*TAPES*' 7.95)('*CDS*' 12.95)

        1⊃2⊃*PRD*
TAPES

        2 1⊃*PRD*
TAPES

Pick with a left argument of length 2 is like writing two **pick**s with one-item left arguments. Notice the reversal of the numbers.

However, a single number is not enough to identify an item in a higher rank array. For example, for a matrix, two integers are necessary: a row position and a column position. Here is how to select the letter '*O*' out of the matrix *G*:

        G←2 2ρ(4 6ρι24) '*TWO*' (3 3ρ0) (3 4)
        (1 2)3⊃*G*
O

Do you see how this result is computed? The left argument of **pick** is a vector. The first item is again a vector of length 2 and is suitable for selecting from the rank-2 array *G*. Row 1, column 2, of *G* contains the three-item vector '*TWO*'. The second item in the left argument of **pick** is 3 and selects the third item of the character vector, giving the scalar '*O*' as a result.

Suppose you want to select '*TWO*'. You might be tempted to write this:

        1 2⊃G

But this is equivalent to this:

        2⊃ 1⊃G

Using **pick** in this way won't work because the 1 in the left argument is not enough to select from a matrix. You need a left argument that has one item containing two integers. **Enclose** produces just that:

        (⊂1 2)⊃G
    TWO

Why do you need **enclose** in this case when you didn't need it to select '*O*'? The answer is that to select from a matrix using **pick**, you always need a nested left argument.

In conjunction with the **each** operator, **pick** can be used to select a set of arrays from arbitrary positions in an array. Here's how it works:

    If   *I*⊃*A* gives *X*
            J⊃*A* gives *Y*
    and   *K*⊃*A* gives *Z*

    Then   *I J K*⊃¨*A A A*   gives   *X Y Z*

The right argument shown is a three-item vector whose each item is *A*. A scalar on the right of any derived function of **each** is extended. So, using **enclose** to create the scalar, the example looks like this:

        I J K⊃¨⊂*A*

Scalar Functions

The scalar functions extend to arrays of rank 2 or greater in the way you would expect. A monadic scalar function is applied to each item of its argument:

```
      -2 3ρι6
 ¯1 ¯2 ¯3
 ¯4 ¯5 ¯6
```

A dyadic scalar function is applied between corresponding items of its two arguments, which conform if they have the same shape:

```
      (2 3ρι6) + 10 × 2 3ρι6
11 22 33
44 55 66
```

With all arrays, the dyadic scalar functions are extended to permit one argument to be a scalar even though the other argument is not a scalar. The array inside the scalar pairs with each item from the non-scalar array:

```
      1+10×2 3ρι6
11 21 31
41 51 61
```

```
      (⊂1 2 3) + 10× 2 3ρι6
11 12 13   21 22 23   31 32 33
41 42 43   51 52 53   61 62 63
```

In this last example, the right argument has shape 2 3, so the result has shape 2 3:

```
      ρ(⊂1 2 3) + 10× 2 3ρι6
2 3
```

The array inside the scalar is the three-item vector 1 2 3. This vector pairs with each of the items from the other argument. Thus, each item of the result is a three-item vector:

```
      ρ¨(⊂1 2 3) + 10× 2 3ρι6
3 3 3
3 3 3
```

Exercises for Section 5.6

1. Write three different APL2 expressions to produce a simple scalar from a one-item simple vector N.

2. Write an APL2 expression to produce the number of rows in matrix M as a scalar.

3. Given the vector W:

$$W \leftarrow (\text{'}ABC\text{'} \ \text{'}DE\text{'})(\text{'}XY\text{'} \ \text{'}PQR\text{'})(\text{'}K\text{'} \ \text{'}LMNO\text{'})$$

   a. Evaluate the following expressions:

      1) ρW
      2) $\equiv W$
      3) $\rho \in W$
      4) $\equiv \in W$
      5) $\rho, /W$
      6) $\equiv, /W$
      7) $\rho \uparrow, /W$
      8) $\equiv \uparrow, /W$

   b. What does $\uparrow$ do in the expression $\uparrow, /W$?

4. Given the array A as follows:

$$A \leftarrow (\iota 4)(2 \ 3\rho \text{'}ABCDEF\text{'})(\subset \text{'}XYZ\text{'})(6 \ (7 \ 8))$$

   Evaluate the following expressions. State the shape and depth of each result:

   a. A
   b. $\uparrow A$
   c. $A[2]$
   d. $2 \supset A$
   e. $2(1 \ 3) \supset A$
   f. $4 \ 2 \ 1 \supset A$
   g. $3 \supset A$
   h. $3 \ 2 \supset A$
   i. $3(\iota 0)2 \supset A$

5. Suppose you are given these arrays:

$$A \leftarrow 3\ 2\rho\iota6$$
$$B \leftarrow 10 \times \iota3$$
$$C \leftarrow 'APL2'$$
$$D \leftarrow A\ B\ C$$

Fill in the blanks in the following expressions so the indicated result is produced:

a. $\underline{\hspace{2cm}} \supset D$
    $APL2$

b. $\underline{\hspace{2cm}} \supset D$
    P

c. $\underline{\hspace{2cm}} \supset \subset D$
    P

d. $\underline{\hspace{2cm}} \supset D$
    $1\ 2\ 3\ 4\ 5\ 6$

e. $\underline{\hspace{2cm}} \supset D$
    6

f. $\underline{\hspace{2cm}} \supset A$
    6

g. $\underline{\hspace{3cm}}\ A$
    $3\ 4$

6. Evaluate the following expressions:

a. $3\ 2 \supset\ddot{}\ \subset D$
b. $((1\ (3\ 2))\ 3\ 2) \supset\ddot{}\ \subset D$

7. Evaluate the following expressions:

a. $\uparrow 0\rho5\ 'A'$
b. $\uparrow 0\rho(5\ 'A')(\iota3)$
c. $\uparrow 0\rho\ 'A'\ 5$
d. $\uparrow 0\rho('A'\ 5)(\iota3)$
e. $3\uparrow('A'\ 5)(\iota3)$
f. $3\uparrow(5\ 'A')(\iota3)$

Section 5.7 – Other Primitive Operators

You've already seen the two primitive operators **each** and **reduction**. This section introduces these primitive operators:

- **scan**
- **n-wise reduction**
- **outer product**
- **inner product**

Scan

The **scan** (\) operator is defined in terms of **reduction** and, like **reduction**, applies to any dyadic function. It is best understood by analyzing an example:

```
      +\ 1 3 5 7 11 13
1 4 9 16 27 40
```

First, notice that the shape of the result matches the shape of the argument of the derived function. The first item of the result matches the first item of the argument; the second item of the result is the +/ of the first two items. And, in general, the *N*th item of the result is +/*N*↑argument. The last item of the result is the same value as +/ of the data.

Scan can be applied to any dyadic function:

```
      ,\ (10 20)(30 40)(50 60)
  10 20  10 20 30 40  10 20 30 40 50 60

      ρ ,\ (10 20)(30 40)(50 60)
3
```

Scan extends to higher-rank arrays much as **reduction** does: it can be used with an axis; and the symbol ⁺\ implies a **scan** along the first axis:

```
        A←4 6ρι24
        +\[1] A
  1  2  3  4  5  6
  8 10 12 14 16 18
 21 24 27 30 33 36
 40 44 48 52 56 60


        ,\ 3 2ρ'AB' 'CD' 'EF' 'GH'
AB ABCD
ED EFGH
AB ABCD


        ,⁺\ 3 2ρ'AB' 'CD' 'EF' 'GH'
AB      CD
ABEF    CDGH
ABEFAB  CDGHCD
```

N-wise Reduction

N-wise reduction is the dyadic form of the derived function produced by **reduction**. It is best understood by analyzing an example:

```
        3 +/ 1 3 5 7 11 13
 9 15 23 31
```

First, notice that the length of the result is less than the length of the right argument. In general, the length of the result is one plus the difference between the length of the right argument and the value of the left argument.

The first item of the result in the preceding example is +/ of the first three items of the right argument. The Nth item of the result is +/3↑(N−1)↓argument.

The derived function is sometimes called a ***moving-window reduction***. In the preceding example, a window three items wide is moved from left to right across the right argument with a reduction performed at each step.

As an example, suppose that a company has sales figures for the last twelve quarters:

$$SALES \leftarrow 1001\ 2741\ 3081\ 3767\ 3279\ 4015\ 7305$$
$$SALES \leftarrow SALES, 7200\ 7496\ 9247\ 5100\ 7650$$

As you can see, there was a big jump in sales during the tenth quarter followed by a big drop in sales in the eleventh quarter. The chief executive officer would like to smooth out these numbers so the monthly fluctuations are not so dramatic. **N-wise reduction** can do the smoothing:

$$(1 \uparrow SALES), (2 + /SALES) \div 2$$
$$1001\ 1871\ 2911\ 3424\ 3523\ 3647\ 5660\ 7252.5\ 7348$$
$$8371.5\ 7173.5\ 6375$$

The expression just shown replaces every item but the first by the average of it and the preceding quarter. Although there are still peaks and valleys in the data, they are not nearly so drastic. Averaging over more than two items at a time smooths the data even more:

$$(3 \uparrow SALES), (4 + /SALES) \div 4$$
$$1001\ 2741\ 3081\ 2647.5\ 3217\ 3535.5\ 4591.5\ 5449.75$$
$$6504\ 7812\ 7260.75\ 7373.25$$

Another interesting **n-wise reduction** uses **catenate** as the operand. As this example shows, **n-wise reduction** with **catenate** applied to a simple vector returns a vector of the sub-vectors implied by the moving window:

$$3 \ , / \ 'ABCDEFGHI'$$
$$ABC\ BCD\ CDE\ DEF\ EFG\ FGH\ GHI$$

Here's an example where the argument is not a simple vector:

$$2 \ , / \ 'BILLY' \ 'BOB' \ 'TOM' \ 'CAT'$$
$$BILLYBOB\ BOBTOM\ TOMCAT$$

By applying **n-wise reduction** to a vector of scalars instead of a vector of vectors, you can get a vector of pairs of names:

$$2 \ , / \ \subset^{\cdot\cdot} 'BILLY' \ 'BOB' \ 'TOM' \ 'CAT'$$
$$BILLY\ BOB \qquad BOB\ TOM \qquad TOM\ CAT$$

N-wise reduction extends to higher-rank arrays just as **reduction** and **scan** do and can be used with an axis. The symbol $\neq$ implies an **n-wise reduction** along the first axis:

```
        A←4 6ρι24
        2 +/ A
  3   5   7   9 11
 15  17  19  21 23
 27  29  31  33 35
 39  41  43  45 47

        3+/A
  6   9 12 15
 24  27 30 33
 42  45 48 51
 60  63 66 69

        3 2ρ'AB' 'CD' 'EF' 'GH'
 AB  CD
 EF  GH
 AB  CD

        2 ,/3 2ρ'AB' 'CD' 'EF' 'GH'
 ABCD
 EFGH
 ABCD

        ρ2 ,/3 2ρ'AB' 'CD' 'EF' 'GH'
 3 1

        2,≠3 2ρ'AB' 'CD' 'EF' 'GH'
 ABEF  CDGH
 EFAB  GHCD
```

Outer Product

The operator **each** applies a function between corresponding items
of two arrays. You may also want to apply a function between all
pairings of items one from the left argument and one from the right
argument. The operator **outer product** (∘.) creates an "all combinations" derived function. The result of combining items from a
two-item vector *A B* in all combinations with items from a three-item
vector *C D E* looks like this:

$$A\ B\quad ∘.fn\quad C\ D\ E$$

A **fn** *C*	*A* **fn** *D*	*A* **fn** *E*
B **fn** *C*	*B* **fn** *D*	*B* **fn** *E*

Applying **multiplication** (×) between pairs of items in all combinations gives a matrix that looks like an operation table for multiplication on integers:

```
        (ι5)  ∘.×  (ι10)
  1   2   3   4   5   6   7   8   9  10
  2   4   6   8  10  12  14  16  18  20
  3   6   9  12  15  18  21  24  27  30
  4   8  12  16  20  24  28  32  36  40
  5  10  15  20  25  30  35  40  45  50
```

Any dyadic function can be used with **outer product**. Here's **outer
product** applied to the function **take** (↑):

```
        2 3 ¯4 ∘.↑ (5 6 7) 'ABC'
  5 6        AB
  5 6 7      ABC
  0 5 6 7    ABC
```

```
        DISPLAY 2 3 ¯4 ∘.↑ (5 6 7) 'ABC'
```

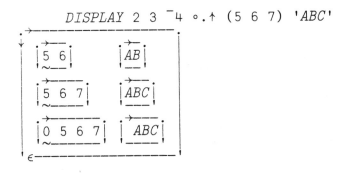

Because the left argument is a three-item vector and the right argument is a two-item vector, the result is a three-by-two array. It is nested because **take** returned a nonscalar array.

The shape of the result of **outer product** is the shape of the left argument catenated with the shape of the right argument. This is stated more formally as follows:

$$\rho \; L \; \circ.F \; R \quad \longleftrightarrow \quad (\rho L),(\rho R)$$

Inner Product

The **inner product** operator (.) applies two functions in a uniform way to arrays. The following example illustrates the way **inner product** applies **addition** and **multiplication** to vectors:

Suppose you have a three-item vector of hours, minutes, and seconds that you want to convert to scalar seconds. You can do this with primitives you already know:

```
      +/3600 60 1 × 2 15 30
8130
```

The left argument is the vector giving the number of seconds in an hour, the number of seconds in a minute, and the number of seconds in a second. The **multiplication** converts everything to seconds, and the **reduction** adds them up. You can write this computation as an **inner product** as follows:

```
      3600 60 1 +.× 2 15 30
8130
```

Inner product on vectors is defined more formally in terms of **reduction** as follows:

$$L \; F.G \; R \quad \longleftrightarrow \quad \subset F/ \; L \; G \; R$$

The **enclose** following the **reduction** in the formal definition is not needed if the **reduction** returns a simple scalar as it did in the first example; but if *G* returns a higher-rank array, the **reduction** would not return a scalar. Here's an example where the **enclose** is required:

```
      3 4,.ρ'ABC'
ABCA BCAB CABC
```

```
      DISPLAY 3 4,.ρ'ABC'
```

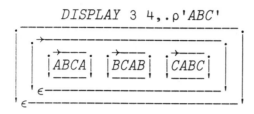

For matrices and higher-rank arrays, **inner product** is defined in terms of **outer product** and **reduction**. The **inner product** $F.G$ applies G between rows of the left argument and columns of the right argument in all combinations. Then each of those results is reduced by F.

Here are some pictures that describe how **inner product** works on matrices:

A B C	F.G	1 2 3
X Y Z		4 5 6
		7 8 9

The arguments are split along the inner axes—the rightmost axis for the left argument and the leftmost axis for the right argument (this is why the operator is called **inner product**). The resulting vectors are given to G in all combinations, with the result reduced by F:

$$F/\ddot{}\quad \boxed{\begin{array}{ccc} A\ B\ C \\ X\ Y\ Z \end{array}}\quad \circ .G\quad \boxed{\begin{array}{c} 1 \\ 4 \\ 7 \end{array}}\ \boxed{\begin{array}{c} 2 \\ 5 \\ 8 \end{array}}\ \boxed{\begin{array}{c} 3 \\ 6 \\ 9 \end{array}}$$

The shape of the result is the shapes of the arguments catenated, with the inner axes removed. This picture shows the result, with an expression to compute each item:

F/A B C G 1 4 7	F/A B C G 2 5 8	F/A B C G 3 6 9
F/X Y Z G 1 4 7	F/X Y Z G 2 5 8	F/X Y Z G 3 6 9

Here is a small example that you should be able to figure out yourself if you are not at a terminal:

```
      I←3 3ρ 14 ¯140 168 ¯40 640 ¯840 27 ¯540 756
      I
 14 ¯140  168
¯40  640 ¯840
 27 ¯540  756

      J←3 3ρ÷⍳9
      J
1           0.5    0.33333333
0.25        0.2    0.16666667
0.14285714 0.125  0.11111111

      I+.×J
3 0 0
0 3 0
0 0 3
```

Depending on the system you are using, the answer could be slightly different from the values shown here. In particular, zero values might be shown as very small numbers (on an IBM 370, in the range of $1E^{-}16$). For most numerical computations, that's close enough to zero compared to the other numbers in the result.

In mathematics, the +.× **inner product** is often called *matrix product*.

The shape of the result of **inner product** is the shape of the left argument without its rightmost axis joined with the shape of the right argument without its leftmost axis. This can be expressed formally for non-scalar arguments as follows:

$$\rho\ L\ F.G\ R \quad \longleftrightarrow \quad (^{-}1\downarrow\rho L),(1\downarrow\rho R)$$

Exercises for Section 5.7

1. State the shape, depth, and value for each of the following
   expressions:

   a. +\⍳5
   b. +\5
   c. +\⊂⍳5
   d. +\(1 2 3)(4 5 6)(7 8 9)
   e. +\(1 2 3)(4 5 6)(7 8 9) 10
   f. +\(1 2 3)(4 5 6)(7 8 9) 10 20
   g. +\(1 2 3)(4 5 6)(7 8 9) (⊂10 20)
   h. +\¨(1 2 3)(4 5 6)(7 8 9)
   i. ,\⍳5
   j. <\0 0 1 0 1 1
   k. ≤\1 1 1 0 0 1 0 1
   l. ≠\1 1 1 0 0 1 0 1
   m. >\(1 0 1 0 1 1)(1 1 1 0 1 1)

2. Determine the value, shape, and depth of the following
   expressions where T is defined as:

$$T ← 3 \ 4 \ ρ \ 3 \ 6 \ 9 \ 1 \ 8 \ 2 \ 4 \ 4 \ 9 \ 7 \ 5 \ 3$$

   a. +\T
   b. −\T
   c. +\[1]T
   d. −\[1]T

3. State the shape, depth, and result of each of the following
   expressions, where

$$A ← 10 \ 5 \ 7 \ 12 \ 4 \ 3$$

   a. 2 +/A
   b. 3 +/A
   c. 5 +/A
   d. 6 +/A
   e. 7 +/A
   f. 0 +/A
   g. 0 ⌈/A
   h. 0 ⌊/A
   i. 2 −/A
   j. ¯2 −/A
   k. 3 −/A
   l. ¯3 −/A
   m. 2 +/¨ A (−A)

4. State the shape, depth, and result of each of the following expressions where:

$$M \leftarrow 4 \ 4\rho 2 \ 4 \ 6 \ 8 \ 1 \ 3 \ 5 \ 7 \ 9$$
$$N \leftarrow 10 \times M$$
$$T \leftarrow 3 \ 3 \ 3\rho\iota 27$$
$$S \leftarrow T$$

  a. `2 +/ M N`
  b. `2 +/¨ M N`
  c. `2 +/[1]¨ M N`
  d. `+/ T S`
  e. `+⌿ T S`
  f. `+/¨ T S`
  g. `+⌿¨ T S`
  h. `+/[2]¨ T S`
  i. `2 +/¨ T S`
  j. `2 +/[1]¨ T S`
  k. `2 +/[2]¨ T S`

5. Given a positive integer N, write an expression to generate the following vector:

$$1 \ \bar{1} \ 2 \ \bar{2} \ 3 \ \bar{3} \ 4 \ \bar{4} \ \ldots \ N \ \bar{N}$$

6. Write a function *CHECK* to produce a Boolean vector with 1's for the rows of numeric matrix M that are in ascending order. Here is an example:

```
          M
      2 3 4 5
      3 1 7 8
      4 7 9 2

          CHECK M
      1 0 0
```

7. Write an expression to produce R, given the result of $+\backslash R$. For example, given the vector N where $N \leftarrow +\backslash \ 2 \ 4 \ 5 \ 7$, produce $2 \ 4 \ 5 \ 7$.

8. Write an expression to generate sets of N consecutive integers where the first item is from ιS. For example, from $N \leftarrow 3$ and $S \leftarrow \iota 4$, you should get the following result:

$$(1 \ 2 \ 3)(2 \ 3 \ 4)(3 \ 4 \ 5)(4 \ 5 \ 6)$$

9. Write a function *MOVING_AVG* to produce the average of each successive group of *N* items from a simple vector of numeric data.

10. Write an expression to convert 3 miles, 6 yards, 2 feet, and 7 inches to inches (1 mile is 1760 yards, 1 yard is 3 feet, 1 foot is 12 inches).

11. Given the following variables:

    $$A \leftarrow 2 \ 4 \ 6$$
    $$B \leftarrow 10 \ 11 \ 12 \ 13$$
    $$C \leftarrow (5 \ 10) \ (1 \ 2 \ 4)$$

    Evaluate these expressions:

    a. $A \circ .+B$
    b. $\rho A \circ .+B$
    c. $A \circ .,B$
    d. $\rho A \circ .,B$
    e. $A \circ .\times C$
    f. $\rho A \circ .\times C$

12. State both the value and shape of the following expressions:

    a. 2 5 10 ∘.* 1 2 3
    b. 1 2 3 ∘.⌈ 1 2 3 4
    c. 1 2 3 4 ∘.⌊ 1 2 3
    d. 3 7 8 ∘.⌈ 5 (6 4)
    e. (3 7)(8 4) ∘.⌈ 5 (6 4)(2 9)
    f. 1 ¯2 2 ∘.↑ 'ABC' (10 20 30 40)
    g. 1 2 3 ∘.⊃ 'ABCD' 'XYZ'
    h. 1 2 3 ∘., 'AB' 'CDE'
    i. 1 2 3 ∘., ⊂¨'AB' 'CDE'

13. Write an expression to produce all nine pairings of the letters *ABC* (including repetitions).

14. Evaluate the following expressions:

    a. (3 4ρ5↑1) +.× 4 3ρ⍳12
    b. (3 4ρ5↑1) ,.× 4 3ρ⍳12

15. The risk level for cardiovascular disease involves *HDL* (high density lipoprotein), *LDL* (low density lipoprotein), triglycerides, and cholesterol. It is measured as the ratio of *LDL* over *HDL*. As the ratio increases, so does the risk and the extent of the treatment:

- 2 or less — Low risk.
- 2-3 — Moderate risk.
- 3-5 — Dietary care indicated.
- 5 or more — Candidate for drug therapy.

A regular blood analysis provides measures of *HDL*, total cholesterol (*TC*), and triglycerides (*TRIG*). The following expressions relate *LDL* to the measured items:

$$LDL \leftarrow TC - HDL + TRIG \div 6$$
$$RISK \leftarrow LDL \div HDL$$

a. Calculate the risk ratio for the following values:

- *HDL*, from 25 to 40 in increments of 5.
- *TRIG*, from 120 to 300 in increments of 10.
- *TC*, from 175 to 225 in increments of 5.

b. Write an expression to produce the values of *LDL* for each possible combination of the given values of *HDL*, *TRIG*, and *TC*.

c. Write an expression to compute the risk values.

Chapter 6

Working with Data

You've seen ways to build collections of data and ways to select subsets of data. In handling data, you may find it useful to compare array items, select particular items in an array, omit items, and search and sort through arrays for specified information. This chapter helps you understand how to use APL2 functions to perform such operations and how to manipulate name assignments to replace values in variables. For work with numeric data, it presents five more computational functions and expands on the **power** function introduced in Chapter 2.

Section 6.1 – Ways of Comparing

This section shows you how to do various comparisons with relational functions, the matching function, and Boolean functions. In APL2, when a comparison is true, the result is 1. When a comparison is not true, the result is 0. One and zero are sometimes called *truth values*. In APL2, truth values are just numbers and can be used in computations just like any other numbers.

Relational Functions

The relational functions are dyadic scalar functions that compare groups of data. The following table summarizes the APL2 relational functions:

Symbol	Name
<	less than
≤	less than or equal
≥	greater than or equal
>	greater than
=	equal
≠	not equal

Table 6.1 APL2 Relational Functions

Here are some examples of the relational functions:

```
      3<2
0

      3 4 5 > 4 10 2
0 0 1

      5 > 4 10 2
1 0 1
```

Since the results of relational functions are numbers, these functions may be used in arithmetic expressions. Here is an example:

```
      R1←10 0 20
      100÷R1+0=R1
10 100 5
```

This expression divides 100 by a vector and avoids an error where the vector contains a zero.

The relational functions are scalar functions. They all work the same way on nested arrays. The function is applied between simple scalars, giving a nested result:

```
      10 20 = (18 10 20) (10 30 20)
 0 1 0  0 0 1
```

Only **equal** and **not equal** can be applied to character data:

```
      'ABCD' = 'ABCE'
 1 1 1 0
      'ABCD' ≠ 'ABCE'
 0 0 0 1
```

Be careful when using **equal** to compare nested character vectors. You might think that the following expression would give the answer 1 0:

```
      'JANE' 'JIM' = 'JANE' 'JOHN'
```

However, when 'JANE' is compared to 'JANE' you get a result of 1 1 1 1, and when 'JIM' is compared to 'JOHN' you get a *LENGTH ERROR*. Even if you fixed the example to avoid the *LENGTH ERROR*, you would not get the result 1 0. Here is an example:

```
      'JANE' 'JIM' = 'JANE' 'JOE'
 1 1 1 1  1 0 0
```

The next section shows how to get the comparison you want.

You must exercise care when using the relational functions with numbers resulting from a computation. Machine arithmetic is not always exact. For example, the result of the expression 1÷3 requires an infinite number of digits to represent it as a decimal fraction. APL2 adjusts the relational functions for small inaccuracies. Here is an example:

```
      .3333333333333 = .33333333333333
 1
```

The numbers are not really equal (the first number has 13 digits and the second, 14 digits), but they are close enough. Exactly how close two numbers need to be before APL2 calls them equal depends on the machine architecture and the APL2 implementation.

The relational functions all do a "close enough" comparison and so they are called *fuzzy functions* and the two numbers in the example just shown are said to be equal within *fuzz* (also called the *comparison tolerance*). This book does not discuss the precise definition of fuzz. Comparisons with zero are never fuzzed, so if you want exact comparisons, compare against zero:

```
      .3333333333333 = .33333333333333
1
      .3333333333333 - .33333333333333
¯3.000377724E¯14
      0=.3333333333333 - .33333333333333
0
```

The above example shows that although the two given numbers are equal within fuzz, their difference is not zero. The actual number you get for the subtraction depends on the system you are using.

Match

The function **match** (≡) is like the relational functions in that it returns a 1 or a 0. It is different because it always returns a single 1 or a single 0 depending on whether its arguments have the same value and the same structure.

On simple scalars, **match** is the same as **equal**:

```
      5 ≡ 5
1
      3 ≡ 4
0
```

On other arrays, **match** returns a 1 only if the two arguments have the same shape and corresponding items match:

```
      'JIM' ≡ 'JOHN'
0
      2 3 (4 5) ≡ 1 + 1 2 (3 4)
1
```

You sometimes want to know whether two arrays (say, X and Y) have the same shape. You might be tempted to write:

$$(\rho X) = (\rho Y)$$

But if X and Y have different rank, this expression will yield a *LENGTH ERROR*. Instead, write this:

$$(\rho X) \equiv (\rho Y)$$

In the discussion of the relational functions, you saw that the following example gave a *LENGTH ERROR* when you wanted the result 1 0:

```
        'JANE' 'JIM' = 'JANE' 'JOHN'
LENGTH ERROR
        'JANE' 'JIM' = 'JANE' 'JOHN'
      ^                ^
```

Can you use **match** to produce the desired result?

```
        'JANE' 'JIM' ≡ 'JANE' 'JOHN'
    0
```

No. **Match** compares the arguments for value and structure. The argument `'JANE'` `'JIM'` does not match the argument `'JANE'` `'JOHN'` in value and structure. Therefore, **match** returns a 0. What you really want is to match items in corresponding positions. To do that, you use **match-each**:

```
        'JANE' 'JIM' ≡¨ 'JANE' 'JOHN'
    1 0
```

Match-each does what your intuition might say **equal** should do. **Equal** is a scalar function so it works like all the other scalar functions.

Boolean Functions

You've just seen a set of functions that return, as results, arrays of truth values—0's and 1's. Such arrays are *Boolean arrays* (named after George Boole, who invented Boolean algebra). The Boolean functions are a set of functions that, given Boolean arrays, produce Boolean arrays. The following tables summarize the Boolean functions:

Symbol	Name	Produces 1 if
∧	**and**	Both arguments are 1
∨	**or**	Either argument is 1
⩑	**nand**	Both arguments are 0
⩒	**nor**	Either argument is 0
=	**equal**	Both arguments are the same
≠	**exclusive or**	Either but not both are 1

Table 6.2 Dyadic Boolean Functions

Notice that = and ≠ can be considered either Boolean or relational. If you think comparisons, ≠ is **not equal**. If you think truth values, ≠ is **exclusive or**.

There is one monadic Boolean function:

Symbol	Name	Produces 1 if
~	**not**	argument is 0

Table 6.3 Monadic Boolean Functions

Here are some examples of the Boolean functions:

```
      0 1 0 1 ∧ 0 0 1 1
0 0 0 1
      0 1 0 1 ≠ 0 0 1 1
0 1 1 0
```

The Boolean functions are easy to implement in electronic circuits, and so they are the functions that describe most of the hardware in a digital computer.

The Boolean functions are useful in making connections between relational expressions. For example, suppose you wanted to know which products cost less than $10 but more than $7:

```
      RETAIL←6.95 7.95 12.95
      RETAIL<10
1 1 0
      RETAIL>7
0 1 1
```

You can connect these into one expression using **and**. Here is an expression that gives 1 for a product that costs more than $7.00 but less than $10:

```
      (RETAIL<10) ∧ (RETAIL>7)
0 1 0
```

In combinations with the **reduction** operator (/), the Boolean functions can answer some interesting questions.

Do all products cost less than $10?

```
      ∧/RETAIL<10
0
```

Does any product cost less than $10?

```
      ∨/RETAIL<10
1
```

Given a Boolean vector, an **exclusive-or-reduction** (≠/) tells you whether there is an odd number of 1's:

```
      ≠/ 1 0 1 1 0 1 0 0
0
      ≠/ 1 0 1 1 0 1 0 0 1
1
```

Checking for an odd number of 1's is a *parity check*. Be sure you can figure out these last two examples. They can help you improve your understanding of **reduction**.

Not (~) can be used to select a complementary set. For example, if you want to produce a 1 when two arrays are not identical, apply **not** to **match**:

      A←'ONE'
      B←'ANOTHER'
      ~A≡B
1

To determine products that don't cost in the range from 7 to 10 dollars, you could enter:

       ~(RETAIL<10) ∧ (RETAIL>7)
    1 0 1

This can be expressed more compactly using **nand**:

       (RETAIL<10) ⊼ (RETAIL>7)
    1 0 1

Some interesting derived functions arise from applying the **scan** (\) operator to Boolean functions.

And-scan (∧\) keeps leading 1's in a Boolean vector. Any 1's after the first 0 are set to 0:

       ∧\1 1 1 1 0 1 0 1 1
    1 1 1 1 0 0 0 0 0

Or-scan (∨\) does a similar operation for 0's; that is, **or-scan** keeps the leading 0's but changes other 0's to 1's.

       ∨\0 0 0 0 1 0 1 0 1
    0 0 0 0 1 1 1 1 1

Exclusive-or-scan or **not equal-scan** (≠\) spreads 1's over 0's until the next 1:

       ≠\0 0 0 1 0 0 1 0 0 0 1 0 0
    0 0 0 1 1 1 0 0 0 0 1 1 1

An **and-scan** (∧\) is used in an expression that deletes leading blanks from a character string. The following example shows the construction of the expression:

```
      TX←'        LEADING BLANKS '
      TX=' '
1 1 1 1 1 1 0 0 0 0 0 0 0 0 1 0 0 0 0 0 0 1

      ∧\TX=' '
1 1 1 1 1 1 0 0 0 0 0 0 0 0 0 0 0 0 0 0 0 0

      +/∧\TX=' '
6
      (+/∧\TX=' ')↓TX
LEADING BLANKS
```

Exercises for Section 6.1

1. Write an expression to count the number of simple scalar 0's in an array.

2. Write an expression to compute the magnitude of a vector without using the **magnitude** function. Test your application with the vector $V←$ ‾21 23 0 ‾1

3. Write the APL2 expression that will produce the results shown in the columns of the following table. Your expressions should contain at most one APL2 relational or Boolean function and either A or B or both A and B. A and B have the following values:

   $$A← \ 0 \ 0 \ 1 \ 1$$
   $$B← \ 0 \ 1 \ 0 \ 1$$

   For example, to compute the result in column 2, use the expression $A∧B$.

A B	1	2	3	4	5	6	7	8	9	10	11	12	13	14	15	16
0 0	0	0	0	0	0	0	0	0	1	1	1	1	1	1	1	1
0 1	0	0	0	0	1	1	1	1	0	0	0	0	1	1	1	1
1 0	0	0	1	1	0	0	1	1	0	0	1	1	0	0	1	1
1 1	0	1	0	1	0	1	0	1	0	1	0	1	0	1	0	1

4. Using the variable $RETAIL$, write an expression to calculate how many products cost less than 10 dollars.

5. Write an expression to return a 1 if a number N is an integer.

6. Investigate the result of applying **less than-scan** ($<\backslash$) to Boolean vectors. How would you describe the function performed?

7. Write a function called *COUNTVOWELS* to count the number of vowels in a character string and calculate the ratio of vowels to characters in the string. Display the result as a three-column table. The first column should be the vowels (AEIOUY); the second column should be the number of occurrences of that vowel in the string; and the third column should display the ratio as a percentage truncated to a whole number. Your function should produce a result as follows:

```
      COUNTVOWEL 'A ROSE IS NOT A DAISY'
   NUMBER PERCENT
A      4       17
E      1       4
I      2       8
O      2       8
U      0       0
Y      1       4
```

8. Predict the result, shape, and depth of the following expressions. Explain any errors that would occur:

   a. `'SMITH'='SMITH'`
   b. `'SMITH'='SMYTH'`
   c. `'SMITH'='SMITHY'`
   d. `'SMITH'≡'SMITH'`
   e. `'SMITH'≡'SMYTH'`
   f. `'SMITH'≡'SMITHY'`
   g. `'APL2'≡'APL2'`
   h. `'APL2'≡'APL2 '`
   i. `1 2 3 4 5 ≡ 1 2 3 4 5`
   j. `1 2 3 4 5 ≡ 1 2 3 (4 5)`
   k. `1 2 3 'AB' ≡ 1 2 3 ('AB')`
   l. `'ABC' (4 5)≡(4 5) 'ABC'`
   m. `'ROY' 'SMITH' = 'ROB' 'SMITH'`
   n. `'ROY' 'SMITH' ≡ 'ROB' 'SMITH'`
   o. `'ROY' 'SMITH' ≡̈ 'ROB' 'SMITH'`
   p. `'ALAN' 'RAY' = 'A'`

9. In logic, the statement "If P is true, then Q is true" is called *implication*. Another way of phrasing this statement is "If P is false, then Q may be either true or false."

   a. Write an expression to compute the truth table for implication using the functions ∨ and ~.

   b. What single APL2 function also yields implication?

10. Write an expression that produces an array with the same values as *M* except that 0's are replaced by 1's.

11. Write an expression to round up any positive number as follows:

   a. To the next higher multiple of .5.

   b. To the nearest multiple of .5.

   For example,

   $$V←2\ 2.3\ 2.5\ 2.7\ 3\ 3.1$$

   (a) results in 2.5 2.5 3 3 3.5 3.5
   (b) results in 2 2.5 2.5 3 3 3

Section 6.2 — Selecting Subsets of Arrays

Selecting and working with subsets is a fundamental activity when you deal with array data structures. This section discusses these operations for selecting and working with subsets:

● **indexing**
● **replicate**
● **expand**
● **without**
● **selective assignment**

Indexing

As you have learned, APL2 arrays are ordered collections of data. In a vector, there is conceptually a first item, a second item, and so forth. In a matrix, there is conceptually a first row, a first column, a second row, a second column, and so forth. This ordering makes it possible to identify any item in an array by using a set of integers to indicate the position in the array. This set of integers is the *index* of the item in the array. Mathematicians use the term ***subscript*** for the same concept.

Chapter 2 explained **indexing** applied to vectors. Here is an example:

```
      'TAPES'[3 2 5 1 4]
PASTE
```

```
      'TAPES'[1 4 2]
TEA
```

When you want to index a rank-*N* array, you must specify an integer for each of the axes. With the **indexing** function, these *N* numbers are written inside the square brackets and are separated by semicolons. For example, to select the item in row 2, column 3, of a matrix, you enter

```
      AC← 3 4ρ'ABCDEFGHIJKL'
      AC
ABCD
EFGH
IJKL
```

```
      AC[2;3]
G
```

To select a cross-section of items, you specify a vector of indices in one or more of the index positions. Here's an expression that selects both column 1 and column 3 from row 2 of matrix *AC*:

```
      AC[2;1 3]
EG
```

When you specify more than one number in any index position, you are requesting that these numbers be used together with the numbers in the other index positions in all combinations. Therefore, if you index two of the rows and three of the columns in a matrix, you select six items:

$$AC[2\ 3;2\ 3\ 4]$$

FGH
JKL

Here is a diagram of this selection:

You can, of course, select an entire row of a matrix by specifying that row and every column in order:

$$AC[2;1\ 2\ 3\ 4]$$

EFGH

You can indicate the selection of every item along some axis more concisely by putting no value in the index position. Using this notation, you can select every item in row 2:

$$AC[2;]$$

EFGH

Here's an example that selects every row of columns 1 and 3:

$$AC[;1\ 3]$$

AC
EG
IK

Leaving out an index is equivalent to writing a vector of integers from 1 up to the length of the axis.

In the preceding two examples, the indices left out are equivalent, respectively, to these expressions:

```
      ι(ρAC)[2]
1 2 3 4
```

```
      ι(ρAC)[1]
1 2 3
```

Eliding an axis selects all items along the corresponding axis. Therefore:

$$AC[2;] \longleftrightarrow AC[2;ι(ρAC)[2]]$$
$$AC[;1\ 3] \longleftrightarrow AC[ι(ρAC)[1],1\ 3]$$

So far, the examples of **indexing** have used only scalars and vectors as indices. Higher rank arrays may also be used as indices. Here are two examples where a matrix is used to index a matrix:

```
      AC[2;2 2ρ 1 3 1 2]
EG
EF
```

```
      AC[2 1;2 2ρ 1 3 1 2]
EG
EF

AC
AB
```

With such generality in the indices, it may seem difficult to predict the kind of array that a given application of **indexing** produces. In fact, however, computing the result of **indexing** is easy if you remember the following rules about rank and shape.

1. Rank of **indexing**: The rank of the result of **indexing** is the sum
    of the ranks of the indices. The rank of an elided index is one.

The following examples show this rule applied to some of the
previous examples:

Expression	Rank	Reason
AC[2;3]	0	(ρρ2)+(ρρ3) 0 + 0
AC[2;1 3]	1	(ρρ2)+(ρρ1 3) 0 + 1
AC[2 3;2 3 4]	2	(ρρ2 3)+(ρρ2 3 4) 1 + 1
MI←3 4ρ 1 3 4 2 1 AC[2 1;MI]	3	(ρρ2 1)+(ρρMI) 1 + 2
AC[;2 3]	2	((ιρρAC)[1])+(ρρ2 3) 1 + 1

2. Shape of **indexing**: The shape of the result of **indexing** is the
    catenate of the shapes of the indices. The shape of an elided
    index is the length of the axis corresponding to that index.

The following examples show this rule applied to the same
expressions as the examples for rule 1:

Expression	Shape	Reason
AC[2;3]	ι0 (empty)	(ρ2),(ρ3) (ι0),(ι0)
AC[2;1 3]	,2	(ρ2),(ρ1 3) (ι0),(,2)
AC[2 3;2 3 4]	2 3	(ρ2 3),(ρ2 3 4) (,2) ,(,3)
MI←3 4ρ 1 3 4 2 1 AC[2 1;MI]	2 3 4	(ρ2 1),(ρMI) (,2) ,(3 4)
AC[;2 3]	3 2	(ρAC)[1],ρ2 3 3 , (,2)

3. Values selected by **indexing**:   Once you know the rank and shape of the result, you can easily compute the values. The first item of the result is the item indicated by the first item of each index. The remaining items of the result come from using the indices in order. A given index has all its values used for a fixed value from the index to its left.

Here is a diagram in the shape of the result of the operation *AC*[2 1;*MI*]. Each position is labeled with the row and column index used to select an item for the result:

2 1	2 3	2 4	2 2
2 1	2 1	2 3	2 4
2 2	2 1	2 1	2 3

1 1	1 3	1 4	1 2
1 1	1 1	1 3	1 4
1 2	1 1	1 1	1 3

```
      AC←3 4ρ'ABCDEFGHIJKL'
      MI←3 4ρ 1 3 4 2 1

      AC[2 1;MI]
EGHF
EEGH
FEEG

ACDB
AACD
BAAC
```

An attempt to select an item that doesn't exist gives the message *INDEX ERROR*:

```
      'ABC'[5]
INDEX ERROR
      'ABC'[5]
      ∧       ∧
```

You can use **indexing** to plot simple graphs. For example, suppose the variable *SALES* represents the number of computer systems that a company sold each month in its first year of operation:

SALES←1 0 3 5 2 7 10 7 10 5 3 2

Comparing these monthly sales numbers in all combinations with the integers from 1 to 10, gives an array of 1's and 0's that, if you squint your eyes, looks like a graph:

```
        (ι10)∘.≤SALES
  1 0 1 1 1 1 1 1 1 1 1 1
  0 0 1 1 1 1 1 1 1 1 1 1
  0 0 1 1 0 1 1 1 1 1 1 0
  0 0 0 1 0 1 1 1 1 1 0 0
  0 0 0 1 0 1 1 1 1 1 0 0
  0 0 0 0 0 1 1 1 1 0 0 0
  0 0 0 0 0 1 1 1 1 0 0 0
  0 0 0 0 0 0 1 0 1 0 0 0
  0 0 0 0 0 0 1 0 1 0 0 0
  0 0 0 0 0 0 1 0 1 0 0 0
```

You can use **indexing** to change the 0's and 1's into blanks and symbols so the data is easier to analyze:

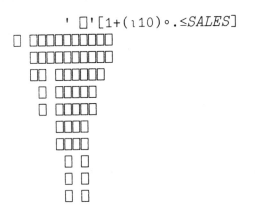

```
        '  □'[1+(ι10)∘.≤SALES]
```

A graph like this is a *histogram* or a *bar chart*. Most often, in a histogram you want the stacks to build upward not downward. One of many ways to build upward is to do the comparison with the integers from 10 to 1 instead of 1 to 10:

      ' ☐'[1+(11-ι10)∘.≤*SALES*]

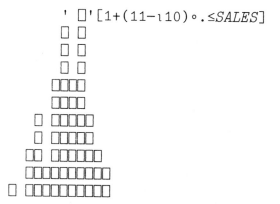

Note: IBM's APL2 Release 3 adds the function **indexing** (☐) as an alternative form of indexing. For information on this new function, see Appendix F.

Selecting Items with a Mask: Replication

Indexing can select zero or more of each item of a vector. If you do not specify the index to an item, **indexing** doesn't select the item at all. If you specify the index once, the item is selected once. Specify the index twice and you get the item twice; and so forth:

      CV1←'*SANDY*'
      CV1[2 2 3 5 5 5]
  AANYYY

The APL2 operator **replicate**—often called **compress**—gives a different way of doing this kind of selection. The left operand is a vector as long as the right argument and indicates how many times to select the corresponding item from the right argument:

      0 2 1 0 3/*CV1*
  AANYYY

A left operand of only 1's and 0's is very useful in selecting a subset of items. For example, if *SALARY* is a vector of salaries, you can select all salaries greater than 5000 with the following expression:

      SALARY←6500 4200 3700 9200 6700
      (*SALARY*>5000)/*SALARY*
  6500 9200 6700

SALARY>5000 evaluates to true (1) or false (0) for each item of salary:

            SALARY>5000
      1 0 0 1 1

Thus, the expression is equivalent to

            1 0 0 1 1/*SALARY*
      6500 9200 6700

A vector of 1's and 0's used as the left operand of **replicate** is often called a *mask*. Here's an example of a mask generated by Boolean functions that is then applied to a nested array:

            RETAIL←6.95 7.95 12.95
            WHAT←'*LPS*' '*TAPES*' '*CDS*'

            (*RETAIL*<10) ∧ (*RETAIL*>7)
      0 1 0
            ((*RETAIL*<10) ∧ (*RETAIL*>7))/*WHAT*
      TAPE

You can use **replicate** to double the quotation marks in a character vector. Remember that to get one quotation mark on input of a character string, you must enter two quotation marks:

```
      CV2←'DON''T'
      CV2
DON'T


      ρCV2
  5


      CV2='''' ←——right argument is a scalar quotation mark
  0 0 0 1 0


      1+CV2=''''
  1 1 1 2 1


      (1+CV2='''')/CV2
DON''T


      ρ(1+CV2='''')/CV2
  6
```

Replicate also applies to higher-rank arrays by the use of an axis specification. The right argument is split along the specified axis, the vector definition of **replicate** is applied, and the pieces are put back together again. When an axis is not written, it defaults to the rightmost axis:

```
        A← 4 6ρι24
        A
   1  2  3  4  5  6
   7  8  9 10 11 12
  13 14 15 16 17 18
  19 20 21 22 23 24


        1 0 0 0 3 2/A
   1  5  5  5  6  6
   7 11 11 11 12 12
  13 17 17 17 18 18
  19 23 23 23 24 24
```

Notice that column 1 is selected once, column 5 is selected three times, and column 6 is selected twice.

Replicate along the first axis selects selects rows of a matrix:

      NAMES←4 4ρ'JOHNJIM EV MIKE'

      1 0 1 0/[1] *NAMES*
JOHN
EV

You can use the symbol ≠ for **replicate**, in which case the axis defaults to the leftmost axis:

      1 0 1 0≠*NAMES*
JOHN
EV

Note: **replicate** is an operator, not a function. It is the first operator you've seen that takes an array as an operand. **Replicate** is the same operator as **reduction**. The name varies according to whether the operand is an array or a function:

      array /   — **replicate**
      function /   — **reduction**

In simple cases, you can think of **replicate** as a function. But in expressions with other operators, you must treat **replicate** as an operator. Here is an example:

      1 0 1/¨ '*ABC*' (1 2 3)
AC 1 3

If you add redundant parentheses, this expression looks like this:

      (1 0 1/)¨ '*ABC*' (1 2 3)
AC 1 3

The operator / applies to its operand 1 0 1 to produce a derived function, which might be called the **1 0 1-replicate** function. This monadic derived function is then the operand of the **each** operator, which applies it to each item of the argument:

      (1 0 1/'*ABC*')(1 0 1/1 2 3)
AC 1 3

Applying two masks to two vectors requires some special thought. If you want to apply two masks to two vectors, you might be tempted to try this:

```
      (1 0 1)(1 1 0)/¨ 'ABC' (1 2 3)
DOMAIN ERROR
      (1 0 1)(1 1 0)/¨ 'ABC' (1 2 3)
      ∧                   ∧
```

The expression looks as though it should work, but the operator / applies to the operand (1 0 1)(1 1 0) first, and **replicate** is not defined on a nested left argument. If you want to apply two masks to two vectors, you must write a defined function that does only the replication and then apply that function using **each**. The following is an example:

```
      ∇Z←L REP R
[1]   ⍝ replicate function
[2]   Z←L/R
[3]   ∇
```

```
      (1 0 1)(1 1 0) REP¨ 'ABC' (1 2 3)
AC  1 2
```

REP works where /¨ fails because *REP* is a function and / is an operator.

Selecting Items with a Mask: Expansion

The APL2 operator **expand** (\) takes a Boolean mask as its left operand. The mask specifies a pattern for building the result. There is a one in the mask for each item in the right argument. Ones in the mask identify where items from the right argument are placed in the result. Zeros in the mask identify where the result should be padded with a fill value:

```
      1 1 0 1 0 1\1 2 3 4
1 2 0 3 0 4
      1 1 0 1 0 1\'ABCD'
AB C D
```

When you apply **expand** to a nested array, the result is padded with items that look like the first item but with numbers replaced by zeros and characters replaced by blanks:

```
      1 0 1\(2 'A' 3)(19 'B' 21)
  2 A 3  0   0  19 B 21
```

```
      DISPLAY 1 0 1\(2 'A' 3)(19 'B' 21)
```

Here's a practical example of **expand**. Given a vector A, insert between each pair of numbers the average of the pair. For example, with the given array A the desired result *NEWA* is shown here:

```
  A←10 12 15 17 16 8
```

```
  NEWA←10 11 12 13.5 15 16 17 16.5 16 12 8
```

Solving this problem mainly requires **n-wise reduction** and **expand**. You can easily compute the average of adjacent numbers using **n-wise reduction**:

```
  AV←(2+/A)×.5
  AV
11 13.5 16 16.5 12
```

Expand with the appropriate mask puts the original numbers into their proper positions in the longer result:

```
    1 0 1 0 1 0 1 0 1 0 1\A
 10 0 12 0 15 0 17 0 16 0 8
```

If you don't know the shape of A, you can compute the mask instead:

```
  M←(¯1+2×ρA)ρ1 0
  M
1 0 1 0 1 0 1 0 1 0 1
```

```
  M\A
10 0 12 0 15 0 17 0 16 0 8
```

The **not** of the mask puts the average values in their proper place:

```
  (~M)\AV
0 11 0 13.5 0 16 0 16.5 0 12 0
```

The desired result is achieved by adding the two parts together:

$$(M\backslash A)+(\sim M)\backslash AV$$
```
10 11 12 13.5 15 16 17 16.5 16 12 8
```

When you apply **expand** to a higher-rank array, an axis may be specified. If no axis is specified, APL2 assumes the rightmost axis. The right argument is split into an array of vectors along the indicated axis, and the vector definition of **expand** is applied to each vector. Here is an example:

```
CH←3 5ρ'ABCDEFGHIJKLMNO'
CH
ABCDE
FGHIJ
KLMNO


1 1 0 0 1 0 1 1\CH
AB  C DE
FG  H IJ
KL  M NO


1 1 0 1\[1]CH
ABCDE
FGHIJ

KLMNO
```

The symbol ⍀ may be used to signify expansion along the first axis.

Note: Like **replicate**, **expand** is an operator, not a function.

Without

It is possible to select items from a vector by specifying the items not wanted. The function **without** (~) returns its left argument with any occurrences of items from the right argument deleted:

```
      'THIS AND THAT'~'HT'
IS AND A
      'BILLY JOE ' ~ ' '
BILLYJOE
```

The example shows a quick way to remove blanks from a character vector. These blanks could arise because of the use of an **enclose**, as in this example:

```
      NAMES←4 4ρ'JOHNJIM EV  MIKE'
      ⊂[2] NAMES
 JOHN JIM  EV   MIKE
```

Because these vectors came from a 4-by-4 matrix, each is a vector of length 4 and some have trailing blanks. The following expression deletes the blanks from each item:

```
      (⊂[2]NAMES)~¨' '
 JOHN JIM EV MIKE
```

Finally, **without** can compute the intersection of two arrays (that is, the items that occur in both arrays) as follows:

```
      X~X~Y
```

Here is an example:

```
      1 3 5 7 9 ~ 1 3 5 7 9 ~ 3 7 11
 3 7
```

Selective Assignment

APL2 supplies a variety of ways to organize and extract parts of an array for those situations when you don't want to operate on the entire array. These functions include **reshape**, **ravel**, **enclose**, **take**, **drop**, **pick**, and **indexing**. They can be used in combination to express a wide variety of selections. Here is an expression that selects one corner of a matrix that is an item in a nested array:

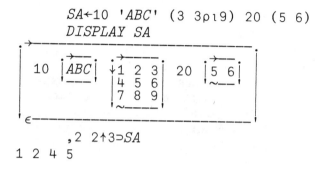

```
      SA←10 'ABC' (3 3ρι9) 20 (5 6)
      DISPLAY SA
```

```
      ,2 2↑3⊃SA
1 2 4 5
```

You can write any expression that results in a selection of all or part of an array in parentheses on the left of an assignment arrow. APL2 replaces the values selected by that expression with values from the array on the right of the arrow:

```
      (,2 2↑3⊃SA)←'WXYZ'
      DISPLAY SA
```

If the preceding example does not work on your system, your implementation may not support selective assignment.

An assignment with a selection expression on the left is a *selective assignment*. The variable whose value is altered is the one whose name appears at the right end of the selection expression (if you ignore square brackets used for **indexing**).

In these expressions, *SA* is the only variable whose value is altered:

```
(2↑SA)←(10 20)(⍳3)
(SA[4])←⊂2.3 3,4
((5⊃SA)[2])←'S'
((⍳0)⊃SA)←0
```

As with any assignment, the explicit result of a selective assignment
is the array on the right and does not print. It is, however, available
for further computation:

```
     1+(2↑SA)←(10 20)(⍳3)
11 21   2 3 4
```

There are three guidelines to help you evaluate an indexed
assignment. These guidelines work if the selection expression does
not contain any functions that add depth (like **enclose**), and does
not contain operators (like **each**). You should apply the first
guideline that fits the expression you are analyzing. Consult the
documentation that comes with your system for a more complete
description.

1. If the leftmost function in the selection expression is **first** or
    pick, the item selected is replaced by the array on the right of
    the assignment arrow:

```
          W←'LPS' 'TAPES' 'DISKS'
          (3 4⊃W)←'C'
          W
LPS TAPES DISCS

          SA←10 'ABC' (3 3⍴⍳9) 20 (5 6)

          (↑2↓SA)←¯1 ¯2

          DISPLAY SA
```

SA←10 '*ABC*' (3 3ρι9) 20 (5 6)

(3 (2 2)⊃*SA*)←'*MID*'

DISPLAY SA

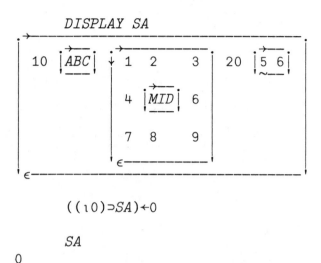

((ι0)⊃*SA*)←0

SA

0

This last selective assignment of *SA* is like an ordinary assignment (*SA*←0) except the variable *SA* must already have a value (even though that value is ignored).

2. If the array on the right of the assignment is a scalar, it replaces each item selected by the selection expression:

SA←10 '*ABC*' (3 3ρι9) 20 (5 6)

SA[1 4 5]←0

DISPLAY SA

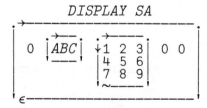

(2 2↑3⊃SA)←0

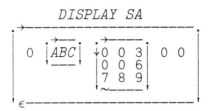

DISPLAY SA

Neither the rank nor the shape of the selected array changes.

3. Each value from the array selected is replaced by the corresponding value from the array on the right of the assignment arrow:

SA←10 'ABC' (3 3ρι9) 20 (5 6)

SA[1 5]←'ONE' 'FIVE'

DISPLAY SA

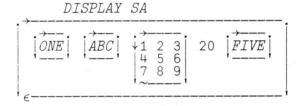

(,2⊃SA)←ι3
DISPLAY SA

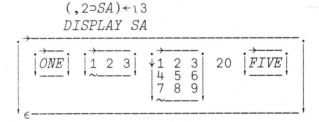

Neither the rank nor the shape of the selected array changes:

● The array selected and the array on the right must have the same rank or APL2 produces a *RANK ERROR*.

● The array selected and the array on the right must have the same shape or APL2 produces a *LENGTH ERROR*.

Note on scalar extension and conformability: APL2 relaxes the conformability rules for selective assignment by ignoring 1's in shape vectors. If you select a subset whose shape is 1 5, you may replace the subset by replacement values of shape 5 1. Ignoring 1's, each array has shape 5. In particular, if the array on the right contains only one item, it is treated as a scalar and extended no matter how many 1's are in its shape.

While any expression that does a selection from an array is permitted on the left of an assignment arrow, implementations may not support them all. Consult the documentation that comes with your system or experiment to see which selections are supported.

Exercises for Section 6.2

1. Given the matrix:

    $$SA \leftarrow 5\ 10\rho\iota50$$

    Evaluate the following expressions in order and show the value of SA after each is complete. If any expression results in an error, say what causes the error:

    a. $SA[2;10]\leftarrow'X'$
    b. $SA[3;10]\leftarrow'XYZ'$
    c. $SA[4;10]\leftarrow\subset'XYZ'$
    d. $SA[;3]\leftarrow0$
    e. $SA[;]\leftarrow'\ '$
    f. $(0\ 1\ 0\ 1\ 0\neq SA)\leftarrow2\ 10\rho-\iota20$

2. Given the vector:

    $$TM \leftarrow (2\ 2\rho'ABC'\ 'DE'\ (\iota^{..}\iota2)\ 10)\ 'ABC'$$

    What is the difference between $TM[1]$ and $\uparrow TM$?

3. Write an expression to replace all 0's in a numeric matrix with the character vector N/A. Here is an example:

1	0	becomes	1	N/A
0	5		N/A	5

4. A manufacturing company has just issued a list of serial numbers of their product for recall. These numbers are in the vector $RLIST$. Write an expression to list which of the company's products in your inventory vector $INVENTORY$ are on the recall list.

5. Given simple numeric vector V, write an expression to replace all the numbers in V that are greater than 10 with the character X, leaving the other items alone.

6. Given two simple arrays M and N with the same rank and shape, write an expression to replace by a blank all items of N different from the corresponding items in M.

7. Explain why the following expression does not expand each item of B using the corresponding mask from M:

$$M \leftarrow (1\ 1\ 0\ 1)(0\ 1\ 0\ 1)$$
$$B \leftarrow 'ABC'\ 'DE'$$
$$M \backslash^{..} B$$

8. Evaluate the following expressions. For each, determine its value and its depth:

   a. `'BYEBYE' ~ 'BY'`
   b. `'BY' ~ 'BYEBYE'`
   c. `'BYEBYE' ~ 'BYEBYE' ~ 'BY'`
   d. `'BYEBYE' ~ ⊂'BY'`
   e. `(⊂'BYEBYE') ~ 'BY'`
   f. `'CAB' 'DAD' ~ 'AB'`
   g. `'CAB' 'DAD' ~`$^{..}$` 'AB'`
   h. `'CAB' 'DAD' ~ ⊂'AB'`
   i. `'CAB' 'DAD' ~`$^{..}$` ⊂'AB'`

9. Evaluate each of the following expressions. For each, state both the result and the depth:

   a. `1 0 1/'APL'`
   b. `1 0 1/⊂'APL'`
   c. `1 2 3/'APL'`
   d. `1 2 3/⊂'APL'`
   e. `1 0 ¯2 3/'APL'`
   f. `1 0 ¯2 3/5 8 9`
   g. `1 0 1/'A' 23 'C'`
   h. `1 0 2/'A' 23 'C'`
   i. `1 2 0/'A' 23 'C'`

10. State the value of each of the following expressions:

    a. `1 0 0 1 1 \ 'APL'`
    b. `1 0 0 1 1 \ 10 20 30`
    c. `((2×ρV)ρ1 0) \ V←'ABCDEF'`
    d. `1 1 0 1 0 1 \ 3 4ρ'ABCD'`
    e. `1 0 0 1 0 1 ＼ 3 4ρι4`
    f. `0 1 0 1 0 1\ 'AB'   (Why?)`
    g. `0\0/ 3 4 5`
    h. `0\0/(3 4) 5`
    i. `0\0/ ('A' 4) 5`
    j. `0\0/ (4 'A') 5`
    k. `1 0 1 0 1 \ 'ABC' (ι4) ('A' 4)`
    l. `1 0 1 0 1 \ (ι4) 'ABC' ('A' 4)`
    m. `1 0 1 0 1 \ ('A' 4) (ι4) 'ABC'`
    n. `1 0 1 0 1 \ (4 'A') (ι4) 'ABC'`

11. Let *M*1, *M*2, *M*3 be three rank-2 arrays having the same shape.

    a. For a given mask *V* where $(ρV) \equiv \ ^-1\uparrow ρM$, write an expression that uses *V* to select the same columns from each of the matrices.

    b. Given three masks *V*1, *V*2, *V*3 and matrices *M*1, *M*2, and *M*3, determine how to use each mask to compress the corresponding matrix. (You will need to create a simple defined function first and then use it in an expression.)

    c. Given three masks *V*1, *V*2, *V*3, apply them each to the matrix *M*, giving three sets of answers. (Note: Use the function defined in part b.)

12. If *M* is a rank-2 array, the following expression replaces all the items of *M* by 12:

    $$M[;]←12$$

    Write an expression to replace all the items in an array of unknown rank by 12.

13. Write an expression to replace all simple scalars in a nested array by 21.

Section 6.3 – Searching and Sorting

To aid in searching for particular items in an array and sorting items, APL2 provides these functions:

- **index of**
- **membership**
- **find**
- **grade up** and **grade down**
- **reverse**
- **rotate**
- **transpose**

Index Of

Index of (ι) is a function that searches a vector left argument for occurrences of items from the right argument. You can search for many items at one time, but you can search only in a vector. The following is an example:

```
LI← 20 40 60 80 40
LIι80 40
```
```
4 2
```

The result always has the same shape as the right argument. Each position in the result is the index position of the first place in the left argument where the item from the right argument is found. Thus, 80 is found at position 4 in *LI* and 40 is found in position 2. The fact that 40 is also found at position 5 is not reported.

If an item searched for is not found, a number one greater than the length of the left argument is returned:

```
LIι100
```
```
6
```

A program can check if a given value is found in another vector by comparing for the number one greater than the length of the vector:

```
(ρLI)<LIι100
```
```
1
```

This expression is true (1) only when the result of **index of** is the "not found" value. See the program *LOOKUP* in the section "More

About Conditional Branching" in Chapter 7 for an example of a program that uses this test.

If the left argument is a nested vector, an item from the right is found if it matches an item on the left:

```
      WHAT←'LPS' 'TAPES' 'CDS'
      WHAT ⍳ 'CDS' 'GUITARS'
  3 4
```

Here `'CDS'` is found at position 3, but `'GUITARS'` is not found at all. Suppose you just want to search for the index of `'CDS'`. You might think that the following expression would find it:

```
      WHAT⍳'CDS'
  4 4 4
```

This is clearly not the answer wanted. Can you figure out why you got the answer 4 4? The right argument is a three-item vector containing the characters `'C'`, `'D'`, and *S*, so you get three answers. Remember that vector notation only works for vectors of length two or longer and here you want a right argument with only one item—the vector `'CDS'`. If you want to search for one item, you must use the function **enclose** (⊂) to make the vector `'CDS'` into a one-item array:

```
      WHAT⍳⊂'CDS'
  3
```

Now **index of** finds the three-item vector `'CDS'` at position 3.

You can use **index of** on character arguments as a way to convert characters to numbers:

```
      ALPH←'ABCDEFGHIJKLMNOPQRSTUVWXYZ '
      ALPH⍳'SECRET MESSAGE'
  19 5 3 18 5 20 27 13 5 19 19 1 7 5
```

These numbers are like a code hiding your message. Of course, your code is easy to break by using **indexing**:

```
      MESSAGE←ALPH⍳'SECRET MESSAGE'
      ALPH[MESSAGE]
  SECRET MESSAGE
```

This example shows that, in some respects, **indexing** is the inverse of **index of**.

You can use **index of** to select the unique items from a vector. Suppose you have the following vector:

$$NV \leftarrow 'JIM' \ 'JOHN' \ 'JIM' \ 'DIETER' \ 'PIER' \ 'JIM'$$

Index of will find only the first occurrence of each name:

```
      NVιNV
 1  2  1  4  5  1
```

Comparing this with the first six integers gives a mask for selecting each name only once:

```
      (NVιNV)=ιρNV
 1  1  0  1  1  0
      ((NVιNV)=ιρNV)/NV
 JIM JOHN DIETER PIER
```

Membership

Index of tells you the index of some given item in a vector. If you want to know only whether an item occurs (as opposed to where it occurs), you can use the function **membership** (ϵ). **Membership** gives a 1 or 0, depending on whether each item of the left argument is (1) or is not (0) found in the right argument:

```
      LI←20 40 60 80 40
      100 40εLI
 0  1
```

Notice that the array in which the search takes place is the right argument (just the opposite of **index of**) and can be any array, not just a vector. In this way, **membership** is similar to (but not the same as) the membership function found in set theory. In the example, 100 is not found (giving 0) but 40 is found (giving 1).

The following examples illustrate a situation where you might want to know if an item exists but not care about its position:

```
      (⊂'CDS')∈WHAT
1
      (⊂'GUITARS')∈WHAT
0
```

Here, **membership** is being used to determine whether the character string in the left argument represents a product stocked by the store. If the answer is **yes,** then you may proceed to look up other information about the product. If the answer is **no,** there is no point in looking further.

An **inner product** using **addition** and **membership** produces a count of the occurrences from the left argument that can be found in the right argument:

```
      I←3 10ρ'1988/05/0413:00:00:1A,B,C,D,E '
      I
1988/05/04
13:00:00:1
A,B,C,D,E

      ρI
3 10
      ρ'.,:;/\'
6
      I +.∈'.,:;/\'
2 3 4
      ρI +.∈'.,:;/\'
3
```

Find

Find (ϵ) is like **membership** except that **find** looks for the whole left argument and you get, for the result, an indication of everywhere that the left argument occurs. Although **find** works for any kind of data, it is most useful (and easiest to demonstrate) on character strings:

$$\text{'}ABC\text{'}\underline{\epsilon}\text{'}ABABCDABCEAB\text{'}$$
$$0\ 0\ 1\ 0\ 0\ 0\ 0\ 1\ 0\ 0\ 0\ 0\ 0$$

This result is the same length as the right argument and has a 1 where the left character string begins. The number of occurrences of the left in the right is:

$$+/\text{'}ABC\text{'}\underline{\epsilon}\text{'}ABABCDABCEAB\text{'}$$
$$2$$

Here's a character vector with some redundant blanks:

$$PHRASE\leftarrow\text{'}NOW\ IS\ \ THE\ \ \ TIME\text{'}$$

You can use **find** to delete the duplicate blanks from *PHRASE* by looking for two blanks:

$$\text{'}\ \ \text{'}\underline{\epsilon}PHRASE$$
$$0\ 0\ 0\ 0\ 0\ 0\ 1\ 0\ 0\ 0\ 0\ 1\ 1\ 0\ 0\ 0\ 0\ 0$$

This result has a 1 for each blank to be discarded. Interchanging the 1's and 0's (with **not**) gives the correct mask for **replicate**.

$$(\sim\text{'}\ \ \text{'}\underline{\epsilon}PHRASE)/PHRASE$$
$$NOW\ IS\ THE\ TIME$$

Grade Up and Grade Down

In Chapter 5, you saw **catenate with axis** used to build a matrix of possible purchases:

```
      PURCHASES
LPS          .9   6.95
TAPES        .9   7.95
CDS         1    12.95
VIDEODISCS  1    19
```

It happens that the retail cost is ordered from least to most expensive. This is an accidental ordering but could be useful. Suppose that you add a fifth row to the matrix:

```
      PURCHASES←PURCHASES,[1]'VIDEOTAPES' 1 13.50
      PURCHASES
LPS          .9   6.95
TAPES        .9   7.95
CDS         1    12.95
VIDEODISCS  1    19
VIDEOTAPES  1    13.5
```

Now the price column is no longer in order. APL2 has two functions that order data: **grade up** (⍋), to arrange data in increasing order, and **grade down** (⍒), to arrange data in decreasing order. These functions work on vectors of numbers. Here are the functions applied to the price column:

```
      PURCHASES[;3]
6.95 7.95 12.95 19 13.5

      ⍋PURCHASES[;3]
1 2 3 5 4

      ⍒PURCHASES[;3]
4 5 3 2 1
```

As you can see, these functions do not produce their argument in sorted order. You might have expected to see **grade up** return an answer of 6.95 7.95 12.95 13.5 19. Instead, you get a vector of small integers. In each example, the answer is a rearrangement of the integers from 1 to 5. These integers are indices that reflect the requested ordering. For example, in **grade up**, the answer is

1 2 3 5 4. These indices mean that to get an increasing vector, you select the first and second items, then the third item, and then the fifth and fourth items, giving the vector sorted in ascending order: 6.95 7.95 12.95. 13.5 19. **Indexing** accomplishes this selection:

```
     T←PURCHASES[;3]
     T[⍋T]
6.95 7.95 12.95 13.5 19
     T[⍒T]
19 13.5 12.95 7.95 6.95
```

Why is this extra step required? Why shouldn't the functions just give you the ordered data directly? The answer is that, in practice, you want to rearrange a whole collection of data based on the ordering of one part of the data. The prices sorted in order are not very useful if you can't identify what product they are associated with. Thus, you want to rearrange the whole matrix based on the order of the prices:

```
     PURCHASES[⍋PURCHASES[;3];]
LPS           .9  6.95
TAPES         .9  7.95
CDS          1    12.95
VIDEOTAPES 1    13.5
VIDEODISCS 1    19
```

This example shows the rows of *PURCHASES* rearranged based on the order in the third column.

The grade functions in their dyadic form apply to matrices of character data. The following selects the product names and constructs a matrix from them:

```
     PNAMES←⊃PURCHASES[;1]
     PNAMES
LPS
TAPES
CDS
VIDEODISCS
VIDEOTAPES
```

Before the rows of this matrix can be put in order, you have to decide what you mean by the order of characters. To English-speaking people, the order A to Z looks like a good choice. But there are lots of alphabets in the world that use characters not in this set. Even in the roman alphabet, you have to decide where lowercase letters belong. Is a lowercase "a" greater or less than an uppercase "Z"? Whatever you decide, you should code your decision as the left argument of the grade functions. The next three examples show left arguments:

$$CS1 \leftarrow ' \; ABCDEFGHIJKLMNOPQRSTUVWXYZ '$$

This sample argument, where all roman letters are written, puts capitalized words first and in order.

$$CS2 \leftarrow ' \; AaBbCcDdEe \; ... \; YyZz '$$

CS2 puts words starting with *A* first, followed by words starting with *a*.

$$CS3 \leftarrow 2 \; 27\rho ' \; ABCDE \; ... \; XYZ \; abcde \; ... \; xyz '$$

CS3 as a left argument orders the rows of a character matrix and ignores capitalization. In a matrix left argument to the grade functions, characters in the same column are treated as though they are the same character. Because the product names are all in uppercase letters, any of the three preceding arrays as left argument gives the same result:

```
      CS3⍋PNAMES
3 1 2 4 5
```

Again, this result is an index vector that rearranges the data.

```
      PNAMES[CS3⍋PNAMES;]
CDS
LPS
TAPES
VIDEODISCS
VIDEOTAPES
```

```
      PURCHASES[CS3⍋PNAMES;]           ⟵ This vector rearranges
CDS          1    12.95                  the whole table
LPS           .9   6.95
TAPES         .9   7.95
VIDEODISCS   1    19
VIDEOTAPES   1    13.5
```

Double **grade up** has some surprising uses. For example, suppose you have these three collections of data:

        A←'XYZ'
        B← 1 2 3
        C← 2.1 2.2 2.3

You want to merge these data collections into the following vector:

    'X' 1 'Y' 2.1 'Z' 2.2 2 2.3 3

Here's a picture of the mapping. The numbers written under the desired answer indicate which variable the corresponding item came from: 1 for *A*, 2 for *B*, and 3 for *C*:

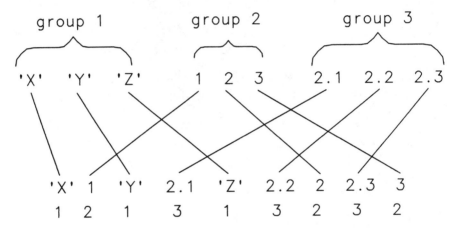

Applying a double **grade up** to the vector of integers in the illustration generates indices that will merge the three vectors in the desired manner:

        MV←1 2 1 3 1 3 2 3 2

        ⍋⍋MV
    1 4 2 7 3 8 5 9 6

        (A,B,C)[⍋⍋MV]
    X 1 Y 2.1 Z 2.2 2 2.3 3

Reverse

Suppose you have a vector and would like to turn it around so the first item is last and the last item is first. Given a four-item vector, you could index with 4 3 2 1:

```
      V←'POTS'
      V[4 3 2 1]
STOP
```

If you don't know the length of the vector to be reversed in advance, you could compute the indices in many ways:

```
      V[1+(ρV)-ιρV]
STOP
      V[⍒ιρV]
STOP
```

The function **reverse** (⌽) turns the items around in one step:

```
      ⌽V
STOP
```

On higher-rank arguments, **reverse with axis** applies. For the rightmost axis, you may elide the axis specification:

```
      A←4 6ρι24
      A
 1  2  3  4  5  6
 7  8  9 10 11 12
13 14 15 16 17 18
19 20 21 22 23 24

      φ[1]A
19 20 21 22 23 24
13 14 15 16 17 18
 7  8  9 10 11 12
 1  2  3  4  5  6

      φA
 6  5  4  3  2  1
12 11 10  9  8  7
18 17 16 15 14 13
24 23 22 21 20 19
```

⊖ is an alternate symbol for **reverse along the first axis**:

```
      ⊖A
19 20 21 22 23 24
13 14 15 16 17 18
 7  8  9 10 11 12
 1  2  3  4  5  6
```

Rotate

The function **rotate** (⌽) shifts the items of a vector by removing items from one side of the vector and reattaching them to the other end. Here is an example:

```
      PHRASE←'NOW IS   THE    TIME'
      2⌽PHRASE
 W IS   THE    TIMENO
```

The left argument gives the number of items for the shift. The name of the function is **rotate** because the items moved out of the left end reappear on the right end.

A negative left argument causes a shift to the right:

```
      ¯2⌽PHRASE
 MENOW IS   THE    TI
```

The character vector *PHRASE* used in these examples has some extra blanks in it. Earlier, you saw an expression using **find** that deletes duplicate blanks. Here's another way to do the same thing, using **rotate**:

```
      P←' '≠PHRASE
      P
 1 1 1 0 1 1 0 0 1 1 1 0 0 0 1 1 1 1

      P ∨ 1⌽P
 1 1 1 1 1 1 0 1 1 1 1 0 0 1 1 1 1 1

      (P∨1⌽P)/PHRASE
 NOW IS THE TIME
```

This selects the non-blank characters and blanks immediately to the left of a non-blank character.

On higher-rank arguments, **rotate with axis** applies. For the rightmost axis you may elide the axis specification. The right argument is split into vectors along the specified axis. If the left argument is a scalar, each vector is rotated that much:

```
      1ϕA
 2  3  4  5  6  1
 8  9 10 11 12  7
14 15 16 17 18 13
20 21 22 23 24 19
```

```
      1ϕ[1]A
 7  8  9 10 11 12
13 14 15 16 17 18
19 20 21 22 23 24
 1  2  3  4  5  6
```

The symbol ⊖ is **rotate along the first axis**:

```
      1⊖A
 7  8  9 10 11 12
13 14 15 16 17 18
19 20 21 22 23 24
 1  2  3  4  5  6
```

You may specify a different rotation amount for each of the vectors in an array. If the left argument is a matrix of rank one less than the right argument, then each vector is rotated by the number corresponding to the vector in the split right argument:

```
      ⁻1 0 1 2ϕA
 6  1  2  3  4  5
 7  8  9 10 11 12
14 15 16 17 18 13
21 22 23 24 19 20
```

Transpose

The monadic **transpose** function rearranges an array so that its shape is reversed. In a matrix, **transpose** turns rows into columns and columns into rows.

```
        AC←3 4ρ'ABCDEFGHIJKL'
        AC
ABCD
EFGH
IJKL


        ⍉AC
AEI
BFJ
CGK
DHL
        ρ⍉AC
4 3
```

The following identity describes the shape of the result of **transpose**:

$$\rho \unicode{x235D} R \quad \longleftrightarrow \quad \phi \rho R$$

The dyadic **transpose** function rearranges its argument and selects a subset of it. The left argument is a list of integers which indicate where in the result the corresponding axis of the right argument should be placed. Here is an example:

```
        T←2 4 3ρι30
        T
 1  2  3
 4  5  6
 7  8  9
10 11 12

13 14 15
16 17 18
19 20 21
22 23 24
```

```
      1 3 2⍉T
  1   4   7 10
  2   5   8 11
  3   6   9 12

 13  16  19 22
 14  17  20 23
 15  18  21 24

      ρ1 3 2⍉T
2 3 4
```

The following picture shows how to predict the shape of dyadic **transpose**—use the left argument to map the argument shape to the result shape:

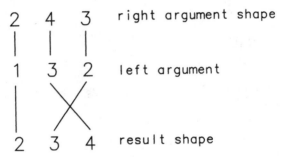

When a number is repeated in the left argument, more than one axis from the argument is mapped to the same axis in the result, with the result length being the minimum of the mapped shapes. Here's an example with a matrix argument:

```
      AC←3 4ρ'ABCDEFGHIJKL'
      AC
ABCD
EFGH
IJKL
      1 1⍉AC
AFK
```

Here is a picture of how the result shape is computed:

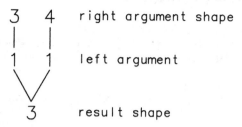

The values selected by this transpose are those where the row index matches the column index: row 1, column 1; row 2, column 2; and row 3, column 3. Now you see why the result shape is the minimum of the axes' lengths. It is not possible to select row 4, column 4 because there are only three rows.

More general transposes on higher-rank arrays are computed the same way.

The symbol for **transpose** looks a lot like the two symbols used for reverse: a circle and a straight line. If you apply any of these three functions to a 3-by-3 matrix, the line tells you which items do not move:

```
      X←3 3ρι9
      X
1 2 3
4 5 6
7 8 9

      (⌽X)(⊖X)(⍉X)
3 2 1    7 8 9    1 4 7
6 5 4    4 5 6    2 5 8
9 8 7    1 2 3    3 6 9

      (⊂X)=(⌽X)(⊖X)(⍉X)
0 1 0    0 0 0    1 0 0
0 1 0    1 1 1    0 1 0
0 1 0    0 0 0    0 0 1
```

Exercises for Section 6.3

1. Write an expression that produces an array having the same shape and depth as array *A* but filled with 0's except where *A* has single digit numbers (that is, between ‾9 and 9) for *A* as follows:

   a. Simple numeric.
   b. Simple but with a mixture of numbers and characters.

2. Write an expression that selects all non-zero numbers from a nested numeric array.

3. Select every item from the array *H* which is not the character string *N/A*.

4. Given simple array *A* which contains numbers and the character string *N/A*, write an expression to replace all the numbers by the number 100.

5. Given simple array *A* which contains numbers and the character string *N/A*, write an expression to replace each number by 100 times that number.

6. Today many cash registers not only print out the cost of each item but also the name of the item. To do this, the system has a *STOCK* database. Suppose each entry in this database is a vector of three-item vectors. Each three-item vector looks like this:

   (inventory number) (product name) (product cost)

   For example, here is a specification of the first three items in *STOCK*:

   ```
   CEREAL ←(112 'ALPHABYTE' 1.89)
   BREAD←(213 'SO_SOFT BREAD' 1.09)
   SOAP←(456 'LIFE GIRL SOAP' 1.75)

   STOCK← CEREAL BREAD SOAP
   ```

   Define a function that will accept a vector of inventory numbers and the name of the stock database, and will produce a matrix listing of the item names and prices that match the inventory numbers.

7. You saw the use of **index of** to delete duplicate items from a vector. Write an expression to delete duplicate rows from a matrix.

8. Given the following matrix:

$$M \leftarrow (\iota 4) \circ . \geq \iota 4$$

```
1 0 0 0
1 1 0 0
1 1 1 0
1 1 1 1
```

Use **reverse** and **transpose** to produce the following arrays:

a.

```
1 1 1 1
0 1 1 1
0 0 1 1
0 0 0 1
```

b.

```
0 0 0 1
0 0 1 1
0 1 1 1
1 1 1 1
```

c.

```
1 1 1 1
1 1 1 0
1 1 0 0
1 0 0 0
```

9. Given the following variables:

$$B \leftarrow \text{'}ABC\text{'} \ \text{'}DEFG\text{'} \ \text{'}IJKLM\text{'}$$
$$W \leftarrow 3 \ 4 \ \rho\text{'}ABCDEFGHIJKL\text{'}$$

Evaluate these expressions:

a. ϕW
b. $\ominus W$
c. $\phi \ominus W$
d. $1 \phi \ominus W$
e. $1 \ 2 \ 3 \ 0 \ominus W$
f. ϕB
g. $\phi^{\cdot\cdot} B$
h. $1 \ 2 \ ^-2 \phi^{\cdot\cdot} B$

10. Given the following array:

    A←3 4ρι12

    Complete the following expressions to produce the stated results:

    a. _____ *A*   e. _____ *A*

    ```
       4   3   2 1                         3   4 1   2
       8   7   6 5                         7   8 5   6
      12  11  10 9                        11  12 9  10
    ```

    b. _____ *A*   f. _____ *A*

    ```
       9 10 11 12                          1   2   3   4
       5  6  7  8                          6   7   8   5
       1  2  3  4                         11  12   9  10
    ```

    c. _____ *A*   g. _____ *A*

    ```
      12 11 10 9                           2  3   4   1
       8  7  6 5                           5  6   7   8
       4  3  2 1                          12  9  10  11
    ```

    d. _____ *A*   h. _____ *A*

    ```
       2  3  4 1                           5   2 11   4
       6  7  8 5                           9   6  3   8
      10 11 12 9                           1  10  7  12
    ```

11. A *palindrome* is a string that reads the same both forward and backward.

    a. Write an expression to determine if a vector *V* is a palindrome.

    b. Given that *V* is a nested vector, write an expression that will determine which of the items of *V* are palindromes.

12. Given a matrix *M*, write an expression to replace the main diagonal of *M* with

    a. The number zero.
    b. The character '*Z*'.
    c. The character string '*DIAG*'.

13. For the matrix T, write an expression to replace with zeros the items on the diagonal just to the right of the main diagonal.

14. Write an expression to test whether a given square matrix S is symmetric (that is, if $S[I;J]=S[J;I]$ for all I and J.)

15. Write an expression that maps numeric vector V so the smallest number maps to 1, the next smallest number maps to 2, and so on until the largest number maps to ρV. For example, the vector 53 47 95 6 77 78 83 13 2 69 should then map to the vector 5 4 10 2 7 8 9 3 1 6.

16. M and N are simple matrices having the same number of columns.

    a. Write an expression to produce a Boolean vector which is 1 when the corresponding row of M is also a row of N.

    b. Write an expression to determine which rows of M match rows in N. Return the row indices of N as the result.

17. Suppose you have the following two character vectors:

    $$FROM \leftarrow 'ABCDEF'$$
    $$TO \leftarrow 'abcdef'$$

    Write an expression using $FROM$ and TO that converts the character string $'CAB'$ to lower case.

18. Given simple scalar S, write an expression to find the first occurrence of S in each row of a matrix. If the scalar is not present, return a number one greater than the number of columns in the matrix.

19. State the shape, depth, and value of the following expressions:

    a. $'ABC'$ $'DEFG'$ ι $'ABC'$
    b. $'ABC'$ $'DEFG'$ ι $\subset'ABC'$
    c. $'ABC'$ $'DEFG'$ ι $\subset'DEFG'$
    d. $'ABC'$ $'DEFG'$ ι $'XY'$
    e. $'ABC'$ $'DEFG'$ ι $\subset'XY'$
    f. $'ABC'$ $'DEFG'$ ι $'XY'$ $'ABC'$
    g. $'ABC'$ $'DEFG'$ ι $\subset'XY'$ $'ABC'$
    h. $'ABC'$ $'DEFG'$ ι $(\subset'XY'),(\subset'ABC')$
    i. $'ABC'$ $'DEFG'$ ι $(\subset'XY')$ $(\subset'ABC')$

20. State the value of each of the following expressions, given:

$$V \leftarrow 20\ 23\ 17\ 30\ 12\ 9$$

   a. $\triangle V$
   b. $\triangledown V$
   c. $V[\triangle V]$
   d. $V[\triangledown V]$
   e. $\triangle \triangle V$

21. State the value of each of the following expressions, given:

$$AV \leftarrow 'ABCD \ldots Z'$$
$$NAMES \leftarrow 5\ 3\rho 'TEETEAATEDADDAB'$$

   a. $AV\triangle NAMES$
   b. $AV\triangledown NAMES$
   c. $NAMES[AV\triangle NAMES;]$

22. The **find** function ($\subseteq$) does not wrap around rows in searching an array. Write an expression to find a character string V in an array A even if the string wraps around in row-major order in the array. For example, searching for XYZ in this array:

```
XYZX
YZXY
ZXYZ
```

produces the following:

```
1 0 0 1
0 0 1 0
0 1 0 0
```

23. Write a dyadic function $BLANKOUT$ whose left argument is a set of characters which, if found in the right argument character string, are to be set to blanks. Here is an example:

```
      ',.''?!' BLANKOUT 'APL2 IS FUN!, ISN''T IT?'
APL2 IS FUN    ISN T IT
```

Section 6.4 — Computation

You've already seen some of APL2's computational functions such as **addition, power,** and **magnitude.** This section contains further discussion of **power** and introduces the rest of the APL2 computational functions:

- **exponential**
- **logarithm**
- **decode**
- **encode**
- **factorial**
- **binomial**
- **trigonometric functions**
- **matrix inverse**
- **matrix divide**

Power and Exponential

Chapter 2 introduced the **power** function. **Power** has some interesting properties that lead to a definition of the function on nonintegers.

Suppose you take the product of two powers of the same number:

$$(2*2)\times(2*3)$$
32

This result is the same as 2*5. Therefore, to compute the product of powers, add the exponents:

$$(X*N) \;\times\; (X*M) \qquad \longleftrightarrow \qquad X*(N+M)$$

Several interesting cases can be derived from this. In each of the examples that follow, add the exponents to determine the results:

$$(2*2)\times(2*3)\times(2*1)$$
64

This example shows that 2*1 is the same as 2 because $(2*2)\times(2*3)$ is $(2*5)$, which is 32. If multiplying also by $(2*1)$ gives 64, then $(2*1)$ must be 2.

$$(2*2)\times(2*3)\times(2*0)$$
32

This example shows that any number to the zero power is 1.
(2*2)×(2*3) is (2*5), which is 32. If multiplying by (2*0) also
gives 32, then (2*0) must be 1.

Power is not limited to nonnegative integer arguments. Here's an
expression with a negative exponent:

        (2*2)×(2*3)×(2*¯2)
    8

(2*2)×(2*3) is the same as (2*5), which is 32. If multiplying by
(2*¯2) gives 8, then (2*¯2) must be the same as dividing by
(2*2), which is 4. Thus, a negative exponent implies division by the
same quantity with the exponent made positive.

Suppose that the exponents are not integers:

        (2*.1)×(2*.5)×(2*.4)
    2

The exponents add to 1 so the answer equals 2*1. Use of fractional
exponents gives rise to some common special cases of **power**.
Consider this:

        (2*.5)×(2*.5)
    2

Again, the exponents sum to 1. But what is 2*.5? It is a number
that when multiplied by itself gives 2. In mathematics, such a
number is a ***square root***. APL2 has no special square root function.
It is just a special case of **power** with a right argument of one-half:

        2*.5
    1.414213562

You may have heard that you cannot take the square root of a
negative number. Try it on your system:

        ¯4*.5

You might get one of two responses. This response means that your
implementation supports only real numbers:

    DOMAIN ERROR
          ¯4*.5
        ∧ ∧

This response means that your implementation supports complex numbers:

    0*J*2

If you get this answer, enter the following:

        0*J*2 × 0*J*2
  ¯4

This result shows that 0*J*2 is the square root of ¯4. The number 0*J*2 is called a complex number. In mathematics, a complex number is often written as an expression like 0 + 2i. Complex numbers are not discussed further in this book.

You indicate cube roots by using **power** with a right argument of one-third:

      64★÷3
  4

In general, in APL2, enter $A \star \div N$ to take the Nth root of a number A.

You saw, in the discussion of **floor** in Chapter 2, that you can compute a 5% interest one time as follows:

    AMOUNT←150.20 331.35 331.25
    AMOUNT×1.05
 157.71 347.9175 347.8125

Suppose one year later you get 5% interest again on your amount. This is, again, 1.05 times the previous new amount:

    AMOUNT×1.05×1.05
 165.5955 365.313375 365.203125

Instead of using multiplication, you can compute the new amount using **power**:

    AMOUNT×1.05★2
 165.5955 365.313375 365.203125

Although there is not much difference between using a power of 2 and multiplication, the difference becomes significant if you require more repetitive multiplications. Suppose you get 5% every year for

four years. Using **power**, you can compute the amount after four
years with no more typing than computing the interest for two years:

AMOUNT×1.05*4
182.5690388 402.7579959 402.6364453

You may want to know your balance on each account at the end of
each of the four years so you can see how your money grows. These
are interest multiplication factors:

(1.05)(1.05*2)(1.05*3)(1.05*4)
1.05 1.1025 1.157625 1.21550625

These can be computed more compactly like this:

1.05*ι4
1.05 1.1025 1.157625 1.21550625

Now you want to multiply each amount by each factor. That is, you
want all combinations of amounts with factors. You should
remember from Chapter 5 that **all combinations** means **outer
product** in APL2. Thus, the desired computation is expressed as
follows:

AMOUNT ∘.× 1.05*ι4
157.71   165.5955   173.875275   182.5690388
347.9175 365.313375 383.5790438 402.7579959
347.8125 365.203125 383.4632813 402.6364453

Finally, you can round these amounts so they are easier to study:

.01×⌊.5+100×AMOUNT ∘.× 1.05*ι4
157.71 165.6   173.88 182.57
347.92 365.31 383.58 402.76
347.81 365.2   383.46 402.64

When **power** is used without a left argument, it is **exponential**.
Exponential is the same as **power** with a left argument of
2.718281828 (rounded to 10 places).

*2
7.389056099

The constant 2.718281828 is often represented in mathematics by the
letter e.

You can use **power** with an integer exponent and with a fractional exponent to express the famous Pythagorean Theorem: "In a right triangle, the length of the hypotenuse is the square root of the sum of the squares of the legs":

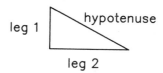

Suppose that the legs are of lengths 3 and 4. The computation of the hypotenuse is follows:

```
LEGS← 3 4
(+/LEGS*2)*.5
```
```
5
```

Logarithm

You've just seen that, in a limited sense, **power** lets you compute products by doing addition (of the exponents). Addition is easy because even if you don't know the algorithm for it, you can compute the sum of 2 and 3 with a ruler by measuring a string of length 2 laid next to a string of length 3. The famous mathematician Napier discovered a way to do the same thing for **multiplication** with a function called **logarithm**.

Napier marked off a ruler so the markings represented the exponents. Now adding lengths is like adding exponents and that is multiplication (as seen in the **power** section). Napier used ivory bars that became known as "Napier's bones." Robert Bissaker adapted the idea and built a ruler called a *slide rule* because it includes a sliding section to make addition of lengths easy. It was the mainstay of engineering calculations until the invention of the electronic calculator.

APL2 implements Napier's function with the symbol ⍟ and calls it **logarithm**. **Logarithm** is certainly less familiar to most people than **addition** and **subtraction**. It is, however, just a function that, given one number, produces another number. All you need to know is what you can do with the function.

Here are some base-10 logarithms:

```
        10⊛100
2
        10⊛325
2.511883361
        10⊛1000
3
        10⊛10000
4
```

Logarithms to the base 10 are sometimes called *common logarithms*.

Logarithm is the inverse of the **power** function:

$$N⊛(N\star X) \quad \text{is } X \text{ for } N \text{ not zero}$$

```
        10⋆10⊛10000
10000
```

In cases where the result is an integer, it is easy to see that **logarithm** is the inverse of **power** because, for example, 4 is the power of 10 that would give 10000.

Every number greater than or equal to 100 but less than 1000 has a logarithm with 2 as an integer part. Given this fact, **logarithm** can be used to compute the number of digits in any decimal number N. When you are programming a report, you can use the computation of the number of digits to determine how much space on a line some data will take. You can compute the number of integer digits by finding the integer part of 1+10⊛N:

```
        1+10⊛100
3
        1+10⊛325
3.511883361
```

Notice that leading zeros on a number have no effect:

```
        1+10⊛00000325
3.511883361
```

By convention, in a decimal number, leading zeros are not written unless there are no other digits.

You already know of a function that takes the integer part of a number—it's **floor**. The following is a more complete expression for the number of digits in a number:

```
      N←345.76
      10⊛N
2.53877475
      ⌊1+10⊛N
3
```

To be completely general, this expression must be augmented in two ways. First, when counting digits in a number, the sign of the number is not relevant. You should apply the expression only to positive numbers. Here is the expression applied only to the **magnitude** of a number:

```
      ⌊1+10⊛|N
3
```

Second, zero is a special case. It is the only number that must be written with a leading zero. Otherwise, it would be written as an empty string of digits. An empty string would, in fact, be more correct, but it is difficult to distinguish it from no number at all. Therefore, we want to count one digit if the number is zero. Here, then, are two expressions for counting the number of integer digits:

```
      ⌊1+10⊛|N+N=0
3
```

```
      ⌊1+10⊛1⌈|N
3
```

The monadic **natural logarithm** (⊛) function is the inverse of the monadic **power** functions:

$$⊛*X \quad \longleftrightarrow \quad X$$

The following is an example:

```
        2*6
64
        2⊛2*6
6
        *6
403.4287935
        ⊛*6
6
```

Decode

In Chapter 5, you saw **inner product** used to convert hours, minutes, and seconds to seconds:

```
        3600 60 1 +.× 2 15 30
8130
```

The left argument had to be computed. **Decode** (⊥) is like **inner product**. (In fact, all the shape rules are identical.) The left argument of **decode** is, however, the units of measurement, not the conversion factors. Thus **decode** can achieve the same result as the above **inner product** as follows:

```
        24 60 60⊥2 15 30
8130
```

The left argument indicates 24 hours in a day, 60 minutes in an hour, and 60 seconds in a minute. Given a vector as an argument to **decode**, the corresponding argument to **inner product** is computed as follows:

```
        ⌽1,×\⌽1↓L
```

Here is an example:

```
        ⌽1,×\⌽1↓24 60 60
3600 60 1
```

From the formula, you can tell that the leftmost number in the left argument is not used and could be anything. The discussion of **encode** gives the reason for including the 24.

In general, the following identity relates **decode** and **inner product**:

$$L\bot R \quad \longleftrightarrow \quad (\phi 1,\times\backslash\phi 1\!\downarrow\!L)+.\times R$$

You might think of time measurement as a counting system, or a *number system*. Seconds count from 0 to 59; then the minutes number increments, and the seconds go back to zero. When the minute count exceeds 59, hours increment. When hours exceed 23, days increment. (A common timekeeping system counts from 1 to 12 for hours, then increments a half-day counter, not from 0 to 1, but from AM to PM. This system takes a little more programming to support.)

A number system that uses a different value in each position is a *mixed radix*, or a *mixed base*, system. More uniform number systems have the same number of values in each position. By far the most common such number system is the Arabic, or decimal number, system based on 10 values in each position. Other common bases for number systems are 2, 8, and 16 (binary, octal, and hexadecimal). These are used mostly by computers. People use base 10 presumably because when the Arabs started using it, people had ten fingers. It's too bad that they didn't have twelve fingers because twelve has twice as many even divisors as ten (2, 3, 4, and 6 compared to 2 and 5). This would have reduced the number of fractions in everyday arithmetic.

APL2 numeric input and output is exclusively base 10.

If you have the digits of a decimal number, you can compute the scalar number they represent using **decode**:

```
      10 10 10 10⊥1 9 8 8
 1988
```

If the number system is not mixed radix, you need not write a vector left argument:

```
      10⊥ 1 9 8 8
 1988
```

This makes alternate number bases easy to convert to decimal. Here are conversions from bases 2 and 16:

```
        2⊥ 0  1  0  1
5
       16⊥ 0  1  9  15
415
```

Any number on the left yields an answer:

```
       137⊥1 2 5 7
2609583
       1.1⊥1 2 5 7
16.251
```

Base 137 is unreasonable and base 1.1 is strange. There is, however, another interpretation of **decode**. Consider the following polynomial:

$$X^3 + 2X^2 + 5X + 7$$

The following expression evaluates the polynomial when X is 137:

```
       +/(137*3) (137*2) 137 1 × 1 2 5 7
2609583
```

You can also write the evaluation of a polynomial as an **inner product** expression:

```
       (137*3) (137*2) 137 1 +.× 1 2 5 7
2609583
```

Finally, you can write the evaluation of a polynomial as a **decode** expression:

```
       137⊥1 2 5 7
2609583
```

On higher-rank arrays, **decode** acts like **inner product** and applies the vector definition between rows from the left argument and columns from the right argument in all combinations:

```
       (2 3⍴24 60 60 10 10 10)⊥3 2⍴2 9 15 8 30 6
8130 32886
 380   986
```

Encode

You may think of **encode** (T) as doing the reverse operation of **decode**. (It's not, correctly speaking, an inverse.) Given the total number of seconds, **encode** can compute the number of hours, minutes, and seconds:

```
      24 60 60 T8130
  2 15 30
```

Notice that this example uses the same left argument the first **decode** example used. Here, however, the 24 is necessary to limit the hours figure to the range 0 to 23. Here's an example where the number of seconds is more than 24 hours:

```
      24 60 60 T813000
  9 50 0
```

Even though 813,000 seconds is more than 24 hours, the answer reflects time less than 24 hours. Two ways are available for you to capture the amount of time lost in this computation. First, you can add another item in the left argument to represent days of the week:

```
      7 24 60 60 T813000
  2 9 50 0
```

This method works only with a right argument that contains less than a week's worth of seconds.

Second, APL2 has a way to let one position in the result of an **encode** get arbitrarily large. A zero in the left argument means "accept any number in the corresponding position in the result":

```
      0 60 60 T 813000
  225 50 0
```

Numbers in the abstract can be arbitrarily large. An indefinite number of digits might be required to represent a number. When you encode numbers, you must know how many digits you want to represent. In a given problem, you usually know.

The following examples use **encode** to reverse the corresponding **decode** examples:

```
      10 10 10 10⊤1988
   1 9 8 8


      2 2 2 2 2⊤5
   0 0 1 0 1



      (4ρ16)⊤415
   0 1 9 15
```

If you are working with polynomials, **encode** takes the value of a polynomial and the value of the variable and computes a set of coefficients:

```
      137 137 137 137 ⊤2609583
   1 2 5 7
```

On higher-rank arrays, **encode** has the same shape rules as **outer product** and applies columns from the left argument against scalars from the right argument in all combinations:

```
      4 2ρ 10 16
   10 16
   10 16
   10 16
   10 16
      (4 2ρ 10 16)⊤137
   0 0
   1 0
   3 8
   7 9
```

Notice that the encoding is along the leftmost axis of the result.

For more detailed information on **encode** with higher-rank arrays, see the documentation that comes with your system.

Factorial and Binomial

Monadic **factorial** and dyadic **binomial** are functions you can use to figure out combinatorial problems. These two functions are discussed in this section.

Factorial

Suppose you have a game consisting of five unique pieces labeled A through E which are arranged in a row. Here is one arrangement of the five pieces:

```
      DISPLAY 'ACBED'
 →─────
|ACBED|
 ──────
```

How many different ways can you arrange these five pieces? For the leftmost position, you could choose any of the five pieces. For the second from the left position, you could choose any of the remaining four pieces. The third position could contain any of the remaining three pieces. The fourth position any of the remaining two pieces. And there is only one choice for the fifth position. The total number of possible arrangements is:

```
      5×4×3×2×1
120
```

or

```
      ×/ι5
120
```

The monadic **factorial** function computes this result directly:

```
      !5
120
```

The number of combinations possible when the pieces are not all distinct can also be computed easily. Suppose of the five pieces, three have the same label:

```
      DISPLAY 'ABAAC'
 →─────
|ABAAC|
 ──────
```

There are still 120 arrangements but some look the same as others.
For fixed B and C, you could choose any A for the first position, any
of the remaining two for the third position, and have only one choice
for the fourth position. Therefore, the number of ways to select the
A's is 3×2×1 which is !3. This is true for every choice of position for
B and C, so the number of distinct arrangements is the total number
of arrangements divided by the number of arrangements not distin-
guishable:

> ```
> (!5)÷!3
> ```
> 20

If you have six white marbles and four black ones, you compute the
number of distinct linear arrangements:

> ```
> (!10)÷(!6)×(!4)
> ```
> 210

> or

> ```
> (!10)÷×/!6 4
> ```
> 210

Note: **factorial** is related to the ***gamma*** function of higher
mathematics as follows:

> $$!A \quad \longleftrightarrow \quad \textbf{\textit{gamma}}~ A+1$$

This relationship is used to define **factorial** on noninteger and
non-positive numbers. The ***gamma*** function is not discussed further
in this book.

Binomial

Suppose you have seven distinct pieces and you select three of them.
How many ways can you select three things from a collection of
seven? You can choose any of the seven for the first selection, any
of the remaining six for the second selection, and any of the
remaining five for the third selection. Thus, the number of
selections is:

> ```
> 7×6×5
> ```
> 210

Factorial 7 is 7×6×5×4×3×2×1. Clearly, if you divide by 4×3×2×1 (which is !7−3), you get the desired result:

$$(!7) \div !7-3$$
    210

In general, to select R things in order from a set of L things, you evaluate the following expression:

$$(!L) \div !L-R$$

If the order of the selected items doesn't matter when selecting three items from a set of seven items, there are !3 different arrangements which contain the same three pieces. Dividing by the number of arrangements giving the same pieces gives the count of the number of different selections ignoring order:

$$(!7) \div (!7-3) \times !3$$
    35

Selecting items from a collection without regard to order is a common operation. The dyadic **binomial** function computes this more compactly:

$$3 !7$$
    35

Formally, **binomial** is defined for all numbers by the following equation:

$$L !R \quad \longleftrightarrow \quad (!R) \div (!R-L) \times !L$$

Note: **Binomial** is related to the mathematical **beta** function.

Trigonometric Functions

APL2 has a full set of trigonometric, hyperbolic, and pythagorian functions whose derivations are based on the analysis of circles. If you have no current use for these functions, you can skip this section.

Pi-times

A fundamental constant related to circles is *pi* (π), which is the number of circle diameters equal to the circumference of a circle. APL2's monadic primitive **pi-times** ($\circ$) computes products of *pi*:

```
      ○1
3.141592654
      ○3
9.424777961
```

The circumference of a circle with radius R is computed with **pi-times** as follows:

```
      ○2×R
```

In science and mathematics, angles are often analyzed by looking at them in a right triangle imbedded in a unit circle with the vertex of the angle in question at the center of the circle:

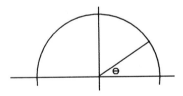

The angle θ is normally measured by measuring the length of the segment of the circumference it intersects. If it intersects a length equal to the radius of the circle, the angle has a measure of one radian. A full circle, therefore, contains 2×*pi* radians. People often measure angles in degrees, and a circle has 360 degrees. The conversion of degrees to radians derives from the fact that 360 degrees is 2×*pi* radians. Thus, one degree is (*pi* radians)÷180.

Using **pi-times**, the following expressions convert 45 degrees to radians:

```
      45×○÷180
0.7853981634
```

          or

```
      ○45÷180
0.7853981634
```

Circular Functions

APL2 includes 25 functions related to circles. Rather than assign each of them a unique symbol, APL2 packages the entire set in the dyadic circular function (○), where the left argument integer specifies which monadic function is desired. The following table summarizes the circular functions available in APL2 Table entries 8-12 apply to complex numbers.

Negative L	L	**Positive** L
$(1-R*2)*.5$	0	$(1-R*2)*.5$
Arc sine R	1	Sine R
Arc cosine R	2	Cosine R
Arc tangent R	3	Tangent R
$(^-1-R*2)*.5$	4	$(1+R*2)*.5$
Inverse hyperbolic sine R	5	Hyperbolic sine R
Inverse hyperbolic cosine R	6	Hyperbolic cosine R
Inverse hyperbolic tangent R	7	Hyperbolic tangent R
$-(^-1-R*2)*.5$	8	$(^-1-R*2)*.5$
R	9	Real R
$+R$ (conjugate)	10	$\|R$
$0J1×R$	11	Imaginary R
$*0J1×R$	12	Phase R

Table 6.4 Circular Functions

Note: If complex numbers are not implemented on your system, the positive numbers above 7 and the negative numbers below ‾7 will not be available.

Many of the relationships between these functions can be seen by looking at a triangle in a unit circle:

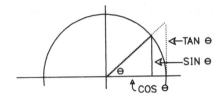

For example, you may have seen this trigonometric equation:

$$1 \leftrightarrow COS^2\theta + SIN^2\theta$$

This equation is tested in APL2 at 30 degrees by the following expression:

```
      +/(1 20030÷180)*2
1
```

If you solve for **sine** in the equation, you get the following:

$$SIN\ \theta \leftrightarrow \sqrt{1-COS^2\theta}$$

This is the value computed by 0O. Thus, given a value of **sine**, you can use 0O to solve for the value of **cosine** for the same angle.

Matrix Inverse

A function *f* is an inverse of function *g* if applying *f* to the result of *g* gives an identity of some kind. For example, in ordinary arithmetic, **multiplication** and **division** are inverses because a number times its reciprocal is 1 which is the identity of multiplication:

```
        N←÷20
        N
  0.05
        N×20
1
```

Multiplication and **division** are scalar functions and extend to arrays like all scalar functions.

```
        N←÷20 10 5
        N
  0.05 0.1 0.2
        N×20 10 5
    1 1 1
```

You've seen **inner product** with operands + and × in Chapter 5. When applied to simple scalars, **inner product** with these operands is like multiplication:

```
      N+.×20
1
```

APL2 has a ⌹ function which is like **reciprocal** on simple scalars and is the inverse of +.×:

```
      N←⌹20
      N
0.05
      N+.×20
1
```

When applied to non-scalars, +.× and ⌹ are not scalar functions:

```
      I←3 3ρ14 ¯140 168 ¯40 640 ¯840 27 ¯540 756
      I
  14 ¯140  168
 ¯40  640 ¯840
  27 ¯540  756
```

```
      ⌹I
0.3333333333   0.1666666667   0.1111111111
0.08333333333  0.06666666667  0.05555555556
0.04761904762  0.04166666667  0.03703703704
```

Inner product with + and × is the algebraic *matrix product*, and ⌹ is the algebraic *matrix inverse* which is APL2's **matrix inverse** function. The +.× **inner product** of any array with its matrix inverse is the *identity matrix* with 1's along the main diagonal and 0's everywhere else:

```
      (⌹I)+.× I
1 0 0
0 1 0
0 0 1
```

Computation of a matrix inverse is a complicated procedure that is subject to numerical errors. The answer given by your APL2 implementation may not lead to a perfect identity matrix for the preceding example. For example, if your computer can store 16 digits, $1E^{-}16$

or $1E^-15$ for off-diagonal items are close to zero when compared to the 1's on the diagonal.

Matrix inverse must be applied to a matrix whose rows are linearly independent (that is, you can't combine some rows by addition, subtraction, and multiplication by a scalar and produce one of the other rows). If the rows are not linearly independent, the matrix is called singular and ⌹ produces a *DOMAIN ERROR*.

You may apply **matrix inverse** to a non-square matrix that has more rows than columns as long as there are as many independent rows as there are columns. In this case, a left inverse is produced:

```
      II← 5 2⍴1 1 1 2 1 3 1 4 1 5

      ⌹II
 0.8   0.5   2.000000000E¯1   ¯0.1  ¯0.4
¯0.2  ¯0.1  ¯4.678201316E¯17   0.1   0.2

      (⌹II)+.×II
1 0
0 1
```

More than one answer which would be a left identity and produce an identity matrix is possible for the result of ⌹ in the above example. APL2 produces the result that, for $M←⌹A$ and $ID←M+.×A$, gives the smallest number in this equation:

$$+/,(ID-A+.×M)*2$$

Producing the result in this way is called a *least squares fit*.

Matrix Divide

Matrix inverse can be used to solve systems of linear equations. Here is an example:

$$X+ \ Y+Z \ = \ 3$$
$$4X+2Y+Z \ = \ 8$$
$$9X+3Y+Z \ = \ 15$$

These equations are satisfied when X is 1, Y is 2, and Z is 0. Here is the solution using **matrix inverse**:

```
      SE←3 3ρ 1 1 1 4 2 1 9 3 1
      SE
 1 1 1
 4 2 1
 9 3 1
      (⌹SE)+.×3 8 15
 1 2 0
```

Matrix divide (⌹) does this computation in a single operation, where the right argument is a matrix of coefficients and the left argument is a vector of results for the equations:

```
      3 8 15⌹SE
 1 2 ¯2.664535259E¯15
```

If the right argument has more rows than columns, the solution APL2 chooses is one that, for $S←B⌹A$, minimizes this equation:

```
      +/,(B-A+.×S)*2
```

Producing the result in this way is also called a *least squares fit*.

Exercises for Section 6.4

1. Suppose you invested one penny in the year 1776 and received 5% interest each year (no rounding). How much money would you have in 1987, 211 years later? Suppose you invested 50 pennies at the same rate. How much money would you have in 1987?

2. You decide to make a trip around the world by balloon and you take with you $100 (USD). You never spend any money, but every time you cross a national boundary, you convert your money into the local currency. You are charged a 5% fee each time you convert money.

   a. Write an expression that computes the amount of money you have after entering the sixth country. Hint: Treat the service charge as negative interest.

   b. It costs one dollar to send a telegram back home. What is the largest number of countries you can visit before sending home for more money? Hint: Use **interval** (ι) for experimentally locating the time when your money would drop below one dollar.

3. Notebooks come in ring sizes that increment by .5 inches. Every .5 inch can accommodate 100 sheets of paper. Define a function called *SIZE* that, given a vector of the number of sheets *S* in a set of manuals, returns the size binder to purchase for each manual.

   Here is a sample execution:

   ```
       SIZE 200 250 263 310
    2 2.5 3 3.5
   ```

4. Write an expression to express an arbitrary integer in base 2. For example, applied to the number 17, you should get 1 0 0 0 1. Hint: Use a base-2 logarithm to compute the number of digits.

5. You saw **indexing** used to produce a histogram. Here is the sales data for a for each month of the year 1987:

   ```
       AMPL← 1005 1011 1017 1009 1023 1024 1021
       AMPL←AMPL,1029 1031 1029 1035 1037
   ```

   a. What is the total number of sales in 1987?

b.   What was the largest number sold in a month?

c.   If one sale represents $137 in profit, what is the total profit for the year?

d.   If each sale is really a lease with a monthly rental, then a sale in January is worth more than a sale in December. What is the total profit for the year, if each sale generates $13 per month starting in the month it is sold?

e.   The sales manager wants to see a histogram of this data. You could easily use **outer product** and **indexing** to plot the graph:

$$ ' \ \square ' [1+(1040-\iota 1039)\circ.\leq AMPL] $$

But a plot over a thousand lines long is not desirable. Scale the data so all of it falls in the range 0 to 20. Using **indexing**, plot a histogram of the resulting data.

f.   The marketing manager wants to show more dramatic growth with the data from part e. Plot just the top of the histogram by subtracting 1000 from the data and then scaling to the range 0 to 20.

6.   Write an expression to convert an integer to a character string that represents an eight-digit signed hexadecimal (base 16) number. Here is an example:

$$
\begin{array}{lll}
12 & \text{converts to} & 0000000C \\
{}^{-}1 & \text{converts to} & FFFFFFFF
\end{array}
$$

7.   Write an expression to convert a character string that represents a hexadecimal number to a signed integer.

8.   Suppose you have a perfectly spherical globe. This globe has a radius of 45 prats (a unit of measure used nowhere in the civilized world).

a.   If you tie a string around the equator on the globe, write an expression to determine the length of the string (ignoring the extra string it takes to tie the knot).

b.   If you want the string to be off the surface of the globe 10 prats over the equator (assuming you have some way of suspending it there), how much string would you have to add?

c. Suppose the planet Xtric is a perfect sphere with a string wrapped tightly around its equator. If you want the string to be 10 prats off the surface over the equator, how much string would you have to add, assuming that the radius of Xtric is 45,000,000 prats?

9. Assume the earth revolves about the sun in a circular orbit. If the distance from the earth to the sun is *DIST* miles, and the earth takes 364.25 days to complete one revolution, at what rate in miles per second is the earth traveling about the sun?

10. The article *"Engineering Voyager 2's Encounter with Uranus"* in the November 1986 issue of **Scientific American** described the remarkable engineering feat of sending a satellite through the solar system past Uranus. As it passed the planet, the satellite transmitted 6000 images of Uranus back to earth. Each of these images consisted of 800 rows of 800 pixels. Because each pixel could represent one of 256 brightness levels, there were 8 bits per pixel, or 5,120,000 bits per image. The data transmission rate was 21.6 kilobits per second. Determine the amount of time that was required to transmit all the images back to the earth. Give this time in terms of weeks, days, minutes, and seconds.

11. In hilly areas, road signs indicate the grade of the road with a pair of numbers such as 1:7. In this pair *a:b*, the first number *a* defines the amount of drop (or climb) vertically that occurs while moving horizontally *b* units. Write a function to accept a pair of grade numbers and determine the angle in degrees from the horizontal of the grade.

12. Evaluate the following expressions:

a. ⌊⊞(ι4)∘.≥ι4
b. ⌊⊞(ι4)∘.≤ι4

13. Suppose one object is traveling at velocity X and another is traveling at velocity Y in the opposite direction. If the objects are moving slow enough, you can just add velocities. If they are on the earth, however, they begin to travel around the curvature of the earth and their relative velocity is less than the sum of their velocities. In space, the relative velocity of two objects traveling in opposite directions is controlled by Lorentz's equation:

$$\frac{X+Y}{1+\sqrt{\dfrac{X+Y}{C^2}}}$$

where C is the speed of light (300,000 meters per second).

Suppose the two velocities are represented in the vector *V*:

a.   Write an expression to compute the relative velocity.

b.   Suppose that each object is traveling at half the speed of light. What is their relative velocity?

By analogy with objects traveling on the earth, Einstein reasoned that, since the relative velocity was less than the sum, space was curved.

14. State the value of each of the following expressions:

a.   10⊥ 2 7 0 5
b.   6⊥ 2 3 4
c.   2 4 6 ⊥2 3 4
d.   10 10 ⊥ 8
e.   10 10 10 ⊥8
f.   2 3 4 ⊥ 8
g.   12⊥5 11
h.   2 12⊥5 11
i.   0 12⊥5 11
j.   2 ⊥ 1 1 0 1 1
k.   5 8 10 ⊥ 2 3 4
l.   (,[' ']5 8 10) ⊥2 3 4
m.   2 ⊥ (1 1 0 1 1)(1 1 0 1)
n.   24 60 60 ⊥ 1 1 30 45

15. State the value of each of the following expressions:

a.   8 ⊤ 123
b.   8 8 ⊤ 123
c.   8 8 8 ⊤ 123
d.   0 8 ⊤ 123
e.   0 8 8 ⊤ 123
f.   24 60 60 ⊤ 1 45 37
g.   0 60 ⊤ 1 45 37
h.   (4 3ρ2 8 10) ⊤ 13
i.   (4 3ρ2 8 10) ⊤ 13 21
j.   (⊂4 3ρ2 8 10) ⊤ 12 21

Section 6.5 – Generating Random Numbers

You saw an encoding of a message that replaced each letter by its position in the roman alphabet. Anyone might guess your method if you encode a message this way. A better way to encode a message would be to use a random arrangement of the alphabet. This section introduces some functions that can be used in this solution.

Deal

Deal (?) generates random numbers. The expression $A?B$ generates A random selections from the set of integers ιB without replacement (that is, no number occurs twice):

```
      5?10
 1 3 6 2 4
      5?10
 3 1 9 5 2
```

Roll

The function **roll** (?) generates one random integer for each integer in the argument. Here is an example:

```
    ? 10 10 10 10 10
 1 5 1 2 4
```

Each selection is independent, so duplicate integers can occur.

You can generate a random roll of a pair of dice as follows:

```
    ?6 6
 3 5
```

Here's a way to encode a message using a random permutation of the alphabet A through Z plus blank:

```
    ALPH1←ALPH[27?27]
    ALPH1
XGNLRUZVB ICOYTDKMQEPJAHSFW
```

The dyadic function **deal** (?) computes 27 (left argument) different random integers from 1 to 27 (right argument). If you try this at your computer, you will probably get different numbers because **deal** does not necessarily produce the same random selection in two consecutive executions.

Using this permuted alphabet, you can get integers that are not related to the position of letters in the roman alphabet:

```
        NUM1←ALPH1ι'SECRET MESSAGE'
        NUM1
 25  20  12  5  20  15  10  18  20  25  25  23  2  20
```

If you would prefer to see some nonsense letters instead of numbers you can turn the integers into characters:

```
        MESS1←ALPH[ALPH1ι'SECRET MESSAGE']
        MESS1
YTLETOJRTYYWBT
```

If you know the encoding alphabet *ALPH*1, the code is easy to break by using indexing:

```
        ALPH1[NUM1]
SECRET MESSAGE
        ALPH1[ALPHιMESS1]
SECRET MESSAGE
```

Now you have an encoding that is not so easy to guess. There are !27 different possible alphabets that could arise from the random selection of 27 items:

```
        !27
1.088886945E28
```

Factorial determines the different possible alphabets because there are 27 choices for the substitution for '*A*', then 26 choices for the substitution for '*B*', and so forth.

Exercises for Section 6.5

1. In each of the following sets of expressions, one expression will satisfy the given statement. Determine which one it is.

   a. Select with replacement two random integers chosen from the set of integers ι10.

      1) ?11 11
      2) ?11 10
      3) ?10 10
      4) 2?10
      5) 2?11

   b. Select without replacement two integers chosen from the set of integers ι10.

      1) ?11 11
      2) ?11 10
      3) ?10 10
      4) 2?10
      5) 2?11

   c. Select with replacement two random integers chosen from the set of integers between ‾5 and 5, excluding both ‾5 and 5.

      1) ‾6+2?10
      2) ‾6+?10 10
      3) ‾5+?10 10
      4) −5+?9 9
      5) ‾5+?9 9
      6) ‾5+2?9
      7) ‾6+2?10

   d. Select without replacement three random integers chosen from the set of integers between ‾5 and 5, inclusive.

      1) ‾6+3?10
      2) ‾6+?10 10 10
      3) ‾5+3?10
      4) ‾5+?10 10 10
      5) ‾5+3?11
      6) ‾5+?11 11 11
      7) ‾6+3?11
      8) ‾6+?11 11 11

2. Write an expression to represent each of the following statements:

   a. The roll of four dice.
   b. The deal of five cards from a standard deck of cards.
   c. A prime number selected at random from the first six prime numbers.
   d. A vector such that its dimension is no greater than 10, and each item is a random integer less than or equal to 25.
   e. A matrix of three rows and four columns containing positive random integers all less than 100.
   f. A two-decimal place random number between 0 and 1. Both 0 and 1 are to be excluded.

3. Given a vector of names *NAMES*, write an expression for each of the following:

   a. Select a name at random to assign to do dishes.
   b. Rearrange the names arbitrarily for a chore list.

   Test your expressions on the following vector:

   $$NAMES\leftarrow \ 'ANNE' \ 'STACY' \ 'SCOTT' \ 'DAVID'$$

Chapter 7

Working with Program Control

You have now been introduced to most of the APL2 primitive functions and operators. The objectives of this text will be complete once you learn more about building and working with programs. This chapter and the next cover several important programming topics:

- Branching
- Debugging
- Controlling input and output
- Iteration
- Recursion

Section 7.1 — Control of Execution: Branching

In the previous chapters, program control was managed with array operations, operators, and the normal sequencing of APL2 expressions in a program from first to last. This is good APL2 style. Sometimes, however, you cannot avoid a requirement to execute the lines of a program in a different order, to execute them repeatedly (a *loop*), or not to execute them at all. For example, before executing a program, you might want to test a user's input for validity and give an error message if there is a problem. Or you might want to repeat a set of lines—perhaps in a drill program that presents a series of exercises to a student.

Branch in a Program

APL2 provides **branch** (→) to request that a specific line be executed next instead of the next line in sequence. The **branch** function used inside a program differs from the other APL2 primitives in two ways:

● It must always be the leftmost symbol in an expression.

● It has no explicit result. That is, it produces no value. Instead, **branch** determines the next line to be executed.

Branch determines the next line to be executed according to the following rules:

1. If the argument is an empty vector, execution continues with the next line in sequence:

      →ι0

2. If the argument is a non-empty vector, execution continues with the line whose number is the first item in the vector. That number must be an integer. This expression is a branch to line 5:

      →5 7 9

3. If the integer line number selected is zero or greater than the number of lines in the program, the program terminates normally. If the program has an explicit result, the result is returned. If the program was called by another program, execution of the calling program resumes. The standard way to request termination of a program is to branch to zero:

    →0

4. If **branch** has no argument, execution of the program terminates and execution of any other programs in the calling sequence also terminate. **Branch** without an argument is sometimes called *escape* or *abort* or *niladic branch*. For example, if program A calls program B, which in turn calls program C, an escape branch (→) in C terminates execution of C, B, and A.

You have used this form of **branch** to clear the state indicator.

As an example of these branching rules, the program *AVGCHK*, which finds the average of the input vector, includes branching to check that the user's input is a simple vector:

```
        ∇ Z←AVGCHK V
[1]     →((1≠ρρV)∨(1≠≡V))/4     ⍝ simple vector?
[2]     Z←(+/V)÷ρV              ⍝ find average
[3]     →0
[4]     'ARGUMENT NOT A SIMPLE VECTOR. TRY AGAIN.'
[5]     ∇
```

AVGCHK has two branch expressions. The first at line [1] is the validity test. It evaluates to 4 if V is not both a vector and simple. Then, according to rule 2, the next line executed is line [4], which displays the error message. If V is a simple vector, the expression at line 1 evaluates to an empty vector. Then, according to rule 1, the next sequential line is executed (line [2] here), which finds the average.

The second branch expression, at line [3], terminates the function execution normally (according to rule 3). If the program did not have this second branch expression, line [4] would be executed even though V was a valid argument.

Labels

There is a problem with branching to a specific line number: Editing can ruin your branch expressions. Look what happens to the first branch expression when a comment line is inserted at the beginning of *AVGCHK*:

```
      ∇ Z←AVGCHK V
[1]   ⍝ finds the average of a simple vector
[2]     →((1≠⍴⍴V)∨(1≠≡V))/4    ⍝ simple vector?
[3]     Z←(+/V)÷⍴V              ⍝ find average
[4]     →0
[5]     'ARGUMENT NOT A SIMPLE VECTOR. TRY AGAIN.'
[6]   ∇
```

The insertion causes the line numbers to change, but the value of the branch expression at line [2] does not change. It is still the constant 4. If the argument is not a simple vector, program execution terminates without the error messages being displayed on line [5]—not what was intended.

The way to avoid this problem is to use line labels. A label is a name written at the left edge of an expression and separated from the expression by a colon. When program execution begins, each label is given as its value the line number where it occurs. For example, suppose the following is line [3] of function *F*:

```
[3]    HERE: any APL2 expression
```

When *F* is called, the local name *HERE* is given the value 3. Elsewhere in *F*, if you want to branch to this line, you code:

```
[10]    →HERE
```

as opposed to:

```
[10]    →3
```

Later, if you insert a line before line [3], and the old line [3] becomes line [4], you won't need to recode anything. On the next execution of the function, *HERE* will mean 4.

Here is the function *AVGCHK* rewritten with a label:

```
      ∇ Z←AVGCHK V
[1]   ⍝ finds the average of a simple vector
[2]     →((1≠⍴⍴V)∨(1≠≡V))/MSG ⍝ simple vector?
[3]     Z←(+/V)÷⍴V              ⍝ find average
[4]     →0
[5]   MSG:'ARGUMENT NOT A SIMPLE VECTOR. TRY AGAIN.'
[6]     ∇
```

Always use labels in your programs. The only exception is when the branch terminates program execution (that is, it evaluates to 0).

The branch expressions used in lines [2] and [4] of *AVGCHK* have a basic difference. Whenever line [4] is executed, the terminating branch to 0 occurs. Such a branch expression is an *unconditional branch*.

In contrast, when line [2] is executed, the branch occurs only if the branch expression is not an empty vector. If the branch expression is an empty vector, there is no branch and the next sequential line is executed. Such a branch expression is a *conditional branch*.

More about Conditional Branching

Any expression that evaluates to an empty vector, a scalar integer, or a vector whose first item is an integer, can be the branch expression. However, the recommended way to write a conditional branch is in this form:

$$→ \text{(condition)} \ / \ \text{label}$$

It is the form used in *AVGCHK*:

```
[2]     →((1≠⍴⍴V)∨(1≠≡V))/MSG ⍝ simple vector?
```

This branch expression uses **replicate** (/). If the condition $((1≠⍴⍴V)∨(1≠≡V))$ evaluates to 1 (true), 1/*MSG* evaluates to *MSG* and the program branches to *MSG* (which is line [5] in the example). If the condition evaluates to 0 (false), 0/*MSG* is an empty vector, and so execution of the program continues with the next sequential line.

This is the most important thing to remember:

$$→ \text{(condition)} \ / \ \text{label}$$

This means "branch to the label *if* the condition is true."

Here's another example using a conditional branch. The program *LOOKUP*, when given someone's name, looks it up in a global list of names. If the name is found, the program returns the index position of the name in the list. If the name is not found, the program appends the name to the list and returns its index:

```
          ∇ Z←LOOKUP NAME
[1]      Z←NAMESιⁿCNAME        ⍝ search for NAME
[2]      →(Z≤ρNAMES)/0         ⍝ if found, all done
[3]      NAMES←NAMES,⊂NAME     ⍝ else add name to list
[4]      ∇
```

The execution of *LOOKUP* is as follows:

● Line [1] searches for the name. Notice that *NAME* is enclosed to treat it as an entity.

● Line [2] exits from the program if the name is found. The explicit result is its index.

● Line [3] appends the name to the end of the list. Z will already be the index to this new name because **index of** (ι) produces a number one larger than the length of the vector if an item is not found.

Although any expression that evaluates to an integer (or to an empty vector) can be used for branching, the standard method shown here makes your programs easier to read and maintain by other people. Occasionally, however, other forms of branch expressions can be used. You will see some of these in programs later in this chapter.

You can use **replicate** to branch to one of a series of labels as in this example:

```
[2]      →((N<0),(N>0))/MSG1 MSG2
```

This expression causes a branch to *MSG1* if N is less than zero, and to *MSG2* if N is greater than zero. If N is equal to zero, the **replicate** function produces an empty vector, and branch to an empty vector means go to the the next line.

More about Unconditional Branching

Unconditional branches have two principal uses:

● Terminate execution of the program.

● Create a branch back to the beginning of a loop.

You have seen the unconditional branch used in *AVGCHK* to terminate execution of the program. The unconditional branch at line [6] in the program *SQRT*, shown next, is used for looping. *SQRT* implements the algorithm for Newton's method of approximating the square root of a positive number:

```
        ∇ Z←SQRT N;EST
[1]     ⍝ square root using Newton's method
[2]     Z←1                   ⍝ guess at root
[3]     REFINE:EST←.5×Z+N÷Z   ⍝ refining the guess
[4]     →(Z=EST)/0            ⍝ quit if no change
[5]     Z←EST                 ⍝ use new guess
[6]     →REFINE               ⍝ repeat
[7]     ∇
```

As long as the value of the result generated continues to differ, the program continues execution, looping from line [6] to line [3].

Stopping Your Program

As soon as you introduce branching into a program, you complicate its execution and open up the possibility for error. For example, you may incorrectly express the condition to terminate a program, potentially causing it to run forever. This condition is called an *endless* or *infinite loop*.

In fact, it is so likely you will run into this situation, that you must learn how to make a program stop at your command before you write programs that include branch expressions.

Attention

You tell the system to stop executing programs with an *attention* signal. Every APL2 system has a way to signal attention. Exactly how this is done is different for different systems and even varies depending on the kind of terminal or keyboard you are using. You need to know the right way to signal attention on the device you are using. Some terminals actually have a button labeled ATTN or BREAK. Pressing this button once signals an attention. On IBM 3270-style terminals, pressing the key labeled PA2 (PA1 in TSO or when session manager not in use) signals attention. If you're using a session manager and your program produces a lot of output, you may have to take some special action to enable the attention key. For example, using the APL2 session manager on an IBM 370 with a 3270-style terminal, you have to press RESET before pressing PA2 if the screen is filled with output.

Here's a pair of programs you can enter and run to help you determine whether you have found the right key:

```
        ∇Z←PROGA X
[1]     Z←1000ρ2
[2]     Z←PROGB X
[3]     ∇


        ∇Z←PROGB X
[1]     BCNT←BCNT+1
[2]     BCNT
[3]     Z←PROGA X
[4]     ∇
```

PROGA sets the local variable Z to a 1000-item vector, then calls *PROGB*. *PROGB* increments a global counter, displays it, then calls *PROGA*. X is passed from function to function but never used. Clearly, once started, these programs will not terminate on their own. They may use up all available space and terminate with a *WS FULL* error, but they won't terminate because of the programming error. In fact, the assignment to Z in *PROGA* is done precisely so space will be used up before you've done too much computing.

When you've located the attention key on the device you're using, enter the following two expressions, wait a few seconds, then signal attention:

```
        BCNT←0
        PROGA 5

1
2
3
4
5
6
7
8
        ⟵(attention signaled)
PROGA[1]
```

You may get a different response from the one shown here. The program name and the line number in the response you get depend on what function and which line of it are being executed when you press the attention key. The rule is that once attention is signaled, program execution terminates as soon as the end of a line has been reached.

The global variable *BCNT* tells you how many times *PROGB* has been executed. If you enter)SIS, you should find many occurrences of *PROGB* in the state indicator and many occurrences of *PROGA* also. Be prepared for a lot of output if you enter)SIS, although on most systems you can also use the attention key to stop output. (On IBM systems using the APL2 session manager, output is terminated by the session manager SUPPRESS command, normally located on the PF5 key.)

If you reset the state indicator—with)*RESET*—and enter the two expressions again, you will probably find that execution stops somewhere else and that *BCNT* has a different value. When you have finished experimenting with these functions, be sure to enter)*RESET* to clear the state indicator.

Interrupt

Sometimes an attention signal is not enough to make a program stop. Here is a program that looks simple but on most systems will execute a long time:

```
        ∇Z←PROGC X
[1]     Z←⍟\10000ρ1
[2]     ∇
```

The expression on line [1] executes almost one hundred million logarithms before reaching the end of line [1]. If you press attention, nothing happens because attention is recognized at end of line.

A second signal, similar to attention, is available to terminate a program immediately without waiting for the end of a line. This signal is an *interrupt*. Typically, pressing the attention key twice signals an interrupt. The interrupt causes a line to terminate before the end is reached, possibly in the middle of executing a primitive function. An interrupt signal produces a response very much like an error in the line.

Call the program *PROGC*, wait a few seconds, then signal an interrupt (two attentions). You should get something like this:

```
      PROGC 5
   ←——(interrupt signaled)
INTERRUPT
PROGC[1]   Z←⊛\10000ρ1
        ∧ ∧
```

Infinite Loops

When you write programs that loop, it is entirely possible you might write a program that just keeps running. Here's an example that creates a loop by the unconditional branch at line [2]. In effect, line [1] is evaluated over and over again:

```
      ∇COUNT;I
[1]   I←0
[2]   L1:I←I+1
[3]   →L1
[4]   ∇
```

Enter the following expression, wait a few seconds, then press attention:

```
      COUNT
   ←——(attention signaled)
COUNT[1]
```

The value of *I* tells you how many times line [1] was evaluated.

As usual, make sure you clean up the state indicator:

)*RESET*

Infinite loops are not necessarily bad. Because APL2 is interactive, you can start a computation and stop it when you want to. Maybe it will even eventually stop itself with an error. Even errors are not necessarily bad. It's alright to write a "quick-and-dirty" program—maybe even with an infinite loop that stops with an error. For example, you write a loop that indexes a vector and does something, then prints a result before incrementing an index and going on to the next item of the vector. This is an infinite loop because you have coded no termination. It will stop because eventually you will index off the end of the vector and get an *INDEX ERROR*. You've got your answers printed out, so who cares about the error? You should *not*, of course, put "quick-and-dirty" programs into an application you're building for others. Use them for your own personal computing only.

Here's an example of a useful infinite loop. You know that to compute an amount of money after receiving 5% interest, you multiply by 1.05. Here is a program that prints out a report of your balance after each year:

```
       ∇ INT AMT;Y
[1]    Y←1
[2]    'YEARS  AMOUNT AT 5% A YEAR'
[3]    LP:'55555   5555555.55555'⍕ Y(AMT←AMT×1.05)
[4]    Y←Y+1
[5]    →LP
[6]    ∇
```

Line [3] uses the **format** function (⍕) to format the output. Section 7.5 discusses **format**.

Here is a sample execution of *INT*:

```
      INT 331.25
YEARS    AMOUNT AT 5% A YEAR
   1       347.8125
   2       365.20313
   3       383.46328
   4       402.63645
   5       422.76827
   6       443.90668
   7       466.10202
   8       489.40712
   9       513.87747
  10       539.57135
  11       566.54991
  ...         ...
```

And the report just keeps on going. When you've seen enough, press attention and)*RESET*.

Good Programming Practices with Branching

In some programming languages, branching is the only means to control the program. In APL2, you often don't need to write branch statements. Instead, the array operations of the language implicitly do looping. If you ever have a choice between using an array operation and writing a loop, use the array operation. When you are beginning to use APL2, it is a good idea to take the time to look for array operations where they are not apparent. You might be surprised how often they arise. Most APL2 systems are optimized for array operations. On these systems, looping is the most inefficient thing you can do. So, if you are about to write a program you think requires a loop, review the problem—maybe you can solve it with **each** or some other operator instead of a loop. Sometimes, however, you cannot avoid looping.

Placing the Test for More Data

If you determine that your solution requires a loop, you must consider where to place the test for more data. This test can be near the end of the program (a *trailing test*) or near the beginning (*leading test*). Here is an outline of the program logic for a trailing test:

1.   Initialize a counter.
2.   Use the counter to select some data.
3.   Apply some computation to the data.
4.   Increment the counter.
5.   Test to see whether there is any more data and go back to step 2 if there is.

The trailing-test logic is common and works for many problems. But when you think about writing a program to solve a problem, you should try to think of some real examples of the data the program will operate on. More often than you might expect, the program will be given empty data. For example, a banking program that selects all the accounts for one person and adds them together might come across someone who is registered with the bank but has no active accounts. The program had better be ready to take the sum of no accounts. Using trailing-test logic will cause the program to fail for this case.

Here is an outline of the program logic for a leading test:

1.   Initialize a counter.
2.   Test to see whether there is any more data and exit if not.
3.   Use the counter to select some data.
4.   Apply some computation to the data.
5.   Increment the counter.
6.   Branch back to step 2.

It is usually better to use a leading test rather than a trailing test even though you think you'll never get an empty case. If you always use this second outline for writing loops, you will have only one scheme to learn to write, and only one scheme to remember when you look at your programs later.

Style of Branch Expressions

Given that you are going to write branch expressions, you have a large choice of possible styles. Any APL2 expression that produces a vector whose leading item is an integer can serve as the right argument of a branch. As mentioned before, however, there is one recommended way of branching: **replicate**. Here are two forms of branching using **replicate**:

- Branch to $L1$ if a condition is true:

    $\rightarrow$(condition)/$L1$

- Branch to $L1$ if a condition is false:

    $\rightarrow$($\sim$condition)/$L1$

These have become the standard forms, but you will often see other forms, like the following:

- Branch to $L1$ if a condition is true:

    $\rightarrow$(condition)$\uparrow L1$
    $\rightarrow$(condition)$\rho L1$
    $\rightarrow L1\times\iota$condition

- Branch to $L1$ if a condition is false:

    $\rightarrow$(condition)$\downarrow L1$

Once you become a proficient programmer, it's all right to deviate from **replicate** now and again; but to the extent you do, other people will experience trouble reading your programs.

Exercises for Section 7.1

1. Rewrite the *SQRT* function to check whether the argument is a positive simple scalar.

2. Write a **branch** expression to branch to *L1* if *I* is 1, to *L2* if *I* is 2, and to *L3* if *I* is 3:

   a. Using **replicate**.
   b. Using **indexing**.

3. Here is a program that simulates a **multiplication-reduction**:

   ```
         ∇Z←TIMESR R;I
   [1]   ⍝ times reduction of a simple vector
   [2]   I←Z←1            ⍝ set result and counter
   [3]   L1:Z←Z×R[I]      ⍝ include next product
   [4]   →((⍴R)≥I←I+1)/L1 ⍝ loop back if more
   [5]   ∇
   ```

   a. Explain why this program fails when given an empty vector.
   b. Rewrite the program to use a leading test.

4. For each of the following expressions, state under what conditions the branch is taken:

   a. →(1≥≡A)/SIM
   b. →(N=⌈N)/INT
   c. →('END'∧.=3↑ANS)/OUT
   d. →(C=5)↑EQ
   e. →(C=5)↓IEQ
   f. →('AEIOU'∨.∈WORD)⍴VOW
   g. →(NEG,EQ,POS)[2+×DATA]
   h. →(0=⍴ANS)/OUT

5. The last four decimal digits of a number can be determined with the following expression:

   $$(4⍴10)⊤N$$

   However, attempting to find the last four digits of the number $2*2*N$, even for a small integer *N*, would exceed the capacity of a computer. However, if you do multiplication in a loop and truncate the result to four digits at each step, you can produce the last four digits easily.

   Write a function *LASTFOUR* which will find the last four digits of $2*2*N$ for any positive integer *N*.

Here are some test cases:

```
      2*2*4
65536
      LASTFOUR 4
5536
      2*2*5
4294967296
      LASTFOUR 5
7296
      LASTFOUR 73
4896
```

Section 7.2 — Debugging Your Program

Once a program stops, either with an error or in response to an attention or interrupt signal, you can look for the error and correct it. Earlier you were told that after an error you should always clean up the state indicator with → or)*RESET*. When you are debugging a program, however, you normally do not clean up the state indicator until after you have determined what has gone wrong. You want to look at the state indicator, and you want to check the values of local variables.

Here are some things to look at and do:

1. Look at the state indicator—)*SIS*—to see how you got to where you are.

2. Look at the arguments of the function that stopped. Are they reasonable values? Are their shapes correct?

3. Look at the values of other local variables to see whether intermediate results are correct. You can look at any name in the workspace, provided a local name does not shadow it. In the course of your investigation, you may enter)*RESET* 1 to remove one line from the state indicator so that you can look at the values of names that are shadowed. In doing so, you will lose the value of some local names.

4. Try sample expressions in immediate execution. If any of them fail, enter → to clear each failed one. Don't use)*RESET* because that would clear everything, including the error you're investigating. If you find the error, you can correct it immediately by editing the function.

Note the difference between use of → and)*RESET* 1. The → clears the state indicator of everything up to an immediate execution line.)*RESET* 1 removes exactly one line from the state indicator.

Here's an example of how the state indicator is used in debugging. Suppose you have a large set of programs. When you execute them you get the following:

```
    START
 LENGTH ERROR
 COMPUTE[3]   Z←X+Y+1
            ∧ ∧
```

You wrote the function *COMPUTE*, and you know it is correct. What could be wrong? Look at the state indicator:

```
      )SIS
 COMPUTE[3]  Z←X+Y+1
            ∧ ∧
 SCALE[5]  TEMP←VALUE÷COMPUTE VALUE
                      ∧∧
 START[1]  SCALE INPUT
           ∧
 *   START
     ∧
```

This looks reasonable to you although you realize you forgot to put a descriptive comment on line 1 of *START*. You make a note to fix that later.

You know that in *COMPUTE*, *X* and *Y* are the arguments and are supposed to be the same length. Check it:

```
      ρX
 3
      ρY
 3
```

You got a *LENGTH ERROR* adding two three-item vectors—very strange. Use the *DISPLAY* function to look at the structures of the arrays:

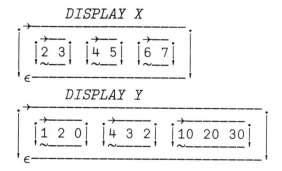

Ask for the shapes of the items:

```
        ρ¨X
  2   2   2
        ρ¨Y
  3   3   3
```

Now you see the problem. X and Y are nested and the items don't match in length. *COMPUTE* is not supposed to be called with nested arguments, so the error must be in the caller of *COMPUTE*.

Now you can begin to look at the caller of *COMPUTE*. Start by removing *COMPUTE* from the state indicator so any variables shadowed by it become visible again:

```
       )RESET 1
       )SIS
SCALE[5] TEMP←VALUE÷COMPUTE VALUE
                  ∧∧
START[1] SCALE INPUT
           ∧
*   START
    ∧
```

And repeat the process, looking at the arguments of *SCALE* and so forth.

Stopping Where You Choose

When APL2 detects an error in a program, it terminates execution and displays a message. When you stop a program with attention or interrupt, execution stops—but where it stops is a matter of chance.

As part of debugging a program called *MYPROG*, you may want your program to stop if it ever reaches lines [3] or [9]. You could edit the function and make an intentional error on lines [3] and [9], but there is a better way. APL2 permits you to request a program stop with the stop facility. The stop facility is indicated by $S\Delta$ and the program name, for example, $S\Delta MYPROG$. To this name, you assign line numbers as in this example:

> $S\Delta MYPROG \leftarrow 3\ 9$

When you execute *MYPROG*, its execution will stop every time line [3] or [9] is selected for execution. Execution stops before anything on the line is evaluated.

You can see what stops are set by entering the following:

> $S\Delta MYPROG$
>
> 3 9

Whenever you set some stops in a program, they replace the old stops.

> $S\Delta MYPROG \leftarrow 5$
> $S\Delta MYPROG$
>
> 5

You can add a stop to existing stops by using **catenate** as follows:

> $S\Delta MYPROG \leftarrow S\Delta MYPROG, 3\ 9$
> $S\Delta MYPROG$
>
> 3 5 9

You can stop on all lines of a function by entering this:

> $S\Delta MYPROG \leftarrow \iota 50$

If there are fewer than 50 lines, the extra requests are ignored. (Of course, if there are more than 50 lines in the function, you didn't enter a large enough integer.)

You remove all stops by setting no stops:

    *S∆MYPROG←*ι0

Restarting Your Program

After you've stopped your program, you may want to start it again. You may have fixed a program error, altered the value of a variable, or, perhaps, made no change at all.

There are two ways to restart a program without starting over from the beginning.

You can restart the execution of the function at the top of the state indicator or at any line of the function by entering a branch arrow (→) followed by the number of the line you want executed next:

    →3

Typically, you want to restart at the line whose number is in brackets in the)*SIS* display. However, you can restart on any line you choose.

You may want to restart execution at the point where execution stopped—perhaps in the middle of a line. You do this by entering:

    →ι0

This is true no matter how the program was stopped, but its use is most appropriate after an interrupt. Here's an example of an expression with an error:

    2+*QQ*×ι10
VALUE ERROR
    2+*QQ*×ι10
      ∧

You can fix this expression by giving a value to *QQ* and entering the expression again:

    →
    QQ←10
    2+*QQ*×ι10
12 22 32 42 52 62 72 82 92 102

Alternately, you can give *QQ* a value and resume the expression from where it left off:

```
     )ERASE QQ
     2+QQ×ι10
VALUE ERROR
     2+QQ×ι10
      ∧

     QQ←10
     →ι0
12 22 32 42 52 62 72 82 92 102
```

Execution stopped because a value for *QQ* could not be located. After *QQ* had a value, →ι0 resumed execution from where it left off without repeating the computation of ι10. Not having to recompute **interval** is a minimal savings. On the other hand, if instead of **interval**, the function that did not need to be reevaluated was a program that runs for an hour, the savings would be more significant.

If function *F* calls function *G* and *G* stops, the state indicator looks like this:

```
     )SIS
G[5]  A←X∗.5
      ∧  ∧
F[7]  Z←G X
      ∧∧
```

You may want to restart execution in *F*, not *G*. To restart on line 7 of *F*, clear the first line in the state indicator before restarting execution:

```
     )RESET 1
     )SIS
F[7]  Z←G X
      ∧∧
     →7
```

You can restart on any line of a program you choose as long as the function is at the top of the state indicator.

Tracing Execution

If you set a stop on every line of a program, you can trace its execution. Each time the program stops, you can branch to resume execution. This approach, while it works, is tedious; so APL2 provides a trace facility (*T*Δ) similar to the stop facility. Unlike the stop facility, the trace facility does not stop execution. Rather, after each line traced has been completely evaluated, output is generated containing the name of the function, the line number, and the last value computed on that line (if any).

The use of *T*Δ is the same as *S*Δ in every respect. To set a trace on lines [3] and [9] of *MYPROG*, enter:

        *T*Δ*MYPROG*←3 9

To remove a trace, assign an empty vector:

        *T*Δ*MYPROG*←⍳0

As an extended example of tracing, consider the *SQRT* program. Here are the request and the result for it:

        SQRT 5
    2.236067977
            (*SQRT* 5)*2
     5

The program clearly works, but you have no idea how many times the program loops before converging on the answer.

You can watch the convergence of the approximations by tracing line [3]:

        *T*Δ*SQRT*←3
        SQRT 5
    SQRT[3] 3
    SQRT[3] 2.333333333
    SQRT[3] 2.238095238
    SQRT[3] 2.236068896
    SQRT[3] 2.236067977
    SQRT[3] 2.236067977
    2.236067977

Tracing functions can generate a lot of output. If you get tired of looking at it, press attention. Attention stops the output and stops the program. You can then remove the traces and restart execution.

Exercises for Section 7.2

1. Modify the initial guess in the *SQRT* function to .5 × *N* and see if the result converges faster.

2. Modify the *SQRT* function and change the estimate of line [2] to Z←1E25.

    a. Put a trace on line [3] and see how many iterations are needed to compute *SQRT* 5.
    b. Try *SQRT* 1E50.
    c. Change the initial guess to 1 and try *SQRT* 1E50.

Section 7.3 – Prompting for Input

Often in the course of running, a program needs some information from the program's user. The program may want the user to choose which of several reports to print or may want to prompt the user to enter data. This section discusses APL2's two styles of input: evaluated input and character input.

Evaluated Input

Putting a **quad** (□) anywhere in an expression except to the left of an assignment arrow causes a request for input. The input request is signaled by □:, after which APL2 expects an entry from the keyboard. Here's an example:

```
      2×□
□:
      10
20
```

Quad is called *evaluated input* because whatever is entered in response to the □: prompt is evaluated as though it were entered in immediate execution mode. It is also sometimes simply called *quad input*.

You can enter a long vector by catenating a **quad** at the end of each line of data to be continued:

```
     MAT←3 12ρ6 8 2 5 9 1 2 5 3 7 5 12 4 6,□
□:
     1 0 9 1 2 3 6 9 3 10 4 7 9 12 5 3 9 0 1,□
□:
     7 3 2

     MAT
6  8  2  5  9  1  2  5  3  7  5  12
4  6  1  0  9  1  2  3  6  9  3  10
4  7  9 12  5  3  9  0  1  7  3   2
```

Inside a program, you can use **quad** to accept an input requested by the program. Here's a program that asks for your age and produces an output that varies with your entry:

```
        ∇Z←AGE;R1;R2;R3 ⍝ GET AGE OF USER
[1]     R1←'You''re not born yet'
[2]     R2←'Thanks'
[3]     R3←'Wishful thinking'
[4]     'Enter your age'
[5]     Z←□
[6]     □←(1++/Z>200 0)⊃R1 R2 R3
[7]     ∇
```

Here are some sample calls:

```
        AGE
Enter your age
□:
        31
Thanks
31

        AGE
Enter your age
□:
        300
Wishful thinking
300
```

```
        AGE
Enter your age
[]:
        ‾1
You're not born yet
‾1
```

Entering a → or)*RESET* in response to a **quad** input request terminates the program. As the user of a program, you can use such a
response to **quad** to stop execution whenever you want. As a
programmer, you cannot prevent a user from stopping a program
this way.

Character Input

A common situation is the need to prompt for character data. For
example, a program may request that the user enter his or her name.
The program *GETNAME* uses **quad** to prompt for input. As soon as
you test it, you will see the problem it creates:

```
        ∇Z←GETNAME   ⍝ PROMPT FOR USER'S NAME
[1]     'Enter your name'
[2]     Z←[]
[3]     ∇

        GETNAME
Enter your name
[]:
        JIM
VALUE ERROR
        JIM
        ∧
[]:
        →
```

The problem is that the user must enter legal APL2 expressions in
response to a **quad** input request. *JIM* has no value, so a *VALUE
ERROR* is reported. Worse would be if *JIM* did have some value.
Your program would get a wrong response. For **quad** input, the
name (a character string) must be surrounded by quotation marks.
People, however, do not use quotation marks when they write their
name. Jim would not think to enter:

```
'JIM'
```

in response to a request for his name. You could, of course, change the prompt to say "Enter your name in single quotes" but this creates extra work for the user and is cumbersome.

To accept character input, APL2 provides **quote-quad** (⍞) input—also called *quad-prime input*. **Quote-quad** used anywhere in an expression, except to the left of an assignment arrow causes a request for input. No characters are displayed, the keyboard just opens for input. Whatever is typed is gathered into a character vector. It is not evaluated. Here is an example:

```
        ∇Z←GETNAME1
 [1]    'Enter your name'
 [2]    Z←⍞
 [3]    ∇
```

```
        GETNAME1
 Enter your name
 JIM         ←——(user typed this)
 JIM         ←——(explicit result prints this)
```

The first *JIM* is the user's typed response. The second *JIM* is the explicit result from *GETNAME*1. It is a three-item character vector. If an APL2 expression is entered in response to **quote-quad** input, it is not evaluated. It is accepted as a character string:

```
        X←⍞
 3+4
        X
 3+4
        ⍴X
 3
```

Quote-quad input can be used to enter a vector of character vectors:

```
        VOFV←⍞ ⍞ ⍞
 JIM
 JOHN
 KAREN
        VOFV
  KAREN JOHN JIM
```

Note the right-to-left execution and its effect on the result. Because the rightmost **quote-quad** is the first processed, you can use the following expression for input of a vector of character vectors:

```
      VOFV←⌽⍞ ⍞ ⍞
JIM
JOHN
KAREN
        VOFV
  JIM JOHN KAREN
```

Applying **reverse** puts the result into the same order as the entries.

Here is a practical example of using **quote-quad**:

```
      ∇INVENTORY;ANS   ⍝ inventory program
[1]   'Need instructions? (Y/N)'
[2]   ANS←⍞
[3]   →('N'=↑ANS)/L1   ⍝ branch if answer is no
[4]   DESCRIBE         ⍝ explain program
[5]   L1:              ⍝ rest of program
[6]   ∇
```

Line [1] prints a question. Line [2] asks for character input. Line [3] checks the input and if the response begins with the letter N, branches to $L1$ (line [5]), skipping the output of the description (an incomplete test but simple and effective). Line [4] prints the contents of the variable named *DESCRIBE*.

Executing Character Input

There is a problem with using evaluated input (⎕) in a program: You have no means of checking the user's input before it is evaluated. For example, the program *MULT* shown next drills the user in the multiplication tables.

```
        ∇MULT N;A;B;ANS;I   ⍝ drill up to N
[1]     NEXT:(A B)←?2ρN
[2]     'How much is' A 'times' B '?'
[3]     I←¯1
[4]     L1:I←I+1              ⍝ count wrong answers
[5]     ANS←⎕                ⍝ prompt for answer
[6]     →(ANS=A×B)/NEXT      ⍝ branch if good answer
[7]     →(I=0 1)/L2 L3       ⍝ three way branch
[8]     'Correct answer is '(A×B)
[9]     →NEXT
[10] L2:'Look at this and try again'
[11]    (−N+5)↑[2]A Bρ'o'  ⍝ picture correct answer
[12]    →L1
[13] L3:'No.  One more try'
[14]    →L1
[15]    ∇
```

Because *MULT* has no means for the user to quit, the user must enter a → in response to ⎕: in order to quit. Here's how the program works:

```
        MULT 12
  How much is 5 times 4 ?
☐:
        20
  How much is 6 times 6 ?
☐:
        36
  How much is 4 times 3 ?
☐:
        10
Look at this and try again
                ooo
                ooo
                ooo
                ooo
☐:
        15
No.  One more try
☐:
        16
  Correct answer is   12
  How much is 5 times 6 ?
☐:
        30
  How much is 5 times 2 ?
☐:
        →
```

Notice the use of **quad** input on line 5 of *MULT*. Knowing that any
APL2 expression works in response to a **quad** input, a clever user
might give 13×2 in response to the problem "How much is 13 times
2 ?" Because this response computes the answer, it defeats the
purpose of the program.

Using **quote-quad** input, you can make the program more immune
to misuse and more friendly as well. Because the user response with
quote-quad input is a character vector, you can check that the
response contains only numbers. The program can even check for
the string *HELP* and branch to a help routine. Once the user's input
is checked, you need a way to *execute* the character vector response
and evaluate the expression represented by the vector.

The APL2 function **execute** (⍎) converts a character string to an executable expression and attempts to execute it, as in this example:

   `⍎'3+4'`

`7`

If you have a character string that represents a vector of numbers, you can use **execute** to get the vector of numbers:

   `CN1←'23.5 1.76 ¯127'`
   `ρCN1`

`14`

   `⍎CN1`
`23.5 1.76 ¯127`
   `ρ⍎CN1`
`3`

You may have a character string representing amounts of money:

   `CN2←'$1.56 $128.50 $2,400.00'`

You can't apply **execute** to this string because it is not the proper representation of an APL2 numeric vector. The dollar signs are illegal and the comma is the APL2 function **catenate**. However, if you remove the illegal characters, you can execute the string:

   `⍎CN2~'$,'`
`1.56 128.5 2400`

Suppose you have a matrix of characters that represents a set of expressions:

   `CN3←2 4ρ'6×ι3ϕ−ι3'`

   `CN3`
`6×ι3`
`ϕ−ι3`

You can't use **execute** on matrices or higher rank arrays—only on vectors and scalars. You can, however, turn a matrix into a vector of its rows, execute each item, and rebuild the matrix:

```
      ⊃⍎¨⊂[2]CN3
 6 12 18
¯3 ¯2 ¯1

      ρ⊃⍎¨⊂[2]CN3
2 3
```

A somewhat different use of **execute** is to extract the value from a variable, given its name. Here is a function that prints information about a variable:

```
      ∇PRINTV NAME;PRINTV
[1]   PRINTV←⍎NAME
[2]   'NAME:' NAME ' DEPTH:' (≡PRINTV)
[3]   'RANK:' (ρρPRINTV) ' SHAPE:' (ρPRINTV)
[4]   ∇

      PRINTV 'CN3'
NAME: CN3  DEPTH: 1
RANK:  2   SHAPE:  2 4
```

There's something new in this function: The name of the function is shadowed. This is done to minimize name conflicts. *PRINTV* can be used to print information about any variable in the workspace except those shadowed by *PRINTV* itself. Thus, you cannot apply the function to either of the names *NAME* or *PRINTV*.

Using **quote-quad** input and **execute**, you can write a new version of the multiplication drill program that is less likely to fail if the user enters an improper answer:

```
      ∇ MULT1 N;A;B;ANS   ⍝ drill up to N
[1]    NEXT:(A B)←?2ρN
[2]     'How much is' A 'times' B '?'
[3]     I←¯1
[4]    L1:I←I+1                ⍝ count wrong answers
[5]    L1R:ANS←⍞               ⍝ prompt for answer
[6]     →(~∧/ANS∊'0123456789')/ER ⍝ only digits
[7]     ANS←⍎ANS               ⍝ get numeric answer
[8]     →(ANS=A×B)/NEXT        ⍝ branch if good answer
[9]     →I↓L2 L3               ⍝ three-way branch
[10]    'Correct answer is '(A×B)
[11]    →NEXT
[12]   L2:'Look at this and try again'
[13]    (-N+5)↑[2]A Bρ'○'  ⍝ picture correct answer
[14]    →L1
[15]   L3:'No.  One more try'
[16]    →L1
[17]   ER:'Please enter an integer'
[18]    →L1R
[19]     ∇
```

The input is now requested using **quote-quad** input. Line [6] checks to ensure that only characters valid in integers were entered.

This function is still not foolproof. For example, a user could enter more digits than possible in the maximum representable integer. To be completely safe, you need error trapping facilities which are not discussed in this book.

Exercises for Section 7.3

1. The *MULT*1 program will fail if the user presses enter in response to the prompt for an answer. This failure occurs because an empty character vector does not contain any invalid characters. The **execute** function will not produce any result and *MULT*1 will get a *VALUE ERROR*. Modify *MULT*1 to check for the empty response.

2. Define a function that converts a given character matrix representation of numeric data to a vector of numbers. Each row of the input character matrix *M* forms one number in the output matrix.

3. Modify *MULT*1 so it does the following:

   a. Checks for the entry *HELP* and prints out instructions.
   b. Checks for the entries *STOP* or *QUIT* and terminates execution.
   c. Offers a congratulatory message when the user enters a correct answer.

4. Variable *N* is a two-item vector of character strings and *AA* and *BB* are two other variables as follows:

$$N\leftarrow'AA'\ \ 'BB'$$
$$AA\leftarrow'VARIABLE\ 1'$$
$$BB\leftarrow\iota\ \ddot{}\ \iota 4$$

   Without mentioning the names *AA* or *BB*, write an expression that will produce a new variable *AABB* which is a two-item vector containing the values of *AA* and *BB*.

5. Replace the following sequence of statements from a program with one expression, using **execute**:

$$\rightarrow(2=\rho,V)/COLN$$
$$T\leftarrow M$$
$$\rightarrow CONT$$
$$COLN:T\leftarrow M[;1\downarrow V]$$
$$CONT:$$

6. Suppose character matrix *M* contains the character representation of a numeric array:

$$M\leftarrow2\ 7\rho'2.1\ 2.22.3\ 2.4'$$

a. Write an expression to convert *M* to the equivalent numeric matrix.

b. If row 1 of *M* contained the representation of two numbers and row 2 contained the representation of three numbers, what error message would be generated by the expression you wrote in part a?

7. State the result of each of the following expressions. State if the result displays or if it is suppressed and where appropriate, give the values of *X* and *Y*.

a.   ⍞'5×3'
b.   ⍞'2','5×3'
c.   ⍞'''5×3'''
d.   ⍞⍞'''5×3'''
e.   ⍞'X←5'
f.   ⍞X←'5×7'
g.   ⍞'X←5×7'
h.   ⍞X,X←'5+3'
i.   ⍞X,X←' .5+3 '
j.   ⍞'X←','5+3'
k.   ⍞X←⍞'5×3'
l.   Y←⍞X←''' 3×5'''

Section 7.4 – Output with Quad and Quote-Quad

You can use either **quad** or **quote-quad** for output by placing the symbol to the left of an assignment arrow.

Quad for Output

□ produces output when it appears on the left of an assignment arrow (←). For an expression that causes output to display, □← makes no difference:

```
      □←150.20×1.05*5
191.6974907
```

But □ is effective when you want to assign a value to a variable and display the value at the same time:

```
      □←T←150.20×1.05*5
191.6974907
```

Quad is also effective in the middle of an expression to display an intermediate result:

        T←150.20×☐←1.05*5
    1.276281562

By using **quad** to display an intermediate result, you can trace the internal execution of an expression.

Quote-Quad for Output

When a value is displayed because of **quote-quad** output, it looks the same as if it had been displayed without the **quote-quad**, but the next output starts at the end of that output instead of on a new line.

Here's an example for vectors:

        ▽*QQO*   ⍝ *quote-quad output*
    [1]   ☐←1 2 3
    [2]   '*ABC*'
    [3]   ▽

        QQO
    1 2 3*ABC*

Programs primarily use **quote-quad** output for output of vectors. You may want to experiment to see what your system does with **quote-quad** output of higher-rank arrays.

Character Input Following Character Output

Output following a **quote-quad** output takes place on the same line as the **quote-quad** output. The same is true for **quote-quad** input. Here's an example:

```
        ∇Z←GETNAME2
[1]     ⍞←'Enter your name '
[2]     Z←⍞
[3]     ∇


        N←GETNAME2
Enter your name JIM

        N
                JIM
        ⍴N
19
```

Using character input after character output you can have a response entered on the same line as the question. The result returned to the program is what was entered. Characters on the line that were not entered become blanks when the value of ⍞ is given to the program.

Exercises for Section 7.4

1. Write a *GETNAME3* function similar to *GETNAME2* shown in the section "Character Input Following Character Output" that deletes leading blanks before returning the result.

2. A programming problem often given in earlier programming language courses was: "Write a program to read in a set of numbers, compute their average, place the result in a variable named *AVER*, and finally display the result." Write an equivalent APL2 expression.

Section 7.5 — Controlling Output

Without applying APL2 functions, you cannot control output. The system—not you—decides how output should look. Output is not, however, undisciplined. APL2 has rules for output, as described in Chapter 5, and if you know the rules, you can exploit them to gain some control. For example, catenating titles onto a table gives you control over spacing of the columns. The individual numbers, however, are always displayed in some default format. By converting numeric arrays into simple character arrays, the **format** function (⍕) gives you control over the appearance of numbers.

Format

In its simplest form, monadic **format** (⍕) produces a simple character array, which displays the same way as the argument array:

```
      AN←3 3ρ1 134.23 100000 0 ¯15.4 ¯14000 1 .65 0
      AN
1 134.23 100000
0 ¯15.4  ¯14000
1   0.65       0

      ρAN
3 3

      ⍕AN
1 134.23 100000
0 ¯15.4  ¯14000
1   0.65       0

      ρ⍕AN
3 15
```

Of course, if you are only going to display the array, there is no point in applying **format**. However, since the result is a simple character array, you can capture the result and modify it any way you want before displaying it. For example, you may want to replace all the blanks with some non-blank character (as is done for check protection):

```
      FM1←⍕AN
((,' '=FM1)/,FM1)←'/'

      FM1
1/134.23/100000
0/⁻15.4//⁻14000
////0.65//////0
```

Format also applies to arrays containing characters:

```
      ⍕'ABC',2 3
ABC 2 3
      ρ⍕'ABC',2 3
7
      ⍕'SMITH' 'JONES'
 SMITH JONES
      ρ⍕'SMITH' 'JONES'
13
```

Format by Specification

When **format** (⍕) has a left argument, the function has either of two different names according to whether the left argument is numeric or character.

If you have a numeric left argument, the function is **format by specification**. If the left argument is two integers, they control the format of every item in the array. The first of the two numbers specifies how many columns in the result **format by specification** produces for each column in the right argument. If the second integer is not negative, it specifies the number of digits to the right of a decimal point:

```
      10 2 ⍕AN
1.00    134.23 100000.00
 .00    ⁻15.40 ⁻14000.00
1.00       .65       .00
```

If you specify the number of digits to the right of the decimal point as zero, then **format by specification** produces no decimal point and displays only integers:

```
      7 0⍕AN
      1     134 100000
      0     ¯15 ¯14000
      1       1      0
```

Notice that, in each case, the numbers are correctly rounded.

A negative integer as the second item of the left argument requests a result in *exponential* or *scientific* notation and the magnitude of the number indicates the number of digits in the mantissa:

```
      10 ¯4⍕AN
   1.000E0  1.342E2    1.000E5
   0.000E0  ¯1.540E1  ¯1.400E4
   1.000E0  6.500E¯1   0.000E0
```

If the first integer in the argument indicates the width is zero, then **format by specification** uses an appropriate width:

```
      0 1⍕AN
   1.0 134.2 100000.0
    .0 ¯15.4 ¯14000.0
   1.0    .7       .0
```

```
      0 ¯4⍕AN
   1.000E0  1.342E2    1.000E5
   0.000E0  ¯1.540E1  ¯1.400E4
   1.000E0  6.500E¯1   0.000E0
```

If the left argument contains a single number, **format by specification** assumes a width of zero:

```
      1⍕AN
   1.0 134.2 100000.0
    .0 ¯15.4 ¯14000.0
   1.0    .7       .0
```

You may indicate a different format for each column by specifying a pair of integers for each column:

```
      3 0 10 2 10 ¯4⍕AN
   1     134.23    1.000E5
   0    ¯15.40    ¯1.400E4
   1       .65     0.000E0
```

Format by Example

Format (⍕) with a character left argument is called **picture format** or **format by example**. The left argument is a character vector that is an example of how a row of the result should appear, except that the numbers in the vector are controls on formatting instead of data. A 5 in the left argument is the only digit that doesn't request any explicit control. Therefore, begin a pattern with all 5's and add controls as they are needed:

```
      PF←'5555.55   555.55   555.555'
      PF⍕ 8743.25 123.46 145.348
 8743.25   123.46   145.348

      ρPF⍕ 8743.25 123.46 145.348
 24
```

Notice that, in this example the result is a character string as long as the left argument.

If the left argument contains only one numeric pattern, **format by example** applies it to each of the numbers in the right argument.

```
      ' 5555.55'⍕ 8743.25 123.46 145.348
 8743.25   123.46   145.35
```

Note that when you request two digits to the right of the decimal point, rounding is done.

By default, neither leading nor trailing zeros are printed. If there are no non-zero digits to the right of the decimal point, then neither the decimal point nor the zeros are produced. If the number is zero (to the requested precision), then nothing is printed:

```
      ' 5555.55'⍕ 8743.25 123   0   145.348
 8743.25   123              145.35
```

A digit 0 in the pattern is a request to fill in leading or trailing zeros from that point until the decimal point.

```
      ' 5505.50'⍕ 8743.25 123   0   145.348
 8743.25   123.00   00.00   145.35
```

A digit 9 in the pattern is the same as a digit 0 unless the value to be formatted is 0, in which case there is no padding:

```
    ' 5595.59'⍕ 8743.25 123    0  145.348
8743.25  123.00              145.35
```

Commas in the pattern are treated as separating symbols as they are in normal U.S. business usage. If a comma would not separate digits in the formatted result, it is not printed:

```
      ' 5,505.50'⍕ 8743.25 123 0  145.348
8,743.25    123.00    00.00   145.35
```

Other non-digits in the pattern are treated as decorations and are copied into the result:

```
      ' 5,505.50 marks '⍕ 8743.25 123 0
8,743.25 marks     123.00 marks      00.00 marks
```

If the data represents amounts of money, you may want a currency symbol before each one:

```
      ' $5,505.50'⍕ 8743.25 123 0  145.348
$8,743.25 $  123.00 $   00.00 $  145.35
```

The dollar sign is just copied into the result in place—it is a decoration. Usually you would want the dollar sign to abut the number without intervening blanks. This is called a floating decoration. There are three digits used to request floating decorations:

1— Float decorator if negative.

2— Float decorator if nonnegative.

3— Float decorator always.

If your numbers really represent money, you probably want the dollar sign always. Therefore, you can use the digit 3 anywhere in the pattern (on the left of the decimal point) to request that the dollar sign be floated:

```
      ' $5,503.50'⍕ 8743.25 123 0  145.348
$8,743.25   $123.00   $00.00   $145.35
```

Picture format rejects any negative numbers unless the pattern provides a place for the negative sign:

```
      '  $5,503.50'⍕ 8743.25 ¯123 0  145.348
DOMAIN ERROR
      '  $5,503.50'⍕ 8743.25 ¯123 0  145.348
      ∧                ∧
```

You allow for negative numbers by specifying you want a decoration floated against the number if it's negative (digit 1):

```
          '  -1,503.50'⍕ 8743.25 ¯123 0 145.348
   8,743.25    -123.00      00.00     145.35
```

Note that in this example the mid-minus character is used to signify a negative number. You can choose any group of characters you like as the negative indication. Here's an example where a dollar sign is attached to every number, but the letters *CR* are attached only to the negative numbers:

```
        '  $5503.10CR'⍕8743.25 ¯123 0 145.348
   $8743.25      $123.00CR   $00.00     $145.35
```

A digit 4 counteracts the action of a 1, 2, or 3, preventing it from affecting the other side of the field, which is then treated as a simple decorator:

```
        '  -5501.40US'⍕8743.25 ¯123 0 145.348
   8743.25US   -123.00US     00.00US    145.35US
```

In a program, a date might be stored in many different ways. For example the date September 23, 1988 might be stored as a single integer 92388 (because it takes less space). Here is an expression that turns an integer into a formatted date with the character / as a separator:

```
      '05/05/05'⍕ 92388
09/23/88
```

Alternatively, a date might be stored as a three-item vector 9 23 88. To format a vector as a date, the digit 6 terminates a field description early. In this example, the placement of 6's in the left argument contains three fields and can format a date stored as a three-item vector:

```
      '06/06/06'⍕ 9 23 88
09/23/88
```

For the use of digits 7 and 8, see the documentation that comes with your system.

Exercises for Section 7.5

1. Write an expression that tests if vector V is a vector of character vectors.

2. Write a function *NUMBER* that attaches bracketed line numbers onto a matrix as in this example:

          NUMBER 2 3ρι6
     [1] 1 2 3
     [2] 4 5 6

3. Determine the value and shape of the following expressions, where V is defined as:

       V← 43.263 9123.468 0 0.739

   a. '5555.55 '⍕V
   b. '5555.55' ⍕V
   c. '5555.50 '⍕V
   d. '5,555.50 '⍕V
   e. '$5,555.50 '⍕$V$
   f. '$0,555.50 '⍕$V$
   g. '5,555.50 *DOLLARS* '⍕V
   h. '$5,535.50 '⍕$V$
   i. '$8,555.50 '⍕$V$
   j. '$_5,535.50 '⍕$V$

4. State the value and the shape of the following expressions, where W is defined as:

       W←93.725 ‾27.8 ‾192.83 6754

   a. '−5,551.55 '⍕W
   b. '$5,551.50*CR* '⍕$W$
   c. '$_5,553.10*CR* '⍕$W$
   d. '$ −5,551.55 '⍕W
   e. '$_−5,551.55 '⍕$W$
   f. '$_5,554.10_*CR* '⍕$W$
   g. '5,555.55 '⍕W

5. Write a function that, given a positive integer, returns the character string containing the representation of that number followed by the appropriate ordinal representation. Here is an example:

        ORDINAL 3
    3RD
        ORDINAL 21
    21ST
        ORDINAL 11
    11TH

Section 7.6 – Control of Execution: Iteration

Applying some computation repeatedly to different sets of data is called *iteration*. The most obvious method for implementing an iteration is to write a loop that selects one set of data, applies the computation to that set, then branches back to select another set.

You have already seen examples where **each** applies a function to every item of a vector. **Each** implements an iteration without looping. Likewise, **reduction** expresses an iteration that reduces a vector to a scalar.

Writing iterative programs without explicit looping is *structured programming* and the mechanisms to express the implicit looping are called *control structures*. In APL2, structured programming is embodied in operators. This section shows how defined operators can be written to provide control structures not available as primitives in APL2. Defined operators defined with explicit branching and looping become the implementation of control structures that are then used without branching and looping.

A Number Operator

APL2 permits numbers and characters in the same array. If you ever want to do arithmetic on such arrays, you must isolate the numeric data from the character data. Suppose you want a function that adds its arguments if they are numeric and doesn't fail if they are character. Here's how you might want it to work:

```
      2 PLUS 3
5
      2 PLUS 'A'
A
```

Here's one way to implement such a function:

```
      ∇ Z←L PLUS R
[1]  ⍝ addition on numbers and characters
[2]     →(0=↑0⍴R)/L1    ⍝ branch if R is numeric
[3]     Z←R             ⍝ result is R
[4]     →0
[5]  L1:→(0=↑0⍴L)/L2    ⍝ branch if L is numeric
[6]     Z←L             ⍝ result is L
[7]     →0
[8]  L2:Z←L+R           ⍝ result is sum
[9]     ∇
```

This function does, in fact, work as advertised. But what if you also wanted a **subtract**, a **maximum**, and so forth. Instead of writing a large set of very similar functions that differ only in the function applied on line [8], write an operator to apply an arbitrary function in the prescribed manner:

```
      ∇ Z←L(FN NUMB)R
[1]  ⍝ FN on numbers and characters
[2]     →(0=↑0⍴R)/L1    ⍝ branch if R is numeric
[3]     Z←R             ⍝ result is R
[4]     →0
[5]  L1:→(0=↑0⍴L)/L2    ⍝ branch if L is numeric
[6]     Z←L             ⍝ result is L
[7]     →0
[8]  L2:Z←L FN R        ⍝ result is computed
[9]     ∇
```

Now, any function can be applied like *PLUS*:

```
      2 +NUMB 3
5
      2 PLUS NUMB 'A'
A
      2 -NUMB 3
 ¯1
      'B' +NUMB 5
B
      'B' -NUMB 5
B
```

The expression ↑0ρ only checks the type of the first item. Therefore, this operator works only for simple scalars. If you try it on vectors, it may fail:

```
      2 3 'A' +NUMB 10 'B' 4
DOMAIN ERROR
NUMB[7]   L2:Z←L FN R
             ∧   ∧
      →
```

It is easy, however, to do the desired operation if you limit the arguments of *+NUMB* to simple scalars. Just apply the function *+NUMB* to each simple scalar in the vector arguments:

```
      2 3 'A' +NUMB¨ 10 'B' 4
12 BA
```

Using **each** in the expression makes the operator work on simple arrays but not nested arrays. Section 7.7 shows you how to write a recursive operator that works on nested arrays as well.

An Each Operator That Quits Early

When you apply a function to a set of data using the **each** operator, the function *fn* applies to each item:

> *fn*¨ data

If there are a thousand items, the function will be applied a thousand times. For example, here's a function that prompts a user for some information and then reads and returns the response:

```
      ∇ Z←READ MSG
[1]   ⍝ prompt with message then read response
[2]    MSG
[3]    Z←⍞
[4]    ∇
```

If you have an application that wants to prompt for a user's name, address, and telephone number, you can write this:

```
      RES←READ¨ 'NAME' 'ADDRESS' 'PHONE'
NAME
Jim
ADDRESS
123 Easy Street
PHONE
555-1234

      ⍴RES
3

      RES
Jim 123 Easy Street 555-1234
```

Users must enter three responses to three prompts. They cannot quit early nor provide extra data.

If you want to prompt for a variable amount of information—say name, address, and names of children—you might try this:

```
      RES←READ¨ 'NAME' 'ADDRESS' 'CHILDREN'
```

But this will stop after one child's name. Here is an operator something like **each** except that it keeps applying the function operand until a certain value is returned:

```
      ∇ Z←(F UNTILV V)R;T
[1]    Z←⍳0
[2]    L1:T←F(↑R)        ⍝ apply F to next item
[3]     →(T≡V)/0         ⍝ quit if V is produced
[4]     Z←Z,⊂T           ⍝ accumulate result
[5]     R←1↓R            ⍝ go on to next item
[6]     →L1
[7]     ∇
```

The *UNTILV* operator runs function *F* using successive items of *R* as arguments. After each application, it checks to see whether the requested value *V* has been returned and quits when it is. At some point, the items of *R* will be exhausted, and *R* will become an empty vector. **First** still works on an empty vector, so the function *F* will continue to be called until the value *V* is produced.

The *UNTILV* operator can be used with the *READ* function by checking for the empty response to the call of *READ*:

```
        R←(READ UNTILV '') 'NAME' 'ADDRESS' 'CHILDREN'
NAME
Jim
ADDRESS
123 Easy Street
CHILDREN
Margaret
Matthew
    ←——(empty response)


        ρR
4

        R
  Jim 123 Easy Street Margaret Matthew
```

Exercises for Section 7.6

1. The operator *NUMB* shown in the section "A Number Operator" works only for simple scalar arguments. Although *NUMB*¨ will work for other simple argument, it can be awkward. Write a *NUMB*1 operator that applies its operand function to simple arguments of any rank.

2. Write a monadic defined function that simulates **interval**.

Section 7.7 – Control of Execution: Recursion

You've seen that any defined function can call any other function by using its name in an expression. A defined function that calls itself is a *recursive function*. Such a function must have a branch that under some condition skips the recursive call, or execution will not stop until some system resource is used up.

A recursive function generally has the following computations:

1. A test to see whether the computation request is simple enough to do without calling the function recursively.

2. A computation of the simple case.

3. A computation of the *n*th case, assuming you have the solution for the *n*-1 case.

These three parts are not necessarily performed in this order nor so neatly partitioned. In particular, there may be more than one recursive call. That's all right as long as each is closer to the simple case than the original arguments.

The first two examples in this section demonstrate the use of recursion to solve computational problems. The first example is a standard mathematical exercise involving a Fibonacci sequence. The second is an entertaining Chinese puzzle called "Tower of Hanoi." The last example in this section shows the development of a recursive operator.

Fibonacci Numbers

Writing a recursive function may or may not be the most efficient way to solve problems that require recurring operations. This section discusses a standard example of a recursive program.

In 1202 A.D., Leonardo Pisano (Fibonacci) published a book, **Liber Abaci**, which was a major influence on the spread of Hindu-Arabic numerals in Europe (Vilenkin). In this book, he posed the following problem:

> Each month the female of a pair of rabbits gives birth to a pair of rabbits one of each sex. Two months later, the female of the new pair gives birth to a pair of rabbits again one of each sex. Find the number of rabbits at the end of the year if there was one pair of rabbits at the beginning of the year.

Of course at the start of the first month there is one pair of rabbits. Assuming that these rabbits are newly born, there is still one pair at the start of the second month. By the start of the third month, there are two pairs—the original pair and their offspring. By the start of the fourth month, the original pair have another pair of offspring bringing the number of pairs to three. One more month and both the original pair and the first offspring have more rabbits. Carrying on this logic leads to the following sequence of numbers:

        1 1 2 3 5 8 13 21 ...

Notice that each integer is the sum of the two preceding integers in the list. Such a sequence of numbers is a *Fibonacci sequence* and the numbers are called *Fibonacci numbers*. The program you are to write must compute the *n*th Fibonacci number, given *n*. Thus, if *n* is 4, the program must compute the fourth Fibonacci number which is 3. Here is the header of the program:

        ∇Z←FIB1 N   ⍝ *find Nth Fibonacci number*

There are two keys to writing a recursive function:

1. You must know how to do the computation for a simple case.

2. You assume that you have already written the function for simple cases and then use it in computing a more complicated case.

Here's how you apply these ideas to the computation of the *n*th Fibonacci number:

1.   If *n* is 1 or 2, you know that the answer is 1.

2.   Assume you have the following function that includes the known case:

```
        ∇Z←FIB1 N   ⍝ find Nth Fibonacci number
[1]     Z←1         ⍝ assume simple case
[2]     →(N∈1 2)/0  ⍝ quit if simple case
[3]
```

Now, write the last lines of the program by making recursive calls. In this case, to get the *n*th Fibonacci number, you have only to add up the previous two Fibonacci numbers. Here then is the whole function with line [3] making the recursive call:

```
        ∇Z←FIB1 N   ⍝ find Nth Fibonacci number
[1]     Z←1         ⍝ assume simple case
[2]     →(N∈1 2)/0  ⍝ quit if simple case
[3]     Z←(FIB1 N-2) + (FIB1 N-1)
[4]     ∇
```

Beware: It's easy to make a mistake and cause your program to go into an infinite recursion. Be prepared to stop execution if no result is produced in a reasonable amount of time.

Iteration or Recursion

As is often the case with recursive functions, you can write the Fibonacci program in a non-recursive, iterative style, as follows:

```
        ∇Z←FIB2 N;P   ⍝ find Nth Fibonacci number
[1]     ⍝ P is previous value
[2]     (P Z)←1
[3]     L1:→(N∈1 2)/0
[4]     (P Z)←Z (Z+P) ⍝ compute next number
[5]     N←N-1
[6]     →L1
[7]     ∇
```

It is a matter of personal preference which program you like better. Many people think recursive programs are more elegant than iterative ones. The iterative program is generally easier to debug because every value being used in the computation can be examined if it stops (or if you stop it). In the recursive program, there is localization at each function call with the same names localized.

For calculating Fibonacci numbers, the iterative program is more efficient because it computes each Fibonacci number up to the *n*th only once. Iterative programs, however, are not necessarily more efficient than recursive ones.

Notice that both programs fail to terminate if called with a noninteger. Try each function with an argument of 1.5 and interrupt execution after a few seconds. Look at the value of local variables and display)*SIS* after each stop. Don't forget to clear the state indicator—)*RESET*—when you have finished.

Closed Formula

As is sometimes the case, both the recursive and iterative versions can be replaced by a *closed formula* that is neither recursive or iterative—it is just an expression. Here is the formula in mathematical notation for the *n*th Fibonacci number:

$$FIB3(N) \ = \ \frac{1}{\sqrt{5}} \left(\left(\frac{1+\sqrt{5}}{2} \right)^{n+1} - \left(\frac{1-\sqrt{5}}{2} \right)^{n+1} \right)$$

When you are deciding on your programming approach to a problem, you must consider all alternatives to determine the best one to use in any particular situation.

Tower of Hanoi

According to legend, when God created the world, he placed sixty-four gold disks on one of three needles, with the disks' diameters decreasing in size as you look up the needle. A succession of priests has been assigned ever since to move disks from the original needle to one of the other needles. Only one disk at a time may be moved, and at no time may a larger disk be placed upon a smaller one. When all the disks have been transferred to a new needle, the world will come to an end.

For those of you who are concerned about the possible truth of this story, keep in mind that ⁻1+2*64 moves are required to complete the transfer. Performing the moves by hand would take a very long time. Doing it with a very fast high-speed computer is more risky.

To develop a program to solve this puzzle, first decide on the arguments of the function you will write. Here is the header of the program and the description of the arguments:

```
      ∇N HANOI NEEDLE
[1]   ⍝ N is the number of disks to be moved
[2]   ⍝ NEEDLE   is a three-item vector
[3]   ⍝      [1] needle containing disks
[4]   ⍝      [2] needle to which disks are moved
[5]   ⍝      [3] a spare needle
[6]   ⍝ program moves from [1] to [2] via [3]
```

Suppose there is one disk left to be moved from needle 1 to needle 2. The program would be called like this:

```
1 HANOI 1 2 3
```

Clearly the solution is to move the one disk from needle 1 to needle 2 and the spare isn't even used. Therefore, the program will contain the following line:

```
'MOVE DISK' N 'FROM' NEEDLE[1] 'TO' NEEDLE[2]
```

Knowing the solution to a simple case, you may now express a more complicated case in terms of the simpler case. Suppose you have *n* disks to move from needle 1 to needle 2. You can move *n*-1 disks to spare needle 3 (and you assume that the *n*-1 case is solved), move the last disk to needle 2, then move the *n*-1 disks from spare needle 3 to needle 2. This process assures that at no time does a disk of larger diameter rest on top of one with smaller diameter.

The complete program, then, must move *n*-1 disks from the current needle [1] to a spare [3] by way of [2]. Here's the expression to do that:

```
(N-1) HANOI NEEDLE[1 3 2]
```

The remaining disk is moved to its final resting place:

```
'MOVE DISK' N 'FROM' NEEDLE[1] 'TO' NEEDLE[2]
```

Then the stack of *n*-1 disks is moved to its final resting place:

```
(N-1) HANOI NEEDLE[3 2 1]
```

The final requirement is a means to stop the recursion. Clearly when *N* is zero, there are no disks to move so the program should do nothing. Here, then, is the complete recursive program that solves the Tower of Hanoi problem:

```
            ∇N HANOI NEEDLE
[1]     →(N=0)/0
[2]     (N-1) HANOI NEEDLE[1 3 2]
[3]     'MOVE DISK' N 'FROM' NEEDLE[1] 'TO' NEEDLE[2]
[4]     (N-1) HANOI NEEDLE[3 2 1]
[5]     ∇
```

Here's the execution of this function for *N*←3.

```
        3 HANOI 1 2 3
MOVE DISK 1 FROM  1 TO 2
MOVE DISK 2 FROM  1 TO 3
MOVE DISK 1 FROM  2 TO 3
MOVE DISK 3 FROM  1 TO 2
MOVE DISK 1 FROM  3 TO 1
MOVE DISK 2 FROM  3 TO 2
MOVE DISK 1 FROM  1 TO 2
```

Recursive Operators

In the section "An **Each** Operator That Quits Early," you saw the defined operator *UNTILV*, which is used to control iteration of a function. It is also common to write operators that control recursion. For example, suppose you wanted to compute the shape of each simple array (depth 0 or 1) in the following nested array:

```
    G1←2 2ρ(3 4ρι12) 'TWO' (3 3ρ0) (3 4)
    DISPLAY G1
```

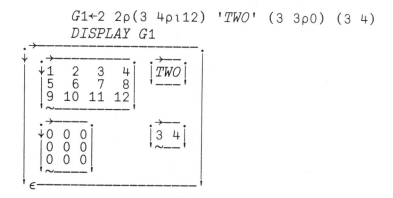

You certainly know how to do this if the given array is a simple array—just apply the **shape** function (ρ). The beginning of the recursive function, then, is to compute shapes of simple arrays in a nested array:

```
      ∇Z←SIMPLESHAPE R
[1]   ⍝ compute shape of each simple array in R
      . . .
[n]   Z←ρR
```

Now, using the standard method for writing a recursive procedure, assume you can handle up to a depth $n-1$ argument. If you're given a depth n argument, you can reduce it to a set of simpler cases by saying:

```
      SIMPLESHAPE¨R
```

Using **each** works because a depth N array contains at least one depth $N-1$ array and no array that is deeper. Thus, the complete recursive function, including the test to stop recursion, is as follows:

```
      ∇Z←SIMPLESHAPE R
[1]   ⍝ compute shape of each simple array in R
[2]     →(1<≡R)/L1         ⍝ branch if not simple
[3]     Z←ρR               ⍝ shape of simple
[4]     →0                 ⍝ exit
[5]   L1:Z←SIMPLESHAPE¨R   ⍝ recur
[6]   ∇
```

Here is the execution of this function on the given data:

```
      SIMPLESHAPE G1
  3 4   3
  3 3   2
```

```
      DISPLAY SIMPLESHAPE G1
```

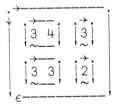

SIMPLESHAPE is an entirely appropriate function, but suppose that you also want a function to **ravel** each simple array and one to apply the **first** function to each simple array. You would have to write a whole set of recursive functions, where each one applied a different monadic function to the simple arrays in a nested array. These functions would all be identical except for the function applied in line [3] (and the comments). Writing such a series of similar functions is a sure sign that it may be more appropriate to write an operator that applies its function operand in the prescribed way.

Here is a defined operator that applies the recursive procedure to any monadic function:

```
      ∇Z←(F MDEPTH)R
[1]   ⍝ apply F to each simple array in R
[2]     →(1<≡R)/L1          ⍝ branch if not simple
[3]     Z←F R               ⍝ apply F to simple R
[4]     →0                  ⍝ exit
[5]   L1:Z←(F MDEPTH)¨R     ⍝ recur
[6]     ∇
```

Notice that the header gives *MDEPTH* as the name of the operator and *F* as the name of the function operand. The rest of the definition is identical to *SIMPLESHAPE* except that *F* is applied in line [3] instead of **shape**.

The next two examples show the operator applied first to **shape** and then to **ravel**:

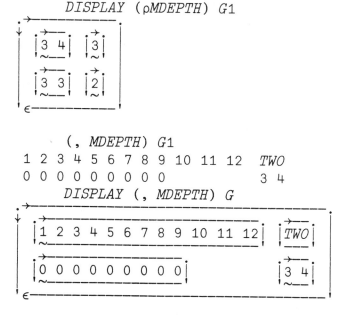

It is a straightforward extension to write a *DDEPTH* operator that does an operation on dyadic functions, similar to *MDEPTH*. Writing this operator is left as an exercise.

Inadvertent Recursion

You may find during testing of a program that you are in a recursive situation when you didn't intend to be. Here's a common way this can happen. Suppose you're defining a program to take an average:

```
        ∇Z←AVG  R
[1]     Z←(+/R)÷ρR
[2]
```

Now you want to execute the function to try it out, and you enter this:

```
[2]     AVG  1  3  5
[3]
```

But you forgot to close the definition. Therefore, the test execution line is accepted as line [2] of the function. If you close the function and then execute it, you'll get an infinite recursion.

Whenever a program takes an unusually long time to execute, press attention and check the state indicator. In this example, a look at the state indicator will show you that recursion is taking place.

Exercises for Section 7.7

1. Write a program that, given an amount of money *AMT* and an integer interest rate, computes and displays the amount after the interest has been added to the amount. The program should then loop (infinitely) listing the amounts for successive years.

2. There are many ways to add up a vector of numbers:

   a. Write a recursive function to add up a vector of numbers.

   b. Write an iterative function to add up a vector of numbers.

   c. Write an expression in closed form to add up a vector of numbers.

3. In Chapter 6 you saw a formula for computing interest after *N* years at a given interest rate. This formula assumed that no rounding was done each time the interest was added.

   a. Write a loop to do the same computation with rounding each time.

   b. If you invested one penny in 1776, how much money would you have in 1987, 211 years later, if interest of 5% is added and rounded every year?

   c. How much money would you have after 211 years if you invested 50 pennies?

4. Write a recursive function that simulates the monadic primitive **interval**.

5. Write a function that implements the closed formula for the *N*th Fibonacci number.

6. Write an expression using *MDEPTH* to compute the rank of each simple array in a nested array.

7. Write a recursive function that applies the function **first** to each simple array in a nested array. Compare the answers produced with those from ↑*MDEPTH* applied to the same argument.

8. Modify *MDEPTH* so that instead of applying its function operand to simple arrays, it applies the function to arrays of depth N where N is another operand of the operator.

9. Write a defined operator *DDEPTHA* that applies a dyadic function to each simple array in a pair of nested arrays. If either argument is a nested array, the program should recur. Here is an example:

```
X←(4 5)(6(7 'B')) (10 11)
  2 (2 3) 'A' +NUMB DDEPTHA X
6 7   8  10 B A
```

10. Write a defined operator *DDEPTHB* that applies a dyadic function to each simple array in the right argument but uses the entire left argument for each application. For example:

$$DISPLAY \ 2 \ 3 \ \rho DDEPTHB \ 'ABC'((5 \ 6)(7 \ 8 \ 9))$$

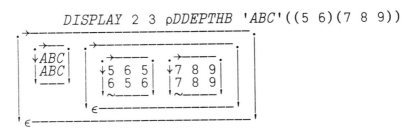

11. Write a recursive program to compute the value of the Ackermann Function on two integers *J* and *N*, where the function is defined mathematically as follows:

$$
\begin{array}{rcl}
0 \ A \ N & \longleftrightarrow & N+1 \\
J \ A \ 0 & \longleftrightarrow & (J-1) \ A \ 1 \\
J \ A \ N & \longleftrightarrow & (J-1) \ A \ (J \ A(N-1))
\end{array}
$$

Chapter 8

Working with
Applications

You've seen many of the pieces of APL2: arrays, functions, and operators. You've learned the fundamentals of programming. In this chapter, you will see the development of three applications. Each shows a different way of using APL2.

The first application is a magazine collector's application. It can be used to keep track of the magazines the collectors own, those they need, the value of their collections, and so on. It is a practical illustration of how easily you can produce a simple working application.

The second application is the simulation of a computer. It shows the suitability of APL2 for simulation and modeling.

The last application makes sophisticated use of nested arrays and defined operators for playing games. It demonstrates APL2's use as a tool in Artificial Intelligence.

Each section illustrates the three development tasks for producing the application:

- Describing the application.
- Designing the application.
- Implementing the application.

Section 8.1 – A Magazine Collection

The magazine collection application allows collectors of magazines to keep track of their collections and make simple inquiries for various kinds of information about their collections. The techniques are the same for a collection of records, stamps, baseball cards, or antiques. For this application, you want to keep track of the popular monthly magazine *APL2 World*.

There are many ways to write a given application. This section contains the programs that illustrate only one way to write the magazine collection application. It is designed for running with simple immediate execution statements. It has no main program that controls the whole application. Most of the programs do little or no validity checking of their arguments. If you call one of these functions with the wrong kind of argument, it will usually just give an error message and suspend.

The programs only use functions and features discussed in this book. Facilities not discussed in this book could make the input and editing phases of the application easier to use. Error-trapping facilities could make the application more foolproof. As you learn more about APL2, you can incorporate these more advanced features into the implementation.

Describing the Application

This application is fairly straightforward. You want to keep track of every issue of the magazine. You want to know the number of copies of each issue you own, the original cost, and the current value. You need a way to enter new data every time a new issue is available, and you need a way to extract subsets of the data for display and computation. You need a way to update information that changes (such as current market value) or that is incorrect.

Designing the Application

For this application, the most important decision is the nature of the data structure for storing the information about the magazine, because virtually every function you write will access the magazine data. A common method for storing this kind of data is a *relational structure*. A relational structure is a matrix. Each row of the matrix contains all the information related to one issue of the magazine—its cost, number of issues owned, date, and so on. Each column of the matrix contains one of the types of information for every magazine—one column contains the cost of each magazine, another contains the publication date of each magazine, and so on.

Without worrying about the exact arrangement of data in the data structure, you must decide what information to store in columns. The first important piece of information is the whole issue number. Most magazines are numbered serially—the first issue being issue 1, the second being issue 2, and so on. In addition, periodicals are organized into volumes. Maybe every six or twelve issues, the volume number is incremented. Issues within a volume are numbered from one. For example, here is the masthead of the first issue of *APL2 World*, which was called *The APL Gazette* when it first appeared:

The January 1987 issue was whole issue number 618. Therefore, to store the information about all the issues up to the this issue, you need a matrix with 618 rows. You might be tempted to let the row index represent the issue number—let the information about whole issue number 200 be in row 200. This organization is not a good idea because later you will be taking various subsets of the matrix. You may also want to order the matrix to put the most valuable issue first. So that each row retains its identity regardless of its position in the matrix, one of the columns should be the issue number. Other columns will contain volume number, number in volume, year of publication, month of publication, cover price, current value, and, most important, the number of copies you own, where a count of zero means you don't have a copy of that issue.

The matrix has the name *MAG*. Here's a portion of the *MAG* matrix representing recent issues:

Issue	Vol	No	Year	Mon	Price	Value	Own
603	57	1	1985	OCT	1.95	1.95	1
604	57	2	1985	NOV	1.95	1.95	1
605	57	3	1985	DEC	1.95	1.95	1
606	57	4	1986	JAN	1.95	1.95	1
607	57	5	1986	FEB	1.95	1.95	1
608	57	6	1986	MAR	1.95	1.95	1
609	57	7	1986	APR	1.95	1.95	1
610	57	8	1986	APR	1.95	1.95	1
611	57	9	1986	JUN	1.95	1.95	1
612	57	10	1986	JUL	1.95	1.95	1
613	57	11	1986	AUG	1.95	1.95	1
614	57	12	1986	SEP	1.95	1.95	1

The design of the entry and edit functions is very important if you want your program to be easy to use. Because this is an application for your own use, simple entry and edit functions are good enough.

Given functions to allow entry of the magazine information, you can build the *MAG* matrix in the format just described. Next you want to be able to do various computations, rearrangements, and selections of the data.

As mentioned before, this application is designed for use in simple immediate execution statements. The various functions are, therefore, constructed to be used together in an expression. Here's a summary of the functions to be provided to the application user:

1. Rearranging function.

    This function takes a matrix of magazines and a column identification and returns that matrix with the rows rearranged with the selected column sorted in decreasing order. The function provided is this:

    ● *SORTDNBY*. Sorts the matrix in decreasing order on the requested column.

2. Subsetting functions.

    These functions take a matrix of magazines and, if appropriate, a selection number, and return a subset of the matrix:

    ● *NEED*. Given a matrix of magazines, returns the matrix subset that contains the rows in which the number of copies owned is zero.

    ● *VOLUME*. Given a volume number and a matrix of magazines, returns the subset matrix that is in the requested volume.

3. Computation functions.

    These functions take a matrix of magazines and perform some computation:

    ● *COST*. Given a matrix of magazines, returns the amount of money spent to purchase them.

    ● *WORTH*. Given a matrix of magazines, returns the current value of the set of magazines.

4. Editing functions.

    These functions add, delete, and modify the magazine database:

    ● *ADD*. Appends new rows to the magazine matrix.

    ● *EDIT*. Modifies rows in the magazine matrix.

In addition, the function *LISTMAG* prints out a matrix of magazines with column headings.

These functions can then be used in combinations in immediate execution statements to do whatever you like. Assume that *MAG* really has information about all the issues of **APL2 World** from the first issue to issue number 618. Here are some expressions you could enter:

● List the contents of volume 41.

```
LISTMAG VOLUME 41 MAG
Issue Vol No Year Mon Price Value Own
  400  41  1 1972 OCT  0.95  5.25   2
  401  41  2 1972 NOV  0.95  5.25   0
  402  41  3 1972 DEC  0.95  5.25   0
  403  41  4 1973 JAN  0.95  5      0
  404  41  5 1973 FEB  0.95  5      1
  405  41  6 1973 MAR  0.95  5      0
  406  41  7 1973 APR  0.95  5      0
  407  41  8 1973 APR  0.95  5      1
  408  41  9 1973 JUN  0.95  5      1
  409  41 10 1973 JUL  0.95  5      2
  410  41 11 1973 AUG  0.95  5      0
  411  41 12 1973 SEP  0.95  5      0
```

● How much money did I spend on volume 41?

```
COST VOLUME 41 MAG
6.65
```

● What are my issues from volume 41 worth today?

```
WORTH VOLUME 41 MAG
35.5
```

● What issues from volume 41 do I lack?

```
LISTMAG NEED VOLUME 41 MAG
Issue Vol No Year Mon Price Value Own
  401  41  2 1972  11  0.95  5.25   0
  402  41  3 1972  12  0.95  5.25   0
  403  41  4 1973   1  0.95  5      0
  405  41  6 1973   3  0.95  5      0
  406  41  7 1973   4  0.95  5      0
  410  41 11 1973   8  0.95  5      0
  411  41 12 1973   9  0.95  5      0
```

● What are the top five most valuable issues?

```
      LISTMAG 5↑[1] SORTDNBY VALUE MAG
   Issue Vol No Year Mon Price Value Own
       1   1  1 1928 JUN  0.05   625   1
       2   1  2 1928 AUG  0.05   600   1
       3   1  3 1928 OCT  0.05   550   1
       4   1  4 1928 DEC  0.05   500   1
       5   1  5 1929 JAN  0.05   500   1
```

You should have a good idea of how your functions are to work together, before you start writing them. In this case, the design of the arguments is heavily influenced by the objective that the functions be used together as shown in the examples.

Implementing the Application

Now you have a pretty good idea of what the application should do. You have listed the main functions to be written and shown examples of the results you expect. Now it is time to start writing programs.

Building and Maintaining the Magazine Matrix

Because the *MAG* matrix has a relational structure, almost every function will refer to the columns of the matrix. Because you have decided that the issue number is column 1 and the volume number is column 2, and so on, you could just use the column numbers in the programs. There are, however, two problems with doing this. First, if you ever want to rearrange the columns of the matrix—maybe because you want to insert a column in the middle that you didn't think about before—you'd have to modify all the functions. Second, even if you don't ever change the column definitions, numbers are not mnemonic. Instead of calling the volume column by the number 2, for example, you should call it *VOL* or some other easy-to-remember name that reminds you of the column's purpose. Therefore, the first function to write is one that is executed only when the column definitions change. Also, because there will be a need to enter months as part of the data, it is also convenient to define global abbreviations for the months. Therefore, the function contains definitions of the columns of the matrix and abbreviations for the months:

```
       ∇DEFINECOLUMNS
[1]    ISSUE←1
[2]    VOL←2
[3]    NO←3
[4]    YEAR←4
[5]    MON←5
[6]    PRICE←6
[7]    VALUE←7
[8]    OWN←8
[9]    ⍝
[10]   JAN←'JAN'
[11]   FEB←'FEB'
[12]   MAR←'MAR'
[13]   APR←'APR'
[14]   MAY←'MAY'
[15]   JUN←'JUN'
[16]   JUL←'JUL'
[17]   AUG←'AUG'
[18]   SEP←'SEP'
[19]   OCT←'OCT'
[20]   NOV←'NOV'
[21]   DEC←'DEC'
[22]   ⍝
[23]   END←'END'
[24]   ∇
```

This function defines eight global variables that assign names to columns of the matrix, twelve globals that can be used when entering months, and a value used to stop editing. If you ever want to add a new column in the middle, you simply edit this function and add a new global column name, adjust the column numbers, and re-execute the function. Most of the other functions will continue to work on the new matrix with little change.

The "Good Programming Practices" section of Chapter 3 advised you to avoid using global variables. This advice still holds. Don't use global variables to pass extra arguments to or extra results from a program. The variables defined in *DEFINECOLUMNS* are really declarations. They are more like global constants. They will never change during the application's execution. You could ensure that no program alters the values of these names by making them defined sequences instead. Here's an example:

```
      ∇Z←ISSUE
[1]   ⍝ Defines issue column number
[2]     Z←1
[3]   ∇
```

By using a defined sequence to hold the global constant, you ensure that an attempt to alter the value of *ISSUE* by assignment leads to an error:

```
    ISSUE←2
SYNTAX ERROR
    ISSUE←2
    ∧     ∧
    →
```

The next step is to build an initial *MAG* matrix which, of course, has no rows:

```
    MAG←0 8⍴0
```

Then you can write a function to list a magazine matrix with headings:

```
      ∇Z←LISTMAG R
[1]   ⍝ R is rows from the MAG matrix
[2]   ⍝ return a labeled display of the issue
[3]     R←(¯2↑1,⍴R)⍴R       ⍝ make R a matrix if it's not
[4]     Z←'Issue' 'Vol' 'No' 'Year' 'Mon' 'Price' 'Value' 'Own'
[5]     Z←Z,[1]R[;ISSUE VOL NO YEAR MON PRICE VALUE OWN]
[6]   ∇
```

The *LISTMAG* function makes displays of subsets of the magazine matrix look like a report.

Next, you need a function to add new data to the matrix and a function to modify an existing row in the matrix. You could simply write two functions: *ADD* to add new entries and *EDIT* to edit existing entries. In the *ADD* function, you would have to check that an issue is not a duplicate, and in the *EDIT* function you would have to check that the issue exists. Instead of checking issues in each function, you can write a function that prompts for the issue number and calls *EDIT* or *ADD* according to whether the issue exists in the *MAG* matrix. Here's such a function:

```
      ∇MAGAZINE;DIS
[1]   L1:'enter issue number or END'
[2]    DIS←□                        ⍝ read issue number
[3]    →(DIS≡END)/0                 ⍝ end request?
[4]    →((ρDIS)≡(⍳0))/OK            ⍝ must be a scalar
[5]    'issue number must be a single integer'
[6]    →L1
[7]   OK:→(DIS∈MAG[;ISSUE])/L2 ⍝ branch if issue exists
[8]    ADD DIS                      ⍝ add new issue
[9]    →L1
[10]  L2:EDIT DIS                   ⍝ edit existing issue
[11]   →L1
[12]  ∇
```

You haven't written the *ADD* and *EDIT* functions yet. But that won't stop you from testing the logic of *MAGAZINE*. You can write dummy *ADD* and *EDIT* functions:

```
      ∇ADD R
[1]   'ADD ROUTINE'
[2]   ∇
```

```
      ∇EDIT R
[1]   'EDIT ROUTINE'
[2]   ∇
```

When either of these functions is called during the test executions of *MAGAZINE*, the identifying message is displayed.

This kind of programming —where you write the top programs in the structure first—is *top-down programming*. It contrasts with *bottom-up programming*, in which you write the lowest-level programs first. The advantages of top-down programming are threefold: it enables you to test the logic of the application before you invest a lot of time writing pieces of code; it enables you to test code repeatedly as you develop additional programs within the structure; and it allows you to demonstrate the running of the application to users when it is still easy to incorporate operational changes.

Once you've tested the logic of *MAGAZINE*, you can write *ADD* and *EDIT* functions. These are straightforward functions:

```
      ∇ADD R;IN
[1]   ⍝ R is the new issue number
[2]   L1:'enter values for issue number ' R
[3]   '      ' 'Vol' 'No' 'Year' 'Mon' 'Price' 'Value' 'Own'
[4]   IN←⎕                    ⍝ read input
[5]   →((,7)≡⍴IN)/OK          ⍝ must be 7 items
[6]   'error - enter 7 items'
[7]   →L1
[8]   OK:MAG←MAG,[1]R,IN       ⍝ add new row
[9]   ∇
```

Notice that even though the month is a character string, it does not need to be entered in quotes because of the global month names.

```
      ∇EDIT DIS;RIDX;CIDX;VAL
[1]   ⍝ edit existing data
[2]    RIDX←MAG[;ISSUE]⍳DIS ⍝ get row number
[3]    'existing data'
[4]    LISTMAG MAG[RIDX;]    ⍝ list current row
[5]    'What do you want to change?'
[6]    CIDX←⎕                ⍝ get col# to change
[7]    'enter new value'
[8]    VAL←⎕                 ⍝ get new value
[9]    MAG[RIDX;CIDX]←VAL    ⍝ replace value
[10]   'new row'
[11]   LISTMAG MAG[RIDX;]    ⍝ list new row
[12]  ∇
```

Taking Subsets of the Magazine Matrix

The functions that select subsets all look alike. You select some column of the data and do some relational operations on the selected data to compute a mask, where a 1 means keep the corresponding row. Then use **replicate** to select those rows.

The first function selects rows for issues you don't own by checking the matrix for zeros in the *OWN* column.

```
      ∇Z←NEED R
[1]   ⍝ R is magazine matrix
[2]    Z←(R[;OWN]=0)⌿R
[3]   ∇
```

The second function selects all rows that match the requested volume number:

```
     ∇Z←VOLUME R;N
[1]   ⍝ R is volume number, matrix
[2]     (N Z)←R
[3]     Z←(Z[;VOL]=N)⌿Z
[4]   ∇
```

Rearranging the Magazine Matrix

To rearrange the matrix, you select the column requested and apply
grade down to get the row indexes of the sorted matrix:

```
     ∇Z←SORTDNBY R;N
[1]   ⍝ R is field to sort on, matrix
[2]     (N Z)←R
[3]     Z←Z[⍒Z[;N];]
[4]   ∇
```

Computations on the Magazine Matrix

The computations necessary for this application require only that
you select the necessary data and perform the desired computation.
Here is a defined function that adds up the cost of all the magazines
in its matrix argument:

```
     ∇Z←COST M
[1]   ⍝ compute cost of magazines
[2]     Z←+/×/M[;PRICE OWN]
[3]   ∇
```

This function yields the total value of the magazines in the matrix
argument:

```
     ∇Z←WORTH M
[1]   ⍝ compute total value of magazines
[2]     Z←+/×/M[;VALUE OWN]
[3]   ∇
```

You can embellish this application with all kinds of features. Try
plotting the total value per volume. Prepare nicely formatted
reports.

Exercises for Section 8.1

1. Define the variable *DESCRIBE* that explains how to use the magazine application.

2. Write a function to sort a requested field in increasing order.

3. Write a function *GAIN* that, given a subset of the matrix, computes the percentage increase in the value of the magazines. Here's an example:

    ```
        GAIN VOLUME 41 MAG
    4.32
    ```

4. Modify the *ADD* function to use **quote-quad** input for input and **execute** to convert the numeric responses into numbers.

5. Modify *EDIT* so that after the new data is supplied, it displays the changed row and asks for verification before making changes in the *MAG* matrix.

6. Modify the application to add another column in which you can put your own comments like "This issue never published" or "This is the 25th anniversary issue" or "This is the last issue with the original name." Modify *DEFINECOLUMNS*, *ADD*, *EDIT*, *LISTMAG*. Don't forget to update the documentation in *DESCRIBE*. Write a function to migrate the existing magazine matrix to the new format.

7. The magazine's name changed with the printing of whole issue number 300. Modify *LISTMAG* so it lists the characters *GAZ* before issues with numbers from 1 to 299, and the characters *WORLD* on other issues.

Section 8.2 – Simulation of a Vector Computer

You can use APL2 to simulate computers. This section discusses a way to write such a simulation.

There are many ways to view a computer's design. Ignoring questions of input and output, here are four ways to look a computer:

1. An application architecture.

   You may view a computer as a special-purpose device that provides some particular application. Point-of-sale computers and banking terminals are examples of special-purpose devices. Users who have no further interest in how the device works take this view.

2. A high-level language architecture.

   You may view a computer as a device that stores arrays and programs and evaluates some high-level language (like APL2). This is the view taken by this book. Very little knowledge of the particular computer you are using is needed to make use of the APL2 language on the computer.

3. A machine-language architecture.

   You may view a computer as a device that has a way of remembering numbers and combining numbers to form new numbers. This machine-language view of a computer is the lowest level of machine architecture that a computer's owner can normally use.

4. An electronic-circuit architecture.

   You may view a computer as a set of electronic switching devices that contains bi-stable relays and electronic paths between logic devices. Electronic engineers who are responsible for constructing a computer look at its design this way.

You can write programs that simulate a computer at any of these levels. In fact, the magazine application takes an application architecture view. It is a simulation of a computer that stores and manipulates a magazine matrix. Since APL2 programs behave like the primitive functions and operators, your programming is, in some sense, designing a computer at the second level—you are extending the APL2 language by providing some facility the designers of the language did not provide.

This section develops a simulation of a computer from a machine language view. The computer architecture simulated is similar to APL2 in that its fundamental arithmetic is vectors. Although the vector computer of this example is a fictitious machine, it is in the style of the IBM 3090 vector facility, which is the first major computer architecture that looks as though it was made for APL2.

Describing the Vector Architecture

You can think of the computer's memory as an ordered list of individual memory cells, each of which can hold one number. This ordered list is often called *main memory* or *main storage*. You can design a computer that does computations on the numbers in the main memory and puts the results back in main memory. In fact, most computers have some specialized high-speed storage areas called *registers* where most computations are performed, because high-speed storage is too expensive to use for main memory. Thus, in a large-scale computer, there may be many millions of memory locations for main memory but only a few for registers (16 on the IBM 370).

With so little memory to hold arguments and results of computational instructions, programs for these computers load one set of scalar values, perform some computations on them, store the result back in main memory, and loop to iteratively process collections of data. Given this architecture for computers, it is not surprising that computer languages are designed to do computations on scalars with various control structures to express looping. APL2, as you have seen, is an array language that expresses computations on collections of data without explicit looping controls.

Vector architectures, which can apply computations to collections of data, now exist. These architectures have a set of vector registers, instructions to move values from main memory into vector registers, perform computations on vector registers, and move results back into main memory. In addition, some control registers record the number of items in the vector registers and other related information.

APL2 programs easily model the structure of these vector architectures.

Designing the Vector Architecture

The first consideration in designing a machine is to come up with a good name for it. The IBM 360 is so called because there are 360 degrees in a circle and that line of machines "covered the full circle of computing needs." Just to have a name, the machine designed here will be called the APL 181. The significance of 181 is that it is a palindrome both horizontally and vertically. (A palindrome is a word, phrase or number that doesn't change when reversed.) A two-dimensional palindrome is an appropriate number for an array-processing machine.

The machine modeled here processes only vectors. You write programs in the machine language to process higher-rank arrays. It would be an interesting exercise to design a machine that processed arrays of any rank.

In preparing to model a computer architecture, the first task—just as it is in developing other applications—is is to define the data structures. In the fictitious machine to be modeled, the objects to be represented are:

- Main memory
- Scalar registers
- Vector registers
- Control registers

You can represent main memory in APL2 as a long vector. You address memory by indexing.

You can represent the scalar registers as a shorter vector. The simple model presented in this section does not use the scalar registers, but a more complete model would.

You can represent the vector registers as a simple matrix, with one row per register and one column per register item. Alternatively, you can represent them as a nested vector with one item per register. It does not make much difference here which representation you choose, but a rule of thumb for choice of data structure is this: If the data can be represented by a rectangular array, do it. Despite this rule, you might still want to use a vector of vectors in the model because you imagine each vector register as an entity. In this model, a simple matrix, not a vector of vectors, represents the vector registers. If you designed a machine where different registers had different lengths, you could not choose a simple matrix and would use a vector of vectors.

Two control registers are needed. The first defines the length of each vector register and is called the *section size* (in the spirit of the

IBM 3090). For a given computer, this number is a constant. On a different model, the section size could be a different constant. The second control register records the number of items actually residing in the vector registers. This number can range from zero up to the section size and is called the *vector count*.

Programs for the APL 181 would really be stored in main memory, but that aspect of the computer is not of interest for this model. Only the effect of the programs on the data in main memory and the registers is of interest.

Suppose you have two vectors in main memory and you want to form their sum. How would you program the APL 181 to perform this computation? Suppose the vectors will fit in a vector register (that is, the length of the vectors is not greater than the section size). Here is the outline of the program:

● Set the vector count to the length of the vectors.
● Load each vector into a vector register.
● Add the vector registers.
● Store the sum back in main memory.

Suppose main memory contains the following:

● Address 2 — Length of the vectors.
● Address 3 — Address of the left argument.
● Address 4 — Address of the right argument.
● Address 5 — Place to store the result.

Here is the program that will perform the vector addition:

```
        ∇EXAMPLE1
  [1]      LOADVCT 2      ⍝ load vector count
  [2]      LOADV 2 3 1    ⍝ load left argument
  [3]      LOADV 3 4 1    ⍝ load right argument
  [4]      ADDV 1 2 3     ⍝ add the vectors
  [5]      STOREV 1 5 1   ⍝ store result in main memory
  [6]    ∇
```

Each line represents one APL 181 machine instruction implemented as a monadic APL2 function. *EXAMPLE1* contains calls to these functions as follows:

Line [1] is the machine instruction that loads the vector count register with the number stored in main memory at location 2. The vector count controls the number of items that take part in each of the instructions that follow.

Line [2] loads vector register 2 by using the address at location 3. The third number in the *LOADV* argument gives the distance between items in main memory. 1 means that the items to be loaded are in adjacent memory locations. (This is sometimes called the *stride*.)

Line [3] loads the right argument for the addition into vector register 3.

Line [4] adds vector register 2 to vector register 3 and puts the sum in vector register 1.

Line [5] puts the sum into storage by taking the sum in vector register 1 and putting it into storage as addressed by location 5 with a stride of 1.

If the vectors are longer than the section size, you need to write a loop as follows:

1. Set the vector count to the minimum of the section size and the number of items left to process in the vectors.

2. Exit from the loop if the count is zero.

3. Load the next section of each vector into the vector registers.

4. Add the vector registers.

5. Store the next section of the sum back in main memory.

6. Loop.

```
        ∇EXAMPLE2
   [1]     LOOP:LOADVCT 2    ⍝ load vector count
   [2]       →(0=VCT)/0      ⍝ exit if count is zero
   [3]       LOADV 2 3 1     ⍝ load segment of left
   [4]       LOADV 3 4 1     ⍝ load segment of right
   [5]       ADDV 1 2 3      ⍝ add segment
   [6]       STOREV 1 5 1    ⍝ store segment of result
   [7]       →LOOP           ⍝ and repeat until done
   [8]     ∇
```

This program is essentially the same as *EXAMPLE1* but illustrates additional effects that some of the instructions must have. *LOADVCT* must set the vector count to the smaller of the number at address 2 and the section size. It must reduce the number at address 2 by the number assigned to the vector count. Suppose that the length of the vector is 8 and the section size is 5. The first time the *LOADVCT* instruction is executed, the vector count is set to 5 and address 2 is set to 3. The second time it is executed, the vector count is set to 3 and address 2 is set to 0.

The two *LOADV* instructions must do more than move data from main memory to vector registers. They must also update the address of the data in storage so the next time they are executed, the next section of the vector is loaded. Suppose the left argument is at machine address 26. The first time the *LOADV* is evaluated, five numbers are loaded into the vector register. The storage address is updated to 31. The next time *LOADV* is evaluated, three numbers are loaded into the vector register and the address is updates to 34. *STOREV* must likewise update the machine's storage address.

With the layout of the machine's memory and registers and the desired properties of the machine instructions identified, you can now implement the model.

Implementing the Vector Architecture

Although the machine could have enormous main memory, lots of registers, and long vector registers, the essentials of the model can be realized with a more modest machine. Here, then, is an APL2 program that defines a machine with a main memory of length 100, six scalar registers, and four vector registers with a section size of five:

```
      ∇ DEFINEMACHINE
[1]   ⍝ define vector machine globals
[2]   MM←100ρ'.'      ⍝ main memory
[3]   SR←6ρ'.'        ⍝ 6 scalar registers
[4]   SS←5            ⍝ section size
[5]   VR←(4 SS)ρ'.'   ⍝ 4 vector registers
[6]   VCT←0           ⍝ vector count register
[7]   ∇
```

The memory and registers are initialized to '.' so it is easy to distinguish items that have been used from items that have not been used. In a real machine, the initial values would probably be zero.

A 100-item vector is used to represent main memory (*MM*), a six-item vector represents the scalar registers, and a matrix with four rows and and a column dimension of the section represents the vector registers. Executing this program defines the machine:

```
      DEFINEMACHINE
```

The program is a defined sequence; it produces no explicit result.

As you develop programs for loading, storing, and doing arithmetic, you need an easy way to look at the machine's contents. The following program depicts the machine's contents:

```
      ∇ SHOWMACHINE;R;N
[1]     N←'MAIN MEMORY' 'VCT'
[2]     R←↑(ρMM)÷25
[3]     N,[.5]((R 1ρ1+25×¯1+ιR),':',R 25ρMM)VCT
[4]     ' '
[5]     N←'SCALAR REGS' 'VECTOR REGS'
[6]     N,[.5](('S',⍕6 1ρι6),SR)(('V',⍕4 1ρι4),VR)
[7]   ∇
```

Here is the execution of this program:

```
            SHOWMACHINE
     MAIN MEMORY                              VCT

       1 :.........................           0
      26 :.........................
      51 :.........................
      76 :.........................

     SCALAR REGS  VECTOR REGS

     S1.          V1.....
     S2.          V2.....
     S3.          V3.....
     S4.          V4.....
     S5.
     S6.
```

This model is not concerned with methods of getting information into and out of the main memory. The APL 181 programs that are presented assume memory has been initialized to the proper values. Here is a function that puts values into memory starting at a specified location:

```
    ∇ A SETMEMORY R
[1]   ⍝ put R into main memory at address A
[2]   R←,R                    ⍝ ignore shape of data
[3]   ((ρR)↑(A-1)↓MM)←R   ⍝ move data to memory
[4] ∇
```

Suppose you want to add two vectors like this:

```
      10 9 8+1 2 3
   11 11 11
```

You need to initialize the machine's memory. First put the values of the two vectors into memory starting at locations 26 and 51 respectively:

```
      26 SETMEMORY 10 9 8
      51 SETMEMORY 1 2 3
```

In addition, the length of these vectors must be stored somewhere. Put it at location 2:

```
      2 SETMEMORY 3
```

Finally, the addresses of the arguments and the result area must be defined. Put the argument addresses at location 3 and 4 and the result address at location 5:

```
      3 SETMEMORY 26
      4 SETMEMORY 51
      5 SETMEMORY 76
```

Here is what memory looks like now:

```
        SHOWMACHINE
MAIN MEMORY                                              VCT

   1 :   .  3 26 51 76 ...................          0
  26 : 10  9  8   .   . ...................
  51 :  1  2  3   .   . ...................
  76 :  .   .   .   .   . ...................


SCALAR REGS   VECTOR REGS

S1.           V1.....
S2.           V2.....
S3.           V3.....
S4.           V4.....
S5.
S6.
```

Before the example programs can be run, you must define a program for each of the desired machine instructions *LOADVCT*, *LOADV*, *ADDV*, and *STOREV*.

LOADVCT must set the vector count (*VCT*) to the minimum of the section size (*SS*) and the length of the vector. The length is decremented by this amount:

```
    ∇ LOADVCT A
[1]    ⍝ load vector count from memory address A
[2]    VCT←SS⌊MM[A]      ⍝ count is min
[3]    MM[A]←MM[A]-VCT   ⍝ reduce storage count
[4] ∇
```

LOADV and *STOREV* take a three-item vector as argument. The first item is the number of the vector register to load or store; the second item is the location in storage that contains the address from which data is fetched or to which data is stored. The third item is the stride. It specifies the distance between items in storage. A stride of 1 causes contiguous storage to be addressed. A stride of 2 causes every other location in storage to be addressed. You can use strides other than 1 to load or store a column of a matrix which is stored in row-major order. For example, a column from a 4-by-3 matrix could be loaded using a stride of 3. Here are the *LOADV* and *STOREV* programs:

```
     ∇ LOADV R;V;A;S
[1]    (V A S)←R
[2]  ⍝ load vector register V
[3]  ⍝  from address in A with stride S
[4]    VR[V;⍳VCT]←MM[MM[A]+S×¯1+⍳VCT]
[5]    MM[A]←MM[A]+VCT
[6]  ∇


     ∇ STOREV R;V;A;S
[1]    (V A S)←R
[2]  ⍝ store vector register V
[3]  ⍝  in address in A with stride S
[4]    MM[MM[A]+S×¯1+⍳VCT]←VR[V;⍳VCT]
[5]    MM[A]←MM[A]+VCT
[6]  ∇
```

The arithmetic functions need only access the vector registers. Here are programs for addition and multiplication. Each takes a three-item vector as argument: the number of the register for the result, the number of the register for the left argument, and the number of the register for the right argument:

```
[0]    ADDV R;V1;V2;V3
[1]    (V1 V2 V3)←R
[2]  ⍝ add vector in V2 to vector in V3
[3]  ⍝ put result in vector V1
[4]    VR[V1;⍳VCT]←VR[V2;⍳VCT]+VR[V3;⍳VCT]
[5]  ∇


     ∇ MULTV R;V1;V2;V3
[1]    (V1 V2 V3)←R
[2]  ⍝ multply vector in V2 by vector in V3
[3]  ⍝ put result in vector V1
[4]    VR[V1;⍳VCT]←×/VR[V2 V3;⍳VCT]
[5]  ∇
```

Now all the pieces are in place for execution of the first sample program:

```
     ∇EXAMPLE1
[1]    LOADVCT 2      ⍝ load vector count
[2]    LOADV 2 3 1    ⍝ load left argument
[3]    LOADV 3 4 1    ⍝ load right argument
[4]    ADDV 1 2 3     ⍝ add the vectors
[5]    STOREV 1 5 1   ⍝ store result in main memory
[6]    ∇
```

The program has no output but does change the registers and memory of the machine. Rather than just execute the program and look at the final state of the machine, you can set stops on the program and examine the machine after the execution of each instruction:

```
     S∆EXAMPLE1←2 3 4 5
     EXAMPLE1
EXAMPLE1[2]
```

The vector count is loaded from address 2 and the contents of address 2 are decremented to zero:

```
     SHOWMACHINE
MAIN MEMORY                                        VCT

  1 :  . 0 26 51 76 ....................            3
 26 : 10 9  8   .   . ....................
 51 :  1 2  3   .   . ....................
 76 :  .  .  .   .   . ....................

SCALAR REGS   VECTOR REGS

 S1.           V1.....
 S2.           V2.....
 S3.           V3.....
 S4.           V4.....
 S5.
 S6.

        →2
EXAMPLE1[3]
```

Resuming execution causes *EXAMPLE*1 to stop after execution of the load for the left argument. Vector register 2 contains the left argument, and the address of the left argument is updated:

```
       SHOWMACHINE
   MAIN MEMORY                                               VCT

     1 :   . 0 29 51 76 ....................                  3
    26 : 10 9  8   .   . .....................
    51 :  1 2  3   .   . .....................
    76 :   .  .   .   .   . .....................


   SCALAR REGS    VECTOR REGS

   S1.            V1  .  .  .  . ..
   S2.            V2 10  9  8 ..
   S3.            V3  .  .  .  . ..
   S4.            V4  .  .  .  . ..
   S5.
   S6.


          →3
   EXAMPLE1[4]
```

Resuming execution causes a stop after the load of the right argument. Vector register 3 contains the right argument, and the address of the right argument is updated:

```
            SHOWMACHINE
   MAIN MEMORY                                          VCT

      1 :  . 0 29 54 76 . . . . . . . . . . . . . . . . . .      3
     26 : 10 9  8   .   . . . . . . . . . . . . . . . . . .
     51 :  1 2  3   .   . . . . . . . . . . . . . . . . . .
     76 :  .   .    .   . . . . . . . . . . . . . . . . . .


   SCALAR REGS     VECTOR REGS

   S1.             V1  .  .  .  . ..
   S2.             V2 10  9  8 ..
   S3.             V3  1  2  3 ..
   S4.             V4  .  .  .  . ..
   S5.
   S6.


            →4
   EXAMPLE1[5]
```

Resuming execution causes a stop after the vector add. The sum is in vector register 1:

```
            SHOWMACHINE
   MAIN MEMORY                                          VCT

      1 :  . 0 29 54 76 . . . . . . . . . . . . . . . . . .      3
     26 : 10 9  8   .   . . . . . . . . . . . . . . . . . .
     51 :  1 2  3   .   . . . . . . . . . . . . . . . . . .
     76 :  .   .    .   . . . . . . . . . . . . . . . . . .


   SCALAR REGS     VECTOR REGS

   S1.             V1 11 11 11 ..
   S2.             V2 10  9  8 ..
   S3.             V3  1  2  3 ..
   S4.             V4  .  .  .  . ..
   S5.
   S6.


            →5
```

Resuming execution causes execution of the store instruction and termination of the example. Now the sum is in memory and the result address is updated:

```
        SHOWMACHINE
MAIN MEMORY                                          VCT

  1 :  .  0 29 54 79 ....................     3
 26 : 10  9  8  .   . ....................
 51 :  1  2  3  .   . ....................
 76 : 11 11 11  .   . ....................


SCALAR REGS    VECTOR REGS

S1.            V1 11 11 11 ..
S2.            V2 10  9  8 ..
S3.            V3  1  2  3 ..
S4.            V4  .  .   . ..
S5.
S6.
```

Notice that each vector operation is controlled by the vector count register. This is why only three numbers were manipulated by each instruction even though a vector register could hold five numbers.

The program *EXAMPLE2* shows how the machine processes vectors that are longer than the section size. Here is the definition of the program again:

```
        ∇EXAMPLE2
[1]     LOOP:LOADVCT 2    ⍝ load vector count
[2]      →(0=VCT)/0       ⍝ exit if count is zero
[3]     LOADV 2 3 1       ⍝ load segment of left
[4]     LOADV 3 4 1       ⍝ load segment of right
[5]     ADDV 1 2 3        ⍝ add segment
[6]     STOREV 1 5 1      ⍝ store segment of result
[7]      →LOOP            ⍝ and repeat until done
[8]     ∇
```

Run *DEFINEMACHINE* again so that the memory of *EXAMPLE1* is lost:

```
        DEFINEMACHINE
```

Suppose you want to add two vectors that are longer than section size, like this:

          10 9 8 7 6 5 4 + 1 2 3 4 5 6 7
     11 11 11 11 11 11 11

Again, you need to initialize the machine's memory. First, put the values of the two vectors into memory starting at locations 26 and 51, respectively:

     26 *SETMEMORY* 10 9 8 7 6 5 4
     51 *SETMEMORY* 1 2 3 4 5 6 7

Put the vector length at location 2:

     2 *SETMEMORY* 7

Finally, put the argument and result addresses at locations 3, 4, and 5:

     3 *SETMEMORY* 26
     4 *SETMEMORY* 51
     5 *SETMEMORY* 76

Put a stop on line 2 of *EXAMPLE2*, so you can look at the state of the machine after each loop:

     S∆EXAMPLE2←2

Now run *EXAMPLE2*:

     EXAMPLE2
     EXAMPLE2[2]

Only the load vector count register has been loaded. The count location in memory has been reduced by the section size:

```
          SHOWMACHINE
MAIN MEMORY                                              VCT

   1 :   .  2 26 51 76 . . ................        5
  26 : 10 9  8  7  6 5 4 .................
  51 :  1 2  3  4  5 6 7 .................
  76 :  .  .  .   .   .  .  .  .................

SCALAR REGS   VECTOR REGS

S1.           V1.....
S2.           V2.....
S3.           V3.....
S4.           V4.....
S5.
S6.
      →2
EXAMPLE2[2]
```

One iteration of the loop is completed. The vector count is set to the number of items left to process. Storage address for the arguments and result have been updated:

```
          SHOWMACHINE
MAIN MEMORY                                              VCT

   1 :   .  0 31 56 81 . .  .................        2
  26 : 10  9  8  7  6 5 4  .................
  51 :  1  2  3  4  5 6 7  .................
  76 : 11 11 11 11 11 . .  .................

SCALAR REGS    VECTOR REGS

S1.            V1 11 11 11 11 11
S2.            V2 10  9  8  7  6
S3.            V3  1  2  3  4  5
S4.            V4  .  .  .  .  .
S5.
S6.
      →2
EXAMPLE2[2]
```

The full result is in memory, the vector count is zero so the program
is ready to terminate:

```
        SHOWMACHINE
MAIN MEMORY                                             VCT

   1 :  .   0  34 59 84   .   . .................        0
  26 : 10   9   8  7  6   5   4 .................
  51 :  1   2   3  4  5   6   7 .................
  76 : 11  11  11 11 11  11  11 .................


SCALAR REGS    VECTOR REGS

S1.            V1 11  11  11  11  11
S2.            V2  5   4   8   7   6
S3.            V3  6   7   3   4   5
S4.            V4  .   .   .   .   .
S5.
S6.
        →2
```

This section introduced enough of a subset so the examples could
be executed on the simulated vector machine. A real vector machine
would have many more instructions.

Exercises for Section 8.2

1. Write a program to simulate a vector multiply instruction.

2. Write programs to simulate loading and storing a scalar register.

3. Write a program that simulates an **addition-reduction** instruction that adds up the contents of a vector register and then adds the sum to a scalar register.

4. Using your new scalar instructions and the reduction instruction, write a loop to compute the **addition-reduction** of a long vector in main storage.

5. Add another register to the machine that is the same length as a vector register that can be used as a mask register. Write a vector comparison instruction that sets the mask register to 1 if the corresponding number in one vector register is less than the corresponding number in another vector register.

Section 8.3 – A Puzzle-Solving Program

The field of Artificial Intelligence (AI) attempts to emulate with computer programs the behavior of humans. Areas of study include recognition of written and spoken natural language, computer vision, robotics, and expert systems. Because human behavior is complicated and not completely understood, the programs are complicated.

AI technologies are also applied in the writing of game-playing programs and puzzle-solving. There are even chess competitions between competing chess-playing programs. Games and puzzles are a good place to begin the study of intelligence because at least the rules are completely understood.

In this section, programs for playing single-person games are developed. In theory, these programs could just try all possible moves from a given position and eventually find a solution. For the simple games considered here, this would even work. For more realistic games, however, no computer is fast enough to carry out all the computations required in a reasonable time. Instead, strategies must be used to reduce the amount of computation. Because strategies are often not completely understood, the programs can become complicated.

APL2 is well suited to writing programs for playing games and for solving puzzles. This section discusses some simple puzzle-solving programs that are general enough to work with most puzzles. One version tries all possible moves and another makes use of some strategies.

Describing the Puzzle-Solving Program

The puzzle to be solved is a simple game consisting of a five-position board containing two white and two black marbles in some initial position:

$$|\overline{WW\_BB}|$$

The goal of the game is to move a marble into the blank spot, making a different blank spot until some given new arrangement such as the following is achieved:

$$|\overline{BBWW\_}|$$

There are 30 different possible arrangements of marbles $((!5) \div (!2) \times !2)$ each of which can be a starting or ending position. This leads to the possibility of 900 different games.

From the starting position, there are four possible first moves. From each of those positions, there are again four possible next moves, and so on. At each step, there are four times as many positions as at the previous step. This set of positions can be represented in an inverted tree structure as follows:

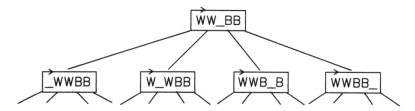

Eventually, at the bottom of the tree, you will find some paths that lead to the desired ending position.

Here are two sequences of moves that each begin with the beginning arrangement on the left and arrive at the final position at the right end by moving one marble at each intermediate step:

```
 .→----.    .→----.    .→----.    .→----.    .→----.
|WW_BB|    |_WWBB|    |BWW_B|    |B_WWB|    |BBWW_|
'_____'    '_____'    '_____'    '_____'    '_____'


 .→----.    .→----.    .→----.    .→----.    .→----.    .→----.
|WW_BB|    |_WWBB|    |BWWB_|    |B_WBW|    |BBW_W|    |BBWW_|
'_____'    '_____'    '_____'    '_____'    '_____'    '_____'
```

The challenge is to write a program which, when given an initial position, computes the path to the final position. You could probably work out an effective strategy to implement this program, but such a program would work only for this game. Instead, a more general scheme will be implemented which, while perhaps not as efficient as a special-purpose program, will work for any game of this type even if you can't figure out a good strategy.

Designing the Puzzle-Solving Program

The parameters of the program are the starting position, the desired ending position, and a function which, given one position, computes all the possible next positions. Because one of the parameters is a function, the program must be a defined operator.

The operator keeps track of a set of paths that have been taken so far. The path at the top of the list is examined to see if it reaches the goal. If it does not, the move function is called to extend the path in its four possible directions, and these new paths are put at the end of the list of paths. Eventually, a path will be identified that reaches the goal, and this path becomes the explicit result of the program. This path will, in fact, be a path of shortest length (perhaps one of many shortest paths).

The operator is perfectly general because it contains no information about the geometry of the puzzle, the way moves are made, or strategies for playing. Anything specific to the problem is given to the operator as a parameter.

The data structure for the puzzle is a simple five-item character vector:

> *BEGIN←'WW_BB'*
> *END←'BBWW_'*

The blank position is represented by an underscore character, so it is easily distinguished from other blanks not part of the data.

The program that computes the next moves must take as argument some position (a five-item character vector), generate all possible next positions, and return them as the result:

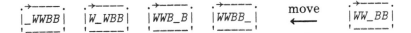

A more complicated data structure is required inside the program so that it can keep track of multiple partially-completed paths. These may be stored in a vector each of whose items is the set of positions that lead from the initial position to the current position. Here is what that internal table would look like after one set of moves from the initial position:

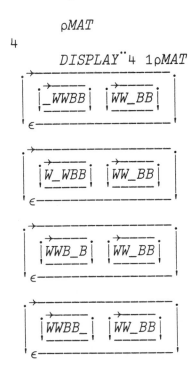

Notice that the paths are stored in reverse order, with the starting path as the second item and each possible next position as the first item. This is so the operator can select the current end of the path using **first** (↑). Each item shown is a two-item vector because one move from the starting position has been taken. In general, the items will be of different lengths.

Implementing the Puzzle-Solving Program

For each puzzle you want the computer to solve, you must write a program that, given some arrangement of the puzzle, computes the set of possible next arrangements. In the case of the marble puzzle, the function will always produce the four possible next arrangements achieved by moving each of the marbles into the blank position. There are many ways to implement this program. The following way is reasonably straightforward:

```
      ∇ Z←MOVECOLOR M;BLI
[1]     ⍝ move generator for color game
[2]     BLI←('_'=M)/⍳⍴M ⍝ get index of blank
[3]     Z←(2⍴⍴M)⍴M
[4]     (1 1⍉Z)←M[BLI]   ⍝ find all permutations
[5]     Z[;BLI]←M        ⍝ of BLI item
[6]     Z←(⊂[2]Z)~⊂M     ⍝ delete start position
[7]   ∇
```

Line [2] gets the index position for the blank.

Line [3] builds a square matrix containing five replications of the input position:

```
      Z←(2⍴⍴M)⍴M
      Z
WW_BB
WW_BB
WW_BB
WW_BB
WW_BB
```

Line [4] moves the blank to each possible next position, one per row of the square matrix:

```
      (1 1⍉Z)←M[BLI]
      Z
_W_BB
W__BB
WW_BB
WW__B
WW_B_
```

Line [5] puts the character replaced by the blank where the blank came from. This effectively swaps the blank position with each other position:

```
      Z[;BLI]←M
      Z
 _WWBB
 W_WBB
 WW_BB
 WWB_B
 WWBB_
```

Finally, line [6] builds a five-item list of these positions, deletes the one that is the same as the input position, and returns the remaining four as the explicit result.

MOVECOLOR works on any size board. You could have 11 positions and 10 marbles. Because the number of possible arrangements is so large, it is best to experiment with small-sized games.

Given the data structures and the *MOVECOLOR* program just described, the general search program can be written in a few lines. Here's how the program is used:

```
      DISPLAY¨BEGIN(MOVECOLOR SEARCH1)END
 .→____.   .→____.   .→____.   .→____.   .→____.
 |WW_BB|   |_WWBB|   |BWW_B|   |B_WWB|   |BBWW_|
 '_____'   '_____'   '_____'   '_____'   '_____'
```

Here is the definition of the search operator:

```
      ∇ Z←STRT(MOVE SEARCH1)G;B;M;NEWP
[1]    ⍝ find path from start to goal
[2]    ⍝ STRT ←→ starting position
[3]    ⍝ G ←→ goal position
[4]    ⍝ MOVE ←→ program to compute next positions
[5]    M←,⊂,⊂STRT          ⍝ initial path is STRT
[6]    Z←⍳0                ⍝ return empty on failure
[7]  LOOP:→(0=⍴M)/0        ⍝ quit no more paths
[8]    →(G≡B←↑↑M)/DONE      ⍝ done if goal
[9]    NEWP←MOVE B          ⍝ compute new positions
[10]   NEWP←(~NEWP∊↑,/M)/NEWP ⍝ keep new positions
[11]   M←(1↓M),(⊂¨NEWP),¨M[1] ⍝ add to paths
[12]   →LOOP                ⍝ back for next path
[13] DONE:Z←⌽↑M             ⍝ return with path
[14]∇
```

Line [5] initializes the internal list of partial paths to the starting position *STRT*.

Line [6] sets the explicit result to empty in case the list of partial paths is exhausted with no solution. This can't happen in the simple game being used as the example but, in general, it can happen.

Line [7] exits if there are no more paths to try.

Line [8] checks to see if the path at the front of the list ends with the desired goal *G*. The first **first** gives the entire first path. The second **first** selects the leading position from the first path.

Line [9] calls *MOVE* (which is the name given inside the program for the *MOVECOLOR* program), giving it the current ending position. *MOVE* is the name in the program for *MOVECOLOR* when the search program is called.

Line [10] checks to see if any of the next positions already exist in a path. Only positions never before reached are accepted. This line contains an interesting subexpression. *M* is a vector of vectors of board positions. To check if the newly generated positions exist already, you want to do membership against the vector of positions already in *M*. The vector of vectors is joined into a single vector by using **catenate-reduction**. Since any reduction on a vector produces a scalar, the result is an enclosed vector. **First** is used to select the vector. Thus the final expression to turn a vector of vectors of positions into a vector of positions is ↑,/.

Line [11] takes the set of new positions and appends them to the front of the old path. **Indexing** is used to select the old path because it returns a scalar which by scalar extension is catenated onto each of the new positions. Finally, the old path is deleted from the list.

Line [12] loops back to process the new first item in the list.

Line [13] returns the path that reached the goal. It is reversed only because you would expect the start position on the left and the final position on the right.

Note: There is absolutely nothing in the search program that uses the fact the game deals with a five-item vector. The start and end positions could be a matrix or any other data structure. As long as you can write a function that can compute the next positions from some given position, the search program will find the goal if any path to the goal exists. If no goal exists, the program may terminate with no more paths to try or may loop forever. If there is a finite number of positions in the game, it will not loop forever.

Without any change to the program, you can use *SEARCH*1 to solve other puzzles of this kind. You define the beginning and ending positions and write a program to compute the moves, and the *SEARCH*1 operator will solve the puzzle.

*SEARCH*1 implements what in AI terminology is a *breadth-first search*. It tries all possible paths in the tree until a path is found. It is guaranteed to find a path if one exists, but it can be horribly inefficient. To solve the simple marbles puzzle requires 26 loops, which is not so bad. If you use more marbles in a longer vector, or try more complicated games, the number of loops rises dramatically.

The next section shows how adding knowledge about the puzzle reduces the number of positions to be examined.

A Puzzle-Solving Program Using Strategy

It is possible to write a search program that is still general but which makes use of information about the problem to reduce the number of paths tried. While only a matter of efficiency, it can make a problem feasible that otherwise could not be computed. This search program using strategy is discussed next.

If you look at the set of all possible next moves from some given position of a game, you expect that some progress toward the goal, some progress away from the goal, and some make no difference. While it is often not possible to measure exactly the amount of progress made toward the goal, it is often possible to come up with a rough estimate. Even a very bad estimate can significantly reduce the number of game positions examined. A good estimate leads to examination of only a few positions not leading to the goal, and a perfect estimate would lead directly to the goal.

If you can write a program that, given a position, computes a number that estimates the distance to the goal, you can pass the program as an operand to a search program.

For the marble puzzle, a simpleminded but effective estimator counts the number of marbles not in their final position. This estimator produces zero only when the goal is reached. Here is a function that implements this estimator:

```
      ∇ Z←GOAL ESTC THIS
[1]     ⍝ GOAL  is the desired goal
[2]     ⍝ THIS  is the position to be estimated
[3]       Z←+/GOAL≠THIS
[4]     ∇
```

The function simply counts the number of marbles out of position.

The estimator shows that the starting position has no marble in its final position:

```
      GOAL ESTC BEGIN
5
```

Applying the function to each of the next positions from the starting position gives the corresponding estimates:

```
 DISPLAY¨ MOVECOLOR BEGIN
 →              →            →            
|_WWBB|    |W_WBB|    |WWB_B|    |WWBB_|
'_____'    '_____'    '_____'    '_____'
```

```
        (⊂END)ESTC¨MOVECOLOR BEGIN
  4  4  5  4
```

Notice the use of **enclose** to provide scalar extension in the call of
ESTC.

Since this estimate does not exactly reflect the number of moves
required to reach the goal, it is not a perfect estimator. Therefore,
using this estimator with a search program, you would expect some
positions to be examined which are not on the path to the goal.
Also, the search program might not choose the shortest solution.

The second version of a search program uses a two-column matrix
of a vector to remember positions. The first column contains the
paths as before. The second column contains the estimates of the
distance from the goal. Here is what the matrix contains after one
move from the start position:

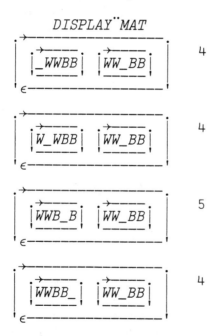

Rather than select the top row of the matrix on each iteration, the
path with the lowest estimator is chosen. This choice increases the
likelihood that each move is closer to the goal. Here is the complete
search program:

```
      ∇ Z←STRT(MOVE SEARCH2 EST)G;B;T;M;NP;IX
[1]    ⍝ find path from start to goal
[2]    ⍝ STRT ↔ starting position
[3]    ⍝ G ↔ goal position
[4]    ⍝ MOVE ↔ program to compute next positions
[5]    ⍝ EST ↔ program to estimate distance to goal
[6]    M←1 2ρ(,⊂STRT)(G EST STRT) ⍝ STRT + estimate
[7]    Z←⍳0                       ⍝ return empty on fail
[8]    LOOP:→(0=↑ρM)/0            ⍝ quit no more paths
[9]    IX←M[;2]⍳⌊/M[;2]           ⍝ index of least est
[10]   →(G≡B←↑IX⊃M[;1])/DONE      ⍝ done if goal
[11]   NP←MOVE B                  ⍝ find new positions
[12]   NP←(~NP∊↑,/M[;1])/NP       ⍝ keep new positions
[13]   T←((⊂¨NP),¨M[IX;1]),[1.5](⊂G)EST¨NP
[14]   M←M[(⍳↑ρM)~IX;],[1]T       ⍝ add to paths
[15]   →LOOP                      ⍝ back for next path
[16]   DONE:Z←⌽↑M[IX;]            ⍝ return with path
[17]   ∇
```

Using *SEARCH2* to solve the same puzzle produces the same path (in this example) as *SEARCH1* but only requires 5 loops instead of 26:

      DISPLAY¨BEGIN (MOVECOLOR SEARCH2 ESTC) END

The improvement in the speed *SEARCH2* over *SEARCH1* is even more dramatic when they are applied to more complicated games. The real challenge is to come up with good enough estimators for those games.

Exercises for Section 8.3

1. Modify the search programs so they count and report the number of loops required to reach the goal.

2. Modify *SEARCH1* so that every 20 loops it stops and asks if you want to continue.

3. Modify the *SEARCH2* program so it keeps track of the number of moves so it can choose the next position based on number of moves plus estimated cost. Actual cost could be just a measure of the number of moves so far.

Exercises 4 to 7 deal with a puzzle called the "eights puzzle." It is a smaller version of the familiar "fifteens puzzle." The "eights puzzle" has eight numbered square tiles on a three-by-three board. There is one blank square. Here's an example:

```
.→──.
↓283|
|164|
|7 5|
'───'
```

The purpose of the game is to slide tiles into the empty space until the following pattern is achieved:

```
.→──.
↓123|
|8 4|
|765|
'───'
```

4. Write a function that, given a position in the "eights puzzle," computes the set of next moves.

5. How many loops does *SEARCH1* require to arrive at the goal?

6. Write an estimator function that counts the number of tiles not in their final position. How many loops does *SEARCH2* require to arrive at the goal using this estimator?

7. Write an estimator function that computes the horizontal plus the vertical distance of each tile from its final position. For example, for the number 8 in the starting position, this number is 2 (1 horizontal plus 1 vertical). How many loops does *SEARCH2* require to arrive at the goal using the second estimator?

Expanding Your APL2 Knowledge

This book has introduced you to most of the important concepts of APL2. You should now be able to write useful programs. A book this size could cover some programming languages in their entirety—but not APL2, which has the richness and power other languages lack. Although you've completed this book, you've just begun to experience APL2's potential.

This postscript summarizes some of the topics not addressed in this book. The bibliography lists other sources for additional information.

System Functions and System Variables

System functions often have to do with interfaces to the implementation or the system. For example, $\square DL$ is a time-delay system function. $\square EX$ is a function that erases an object much like the command)*ERASE*.

System variables provide a way to communicate with the system and often represent user-settable options. For example, $\square PW$ lets you set the width of output. $\square TS$ is a time stamp.

All system functions and system variables are identified by names starting with the character $\square$.

Event Handling

Any program you write may contain an error. Even if you are convinced there is no error in the program's logic, there may be the potential for an error in the way someone uses the program. You may not want to check for all kinds of exceptional conditions. You may not want to check whether a number entered by a user in response to a prompt is correctly formatted. APL2 gives the programmer the ability to trap an error under the program's control. This prevents application users from seeing APL2 error messages that they may not understand.

The primary event-trapping facility in APL2 is the monadic system function $\square EC$. When given an expression represented as a character string, $\square EC$ evaluates the expression and returns either the result of the expression or an indication of what error occurred.

Complex Numbers

Complex numbers are a generalization of the real numbers used in ordinary computation. They often arise in electrical engineering studies and can be used in generating and manipulating two-dimensional graphics. Implementations of APL2 that allow complex numbers extend the domain of the computational functions to complex numbers.

Limiting Cases

There is an algebra of empty arrays that makes APL2 work in limiting cases. It is not usually necessary to make a special case test for empty arguments in APL2 programs. Without special planning on the part of the programmer, programs often work as desired in empty cases.

Shared Variables

Names in a program can contain data or programs. APL2 permits two programs running independently to contain a variable name in common, which is called a *shared variable.* Use of shared variables permits independently running programs in different active workspaces to communicate because the value given to the variable by one program can be accessed by the other program.

Auxiliary Processors

Applications often need access to data not in an APL2 workspace. An APL2 program may also need to create or modify such data. The APL2 system uses programs called *auxiliary processors* to read and write files. These programs communicate with the APL2 program by using shared variables. The auxiliary processors can run asynchronously from the programs in the workspace.

External Names and Associated Processors

You can use APL2 in combination with programs written in other languages. These programs are represented by external names— names whose definitions are not in the workspace. You can have an application where most of the programs are written in APL2, but some of the programs are written in FORTRAN or some other language. You can access existing libraries of programs written in other languages and use them as though they were APL2 programs. You can apply all the APL2 operators to these programs.

You can also establish external names to other collections of APL2 programs. This allows use of an APL2 application without bringing the application into your active workspace and, possibly, creating name conflicts with objects you have defined.

Associated processors handle the communication between APL2 and programs in other languages. Associated processors differ from auxiliary processors in that they are fully synchronous.

The *DISPLAY* Function

The following is the *DISPLAY* function as distributed by IBM in APL2 Release 2, Program number 5668-899.

On most APL2 systems that provide the *DISPLAY* function, you can find it in library 1 by entering:

```
)COPY 1 DISPLAY DISPLAY
```

This function uses characters from the APL2 character set to draw the best box it can. Sometimes a second function *DISPLAYG* is provided that uses non-APL graphic characters to draw better boxes on suitably-equipped terminals.

```
      ∇ D←S DISPLAY A;⎕IO;R;C;HL;HC;HT;HB;VL;VB;V;W;N;B
[1]   ⍝ (C) SEE COIBM.   5668-899 DISPLAY (DISPLAY)
[2]   ⍝ NORMAL CALL IS MONADIC.  DYADIC CALL USED ONLY IN
[3]   ⍝ RECURSION TO SPECIFY DISPLAY RANK, SHAPE, AND DEPTH.
[4]   ⎕IO←0
[5]   ⍕(0=⎕NC 'S')/'S←⍴A'
[6]   R←↑⍴,S                    ⍝ PSEUDO RANK.
[7]   C←'..''''''              ⍝ UR, UL, LL, AND LR CORNERS.
[8]   HL←'-'                    ⍝ HORIZONTAL LINE.
[9]   HC←HL,'⊖→',HL,'~+∊'       ⍝ HORIZONTAL BORDERS.
[10]  HT←HC[(0<R)×1+0<↑¯1↑,S]
[11]  W←,0≡¨↑0⍴⊂(1⌈⍴A)↑A
[12]  HB←HC[3+3⌊(∨/W)+(∧/0 1∊W)+3×1<⍴⍴S]
[13]  VL←'|'                    ⍝ VERTICAL LINE.
[14]  VB←VL,'⌽↓'                ⍝ VERTICAL BORDER.
[15]  V←VB[(1<R)×1+0<¯1↑¯1↓,S]
[16]  ⍕(0∊⍴A)/'A←(1⌈⍴A)⍴⊂↑A'   ⍝ SHOW PROTOTYPE OF EMPTIES.
[17]  →(1<≡A)/GEN
[18]  →(2<⍴⍴A)/D3
[19]  D←⍕A                      ⍝ SIMPLE ARRAYS.
[20]  W←1↑⍴D←(¯2↑1 1,⍴D)⍴D
[21]  N←¯1+1↓⍴D
[22]  →(0=⍴⍴A)/SS
[23]  D←(C[1],V,((W-1)⍴VL),C[2]),((HT,N⍴HL),[0]D,[0]HB,N⍴HL),C[0],(W⍴VL),C[3]
[24]  →0
[25]  SS:HB←((0 ' ')≡↑0⍴⊂A)/' -'
[26]  D←(B,B,((W-1)⍴B),B),(((((⍴HT)⍴B),N⍴B),[0]D,[0]HB,N⍴B),B,(W⍴B),B←' '
[27]  →0
[28]  GEN:D←⍕DISPLAY¨A          ⍝ ENCLOSED ...
[29]  N←D∨.≠' '
[30]  D←(N∨~1⌽N)⌿D
[31]  D←(∨⌿~' '⍷D)/D
[32]  D←((1,⍴S)⍴S)DISPLAY D
[33]  →(2≥⍴,S)↓D3E,0
[34]  D3:D←0 ¯1↓0 1↓⍕⊂A         ⍝ MULT-DIMENSIONAL ...
[35]  W←1↑⍴D
[36]  N←¯1+1↓⍴D
[37]  D←(C[1],V,((W-1)⍴VL),C[2]),((HT,N⍴HL),[0]D,[0]HB,N⍴HL),C[0],(W⍴VL),C[3]
[38]  D3E:N←¯2+⍴,S
[39]  V←C[N⍴1],[0]VB[1+0<¯2↓,S],[0]((((¯3+↑⍴D),N)⍴VL),[0]C[N⍴2]
[40]  D←V,D
[41]  ∇
```

Editing with
the Del Editor

This appendix describes how to enter and alter APL2 programs. The following descriptions refer to defined functions but they hold equally for defined operators and defined sequences. Some editors will also permit editing of arrays.

Selecting an Editor

APL2 provides two editors called the *del editors* and also provides access to a variety of other editors. If you already know how to use one of the editors supplied with your computing system, you can use it and not bother to learn a new editor.

To identify the editor you want to use within APL2, you use the system command *)EDITOR*. For example, if the name of the system editor is XEDIT, enter the system command:

> *)EDITOR XEDIT*

From now on, when you request entry to definition mode via the del ($\triangledown$) in this APL2 session, XEDIT will be used as the editor.

A disadvantage of using a general system-provided editor is that it probably differs on each system you encounter. The APL2 del editors are the same on all supported computers. The del editors are similar except that editor 1 is a line editor that operates on one line at a time and editor 2 is a full-screen editor, operating on a set of lines at a time.

The command *)EDITOR* 1 selects the line editor, and the command *)EDITOR* 2 selects the full-screen editor.

The current editor is the one selected by the most recent *)EDITOR* command. If you don't select an editor, your system chooses some default editor, normally editor 1. You can determine which editor is currently in use as follows:

> *)EDITOR*
> *IS* 1

Displaying an Existing Definition

No matter what editor you select, you often want to see the definition of an existing function. You request the display of an existing definition the same way with any editor:

> *$\triangledown MYCOST$[$\square$]$\triangledown$*

Entering Definition Mode Using the Current Editor

All editors are entered the same way. You edit an existing program by entering del (∇) and the function name:

> ∇*MYCOST*

The response depends on the editor selected.

To begin editing of a new function, enter del (∇) and the header of the function:

> ∇*Z←NEWFN X;Y*

Again the response to this request depends on the editor selected.

The APL2 Full-Screen Editor:)*EDITOR* 2

After entering the full-screen editor, you will see displayed as many lines of the definition as will fit on the screen (the whole program, if it is short). If you're defining a new program, you see only an information line preceded by the three characters [ᴀ] and the header preceded by the three characters [0].

Here's an example of the screen after you have entered editing of an existing program:

```
[ᴀ]
[0]   Z←EXISTINGFN X
[1]   ᴀ a simple function
[2]   existing line 2
[3]   existing line 3
[4]   existing line 4
```

If you want to change an existing line, enter the change on top of the existing line, without changing the line number, and press enter.

```
[ᴀ]
[0]   Z←EXISTINGFN X
[1]   ᴀ a simple function
[2]   modified line 2
[3]   existing line 3
[4]   existing line 4
```

To delete an entire line, type [∆*number*] at the left edge of the screen. Anywhere on the left edge is OK, but doing it on the line to be deleted is convenient. (The editor has no "un-delete" command.) The first example coming up shows the screen with the delete command on it, and the second example shows the screen after you press enter and the deletion has been processed:

Delete command typed following line [2]:

```
[⍙]
[0]    Z←EXISTINGFN X
[1]    ⍝ a simple function
[2]    modified line 2
[∆3]   existing line 3
[4]    existing line 4
```

After pressing enter:

```
[⍙]
[0]    Z←EXISTINGFN X
[1]    ⍝ a simple function
[2]    modified line 2
[4]    existing line 4
```

To add lines at the end of the function, type them in after the end of the function. Line numbers are not necessary. After you press enter, APL2 numbers the lines. The first example coming up shows the screen with the lines entered, and the second example shows the screen after you press enter:

New lines typed:

```
[⍙]
[0]    Z←EXISTINGFN X
[1]    ⍝ a simple function
[2]    modified line 2
[4]    existing line 4
new line 5
new line 6
```

After pressing enter:

```
[⍙]
[0]   Z←EXISTINGFN X
[1]   ⍝ a simple function
[2]   modified line 2
[4]   existing line 4
[5]   new line 5
[6]   new line 6
```

To add lines in the middle of the function (say between lines 4 and 5), just type over line [5] (on top of the line number) and the following lines (again no line number is necessary). The existing lines are unaffected.

Insert lines typed:

```
[⍙]
[0]   Z←EXISTINGFN X
[1]   ⍝ a simple function
[2]   modified line 2
[4]   existing line 4
inserted line 1
inserted line 2
```

After pressing enter:

```
[⍙]
[0]     Z←EXISTINGFN X
[1]     ⍝ a simple function
[2]     modified line 2
[4]     existing line 4
[4.1]   inserted line 1
[4.2]   inserted line 2
[5]     new line 5
[6]     new line 6
```

To exit from editing and record the changes to the function in the workspace, enter a del (∇) on a line by itself. (Some systems define a program function key that you can use to exit from editing.) To exit from the editor and discard any changes made to the function, enter the three characters [→] at the left edge of the screen.

You can learn other features of editor 2 that this book does not discuss by reviewing the APL2 reference manual included with your system. Some features you might want to look up are summarized here. You enter each at the left edge of the screen:

● [□3-5] — Display a set of lines.

● [/*ABC*/] — Display all lines containing the string *ABC*.

● [/*ABC*/*DEF*/] — Change first occurrence of *ABC* to *DEF* on all lines.

● [/*ABC*/*DEF*/¨] — Change *ABC* to *DEF* everywhere.

● [/*ABC*/*DEF*/3-] — Change *ABC* to *DEF* on line 3 and on all succeeding lines.

● [∇] — Record changes to program in workspace but stay in definition mode.

● ∇ — Begin defining another program. Screen is split at this point and you are editing two functions at the same time.

● [⍎] — Execute an expression and display its result.

The APL2 Line Editor:)*EDITOR* 1

The line editor is similar to the full-screen editor except that it operates on one line at a time. After entering the line editor, you are prompted with a line number. Let *EXISTINGFN* be as it was before the editing done in the previous section. The editor will prompt you for line [5]. The following examples show the progression of an editing session. The only changes occur at the bottom of each example.

```
      ∇EXISTINGFN
 [5]
```

If you want to add a line at the end of the function, enter it after the prompt:

```
      ∇EXISTINGFN
 [5]  new line 5
 [6]  new line 6
 [7]
```

To add a line in the middle of the function, enter a fractional line number in square brackets. In this example, [4.1] indicates that the line should be inserted between lines [4] and [5]:

```
       ∇EXISTINGFN
 [5]    new line 5
 [6]    new line 6
 [7]    [4.1] inserted line 1
[4.2]
```

The next prompt number continues the fractional sequence.

To delete a line, enter a delta (∆) and the line number in square brackets:

```
       ∇EXISTINGFN
 [5]    new line 5
 [6]    new line 6
 [7]    [4.1] inserted line 1
[4.2]   [∆3]
 [3]
```

You will always be prompted for a new line. You can always follow this with another line number in brackets and that line will be the one added, deleted, or inserted.

To see the whole function as currently defined, enter a ☐ inside square brackets:

```
       ∇EXISTINGFN
 [5]    new line 5
 [6]    new line 6
 [7]    [4.1] inserted line 1
[4.2]   [∆3]
 [3]    [☐]
 [0]    Z←EXISTINGFN X
 [1]    ⍝ a simple function
 [2]    existing line 2
 [4]    existing line 4
[4.1]   inserted line
 [5]    new line 5
 [6]    new line 6
 [7]
```

To exit from the editor and record the changes to the program in the workspace, enter del (∇) in response to the prompt. To exit from the editor and discard the changes to the program, enter the three characters [→] in response to the prompt.

APL Blossom Time

APL2 continues the rich tradition of the APL programming language, first defined and implemented by Kenneth Iverson and Adin Falkoff and their team which included Larry Breed and Dick Lathwell. APL and APL2 advocates have an esprit all their own as evidenced by the following song written by Michele Montalbano. This song encapsulates the early history of APL.

Dedicated to the pioneers of APL
with respect and affection

by

J.C.L. Guest

To the tune of "The Battle of New Orleans"

Back in the old days, in 1962,
A feller named Ken Iverson decided what to do.
He gathered all the papers he'd been writing for a spell
and he put them in a little book and called it APL.

Well!...
> He got him a jot and he got him a ravel
> and he revved his compression up as high as she could go
> And he did some reduction and he did some expansion
> And he sheltered all his numbers with a ceiling and a flo'.

Now Sussenguth and Falkoff, they thought it would be fine
To use the new notation to describe the product line.
They got with Dr. Iverson and went behind the scenes
And wrote a clear description of a batch of new machines.

Well!...
> They wrote down dots and they wrote down squiggles
> And they wrote down symbols that they didn't even know.
> And they wrote down questions when they didn't know the answers
> And they made the Systems Journal in nineteen sixty-fo'.

Now writing dots and squiggles is a mighty pleasant task
But it doesn't answer questions that a lot of people ask.
Ken needed an interpreter for folks who couldn't read
So he hiked to Californ-i-a to talk to Larry Breed.

Oh!...
> He got Larry Breed and he got Phil Abrams
> And they started coding FORTRAN just as fast as they could go
> And they punched up cards and ran them through the reader
> In Stanford, Palo Alto, on the seventy-ninety-oh.

Well, a FORTRAN batch interpreter's a mighty awesome thing
But while it hums a pretty tune, it doesn't really sing.
The thing that we all had to have to make our lives sublime
Was an interactive program that would let us share the time.

Oh!...
    They got Roger Moore and they got Dick Lathwell,
    And they got Gene McDonnell with his carets and his sticks,
    And you should've heard the uproar in the Hudson River valley
    When they saved the first *CLEANSPACE* in 1966.

Well, when Al Rose saw this he took a little ride
In a big station wagon with a typeball by his side.
He did a lot of teaching and he had a lot of fun
With an old, bent, beat-up 2741.

Oh!...
    It typed out starts and it typed out circles
    An it twisted and it wiggled just like a living thing.
    Al fed it a tape when he couldn't get a phone line
    And it purred like a tiger with its trainer in the ring.

Now there's much more to the story, but I just don't have the time
(And I doubt you have the patience) for an even longer rhyme.
So I'm ending this first chapter of the tale I hope to tell
Of how Iverson's notation blossomed into APL.

So!...
    Keep writing nands when you're not writing neithers,
    And point with an arrow to the place you want to be,
    But don't forget to bless those early APL sources
    Who preserved the little seedling that became an APL tree.

●

Live performance at the APL81 Conference in San Francisco by L. Breed, J. Brown, J. Bunda, D. Dloughy, A. O'Hara, R. Skinner, and 900 attendees.

45-RPM recording by J. Brown, M. Wheatley, J. Bunda, and B. Duff.

The Great Empty-Array Joke Contest

Empty arrays are often difficult for people to conceptualize—especially empty arrays containing structure. The example joke that follows was used in many presentations as a way to motivate understanding of APL2 empty arrays. Rather than use the same joke repeatedly, a contest was established to seek out empty-array jokes. Early results of the contest were collected in the *APL Quote Quad*, the journal of the APL special interest group (SIGAPL) of the Association for Computing Machinery. Reprinted here is an abbreviated version of that collection.

APL Quote Quad, Vol. 11, No. 4: June 1981

ANNOUNCEMENT

The Great Empty-Array Joke Contest

I am searching to find the world's best empty-array jokes. They will be edited into a priceless collection (it doesn't seem appropriate to have a non-empty price). Many submissions will be printed in these very pages (or ones similar to these) along with your name (so beware).

Example:

> **Man in restaurant:** May I have coffee without cream?
> **Waiter:** We don't have cream. You can have it without milk!

Entries will be judged according to my mood on the day they are received. Cash prizes (not to exceed $10 each) will be awarded and —best of all—there is no time limit on submissions; take as long as you wish. Submit jokes to:

Jim Brown
APL Joke Editor
P.O. Box 20937
San Jose, Calif. 95169
U.S.A.

APL Quote Quad, Vol. 12, No. 2: December 1981

Empty-Array Joke Column

The Great Empty-Array Joke Contest was announced at SHARE 57 in Chicago and in the pages of this publication, Vol. 11, No. 4. The fact that the table of contents said page 22 while the announcement was on page 26 does not constitute an entry to the contest. Since then, the number of people submitting jokes has been astonishing; they are outnumbered only by the people who did not. Vol. 12, No. 1 contained the first collection of jokes, but unfortunately there were none at that time. Here's the next batch.

Almost before the contest began (that is, only three weeks afterward), I received twelve entries from one (misguided?) person. Here are two of them; you'll be blessed (?) with others in issues to come.

1. First is another version of the sample joke given at the time of the announcement of the contest:

   Customer: I'd like to have strawberries without cream.
   Waiter: We haven't any cream.
   Customer: Do you have any yogurt?
   Waiter: Sure, we have yogurt.
   Customer: Okay, I'll have them without yogurt.

   —E. E. McDonnell

2. I heard the following joke at about the same time as number 1, and have repeated it almost as many times.

   Lady: What price are your pork chops?
   Butcher: $5.98 per pound.
   Lady: That's outrageous! Mr. Schmidt down the street only charges $3.98 per pound.
   Butcher: Why don't you buy them from Mr. Schmidt, then?
   Lady: He's all out of them today.
   Butcher: Lady, when I'm all out of chops, I charge only $2.98 for them.

   —E. E. McDonnell

3. Next is the first submission that involves a nested empty array—an empty vector of two-element vectors.

> **Man to lady at party:** Didn't I meet you in Zanzibar last year?
>
> **Lady:** No, I've never been to Zanzibar.
>
> **Man:** Neither have I. It must have been two other people.
>
> —*Dan Moore*

4. The following story was submitted by several people (including Glenn Schneider ... who labeled the envelope "One Empty-Array Joke," but I think he miscounted). This version was the first one I received.

> —*D. O. Smith*

5. This next joke is questionable, in that only the punch line is empty. I had to include it because every collection of jokes must have one of this type.

> How many empty arrays does it take to screw in a light bulb?
>
> —*Joe Baginski*

That's it for this issue. In review, the rules of the contest are as follows:

- Any story dealing with emptiness, nothingness, the absence of something, something left out, or zeroness (as in the shape of an empty vector) is acceptable.
- Pictures, drawings, and cartoons are acceptable, if not copyrighted....
- Cash prizes will not exceed ten dollars.
- I am the sole judge of the contest.
- There is no time limit on entries.

Keep them coming!

APL Quote Quad, Vol. 12, No. 3: March 1982

Empty-Array Joke Column

The response to the empty-array joke contest continues to be unbelievable; at least, I cannot find anyone who believes it! Duplicate stories are starting to show up as expected. One I didn't expect was Number 5 from the last issue (How many empty arrays does it take to screw in a light bulb?). Jeff Shallit turned in the same one before the first one reached publication. I guess there is no accounting for taste.

6. This entry comes from a person who is editor of a publication which would not consider publishing columns like this one (unless that publication were exactly like this one).

> **Customer:** Your prices are very reasonable. How do you make a profit?
> **Store Owner:** We don't make money on any individual item, but we make up for it in volume.
>
> —*Art Anger*

7. In the last issue we had a joke with an empty punch line. This one apparently does not have an empty punch line. I'm awaiting (breathlessly) the receipt of the punch line.

> **Q:** How do you keep a turkey in suspense?
>
> —*Zeke Hoskins*

8. This is a second submission by someone bent on doing better than his first one (Number 3), which should be easy.

> **Boy:** Mom, I saved 50 cents today!
> **Mother:** How did you do that?
> **Boy:** Instead of taking the bus to school today, I ran behind it.
> **Mother:** Silly, you should have run behind a taxi!
>
> —*Dan Moore*

9. This story puts I. P. Sharp well in the lead with the number of stories. You others need to try harder!

> **98-lb. weakling** (after bully kicks sand in his face and steals his girlfriend): What a show-off! I feel like punching him in the nose again.
> **Incredulous Friend:** You punched him in the nose before?
> **98-lb. weakling:** No. I *felt* like punching him in the nose before.
>
> —*E. E. McDonnell*

10. Finally, we close with a talking-dog story.

> **Boy:** My dog can do arithmetic.
> **Friend:** Oh yeah? Let's see!
> **Boy (to dog):** How much is 2 minus 2?
> **Dog:**
>
> —*Otto Mond*

●

Keep those jokes coming. I don't want to run out of them.

Appendix E

APL2 Character Set

The entire set of displayable APL2 characters is shown in the chart on the next page, along with their common-usage names. The names shown are for the symbols themselves and not necessarily for the operations that they represent.

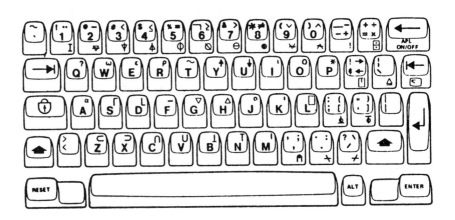

Keyboard for APL2

A B C D E F G H I J K L M N O P Q R S T U V W X Y Z

A̲ B̲ C̲ D̲ E̲ F̲ G̲ H̲ I̲ J̲ K̲ L̲ M̲ N̲ O̲ P̲ Q̲ R̲ S̲ T̲ U̲ V̲ W̲ X̲ Y̲ Z̲

a b c d e f g h i j k l m n o p q r s t u v w x y z

0 1 2 3 4 5 6 7 8 9

<table>
<tr><td>¨</td><td>dieresis</td></tr>
<tr><td>¯</td><td>overbar</td></tr>
<tr><td><</td><td>less than</td></tr>
<tr><td>≤</td><td>less than or equal to</td></tr>
<tr><td>=</td><td>equal</td></tr>
<tr><td>≥</td><td>greater than or equal to</td></tr>
<tr><td>></td><td>greater than</td></tr>
<tr><td>≠</td><td>not equal</td></tr>
<tr><td>∨</td><td>down caret</td></tr>
<tr><td>∧</td><td>caret</td></tr>
<tr><td>−</td><td>minus (bar or midbar)</td></tr>
<tr><td>÷</td><td>divide</td></tr>
<tr><td>+</td><td>plus</td></tr>
<tr><td>×</td><td>times</td></tr>
<tr><td>?</td><td>query</td></tr>
<tr><td>⍵</td><td>omega ★</td></tr>
<tr><td>∊</td><td>epsilon</td></tr>
<tr><td>⍴</td><td>rho</td></tr>
<tr><td>~</td><td>tilde</td></tr>
<tr><td>↑</td><td>up arrow</td></tr>
<tr><td>↓</td><td>down arrow</td></tr>
<tr><td>⍳</td><td>iota</td></tr>
<tr><td>○</td><td>circle</td></tr>
<tr><td>⋆</td><td>star</td></tr>
<tr><td>→</td><td>right arrow</td></tr>
<tr><td>←</td><td>left arrow</td></tr>
</table>

<table>
<tr><td>⍺</td><td>alpha ★</td></tr>
<tr><td>⌈</td><td>up stile</td></tr>
<tr><td>⌊</td><td>down stile</td></tr>
<tr><td>_</td><td>underbar</td></tr>
<tr><td>∇</td><td>del</td></tr>
<tr><td>∆</td><td>delta</td></tr>
<tr><td>∘</td><td>jot</td></tr>
<tr><td>'</td><td>quote</td></tr>
<tr><td>⎕</td><td>quad</td></tr>
<tr><td>(</td><td>left paren</td></tr>
<tr><td>)</td><td>right paren</td></tr>
<tr><td>[</td><td>left bracket</td></tr>
<tr><td>]</td><td>right bracket</td></tr>
<tr><td>⊂</td><td>left shoe</td></tr>
<tr><td>⊃</td><td>right shoe</td></tr>
<tr><td>∩</td><td>cap</td></tr>
<tr><td>∪</td><td>cup</td></tr>
<tr><td>⊥</td><td>base</td></tr>
<tr><td>⊤</td><td>top</td></tr>
<tr><td>|</td><td>stile</td></tr>
<tr><td>;</td><td>semicolon</td></tr>
<tr><td>:</td><td>colon</td></tr>
<tr><td>,</td><td>comma</td></tr>
<tr><td>.</td><td>dot</td></tr>
<tr><td>\</td><td>backslash</td></tr>
<tr><td>/</td><td>slash</td></tr>
<tr><td></td><td>blank (space)</td></tr>
</table>

<table>
<tr><td>⍱</td><td>nor</td><td>∨</td><td>~</td></tr>
<tr><td>⍲</td><td>nand</td><td>∧</td><td>~</td></tr>
<tr><td>⍒</td><td>del stile</td><td>∇</td><td>|</td></tr>
<tr><td>⍋</td><td>delta stile</td><td>∆</td><td>|</td></tr>
<tr><td>⍙</td><td>delta underbar</td><td>∆</td><td>_</td></tr>
<tr><td>⌽</td><td>circle stile</td><td>○</td><td>|</td></tr>
<tr><td>⍉</td><td>circle backslash</td><td>○</td><td>\</td></tr>
<tr><td>⊖</td><td>circle bar</td><td>○</td><td>−</td></tr>
<tr><td>⍟</td><td>circle star</td><td>○</td><td>⋆</td></tr>
<tr><td>⌶</td><td>I-beam ★</td><td>⊥</td><td>⊤</td></tr>
<tr><td>⍫</td><td>del tilde</td><td>∇</td><td>~</td></tr>
<tr><td>⍎</td><td>base jot</td><td>⊥</td><td>∘</td></tr>
<tr><td>⍕</td><td>top jot</td><td>⊤</td><td>∘</td></tr>
<tr><td>⍀</td><td>backslash bar</td><td>\</td><td>−</td></tr>
<tr><td>⌿</td><td>slash bar</td><td>/</td><td>−</td></tr>
<tr><td>⍝</td><td>lamp</td><td>∩</td><td>∘</td></tr>
<tr><td>⍞</td><td>quote-quad (quad-prime)</td><td>⎕</td><td>'</td></tr>
<tr><td>!</td><td>shriek</td><td>.</td><td>'</td></tr>
<tr><td>⌹</td><td>domino</td><td>⎕</td><td>÷</td></tr>
<tr><td>⍂</td><td>quad backslash ★</td><td>⎕</td><td>\</td></tr>
<tr><td>⌻</td><td>quad jot ★</td><td>⎕</td><td>∘</td></tr>
<tr><td>⌷</td><td>squad (squished quad)</td><td>[</td><td>]</td></tr>
<tr><td>≡</td><td>equal underbar</td><td>=</td><td>_</td></tr>
<tr><td>⍷</td><td>epsilon underbar</td><td>∊</td><td>_</td></tr>
<tr><td>⍸</td><td>iota underbar ★</td><td>⍳</td><td>_</td></tr>
<tr><td>⍢</td><td>dotted del ★</td><td>¨</td><td>.</td></tr>
<tr><td>%</td><td>percent ★</td><td>/</td><td>÷</td></tr>
<tr><td>&</td><td>ampersand ★</td><td>|</td><td>∊</td></tr>
<tr><td>¢</td><td>cent ★</td><td>|</td><td>⊂</td></tr>
<tr><td>$</td><td>dollar ★</td><td>S</td><td>/</td></tr>
<tr><td>#</td><td>pound ★</td><td>N</td><td>=</td></tr>
<tr><td>@</td><td>at ★</td><td>Q</td><td>∘</td></tr>
<tr><td>!</td><td>exclamation ★</td><td>'</td><td>∘</td></tr>
<tr><td>|</td><td>vertical bar ★</td><td>|</td><td>⊥</td></tr>
<tr><td>~</td><td>tilde ★</td><td>|</td><td>~</td></tr>
<tr><td>¬</td><td>not ★</td><td>/</td><td>~</td></tr>
<tr><td>¦</td><td>split bar ★</td><td>,</td><td>'</td></tr>
<tr><td>"</td><td>double quote ★</td><td>¨</td><td>'</td></tr>
<tr><td>{</td><td>left brace ★</td><td>−</td><td>(</td></tr>
<tr><td>}</td><td>right brace ★</td><td>−</td><td>)</td></tr>
<tr><td>\</td><td>backslash ★</td><td>\</td><td>⊥</td></tr>
<tr><td>`</td><td>accent ★</td><td>\</td><td>¯</td></tr>
</table>

★ These characters currently have no assigned purpose in APL2, other than their use as decorators.

APL2 Release 3 Functions

In November 1987, IBM announced APL2 Release 3 which contains two new primitive functions:

- **indexing**
- **partition**

This appendix briefly describes these functions. For further information on these functions and the other features of APL2 Release 3, see "*APL2 Programming: Language Reference*" (IBM order number SH20-9227).

Indexing

The **indexing** (⌷) function is like indexing with brackets except that it has the syntax of a dyadic function and can be used with operators. In general terms, indices that would be listed in square brackets separated by semicolons are instead written as the left argument of the **indexing** function. The right argument is the array being indexed:

$$A[I;J;K]$$

is written as

$$I \; J \; K \; ⌷ \; A$$

The length of the vector written on the left of the **indexing** function must match the number of axes in the array being indexed. Thus to index a rank-3 array, you need a three-item left argument. For example:

```
      B←2 3 4ρι24

      B
   1  2  3  4
   5  6  7  8
   9 10 11 12

  13 14 15 16
  17 18 19 20
  21 22 23 24

      B[2 1;1;3 1]
  15 13
   3  1

      (2 1) 1 (3 1) ⌷ B
  15 13
   3  1
```

Because this **indexing** function can be used with operators, you can
apply several indices to one array independently:

$$(1\ 1\ 1)(2\ 1\ 3)\unicode{x2395}^{\cdot\cdot}{\subset}B$$

  1 15

This is sometimes called *scatter indexing* because you can use it to
select arbitrary items from an array as opposed to rectangular
subsections.

You can index each of a set of arrays with the same index as follows:

$$({\subset}(2\ 1)\ 1\ (3\ 1))\ \unicode{x2395}^{\cdot\cdot}\ B\ (10{\times}B)\ (100{\times}B)$$

  15 13   150 130   1500 1300
   3 1   30 10   300 100

When indexing a vector, a scalar left argument is treated as though
it were a vector of length 1:

        V←'*ABCDEFGHI*'
        3⎕*V*
  C

Be careful when you want to select more than one item from a
vector. For example, to select the third and fourth item from the
character vector *V*, you might try the following expression:

        3 4⎕*V*
  RANK ERROR
        3 4⎕*V*
       ∧ ∧
      →

This expression fails because a two-item left argument can only
index a rank-2 array. A nested left argument does the desired
operation:

        ({\subset}3 4)⎕*V*
  CD

The **indexing** function may be used with an axis to indicate elided indices. The following examples contrast indexing with brackets to the **indexing** function:

```
      B←2 3 4ρι24
      B
 1  2  3  4
 5  6  7  8
 9 10 11 12

13 14 15 16
17 18 19 20
21 22 23 24

      B[2 1;;3 1]
15 13
19 17
23 21

 3  1
 7  5
11  9

      (2 1) (3 1) ⌷[1 3] B
15 13
19 17
23 21

 3  1
 7  5
11  9
```

Partition

The purpose of the **partition** ($\subset$) function is to divide up the right argument producing one item in the result for each division. For example, given the vector *'JIM,JOHN,GEORGE,FRED'*, the **partition** function may be used to produce a vector of the four names as follows:

```
        LIST←'JIM,JOHN,GEORGE,FRED'
        M←(LIST≠',')
        M
 1 1 1 0 1 1 1 1 0 1 1 1 1 1 1 0 1 1 1 1

        M⊂LIST
 JIM JOHN GEORGE FRED

        DISPLAY M⊂LIST
```

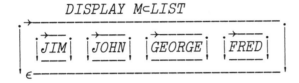

A division is expressed in the left argument as an increase in value. Whenever an item of the left argument is greater than the previous item, a new division is started. Any item in the right argument corresponding to a zero in the left argument does not appear in the result. The magnitude of items in the left argument has no influence on the operation. Only increases in value are relevant:

```
        DISPLAY (2×M)⊂LIST
```

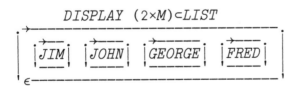

If the left argument does not contain any zeros, then all items from the right argument appear in the result:

```
        DISPLAY (1+M)⊂LIST
```

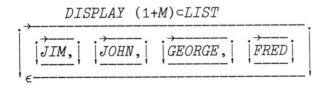

A good way to remember that an increase in the left argument causes the start of a new item in the result is to remember that an increasing arithmetic progression results in a vector of one-item vectors:

```
      (ι5)⊂'ABCDE'
 A  B  C  D  E
          DISPLAY (ι5)⊂'ABCDE'
 ┌→──────────────────────┐
 │ ┌→┐  ┌→┐  ┌→┐  ┌→┐  ┌→┐ │
 │ │A│  │B│  │C│  │D│  │E│ │
 │ └─┘  └─┘  └─┘  └─┘  └─┘ │
 │∊───────────────────────┘
```

Glossary

Active workspace .... Workspace in which APL2 objects can be examined and expressions executed.

Algorithm .... Abstract description of a program. The description of a process or procedure.

Argument .... Array which is input to a function.

Array .... Rectangular collection of zero or more items arranged along zero or more axes. Each item in an array is a single number, a single character, or any other array.

Assignment .... Association of a name and an array.

Attention signal .... Request for a program to stop executing at the end of a line.

Axis .... One of the directions along which data is arranged.

Boolean array .... Array of 1's and 0's.

Boolean function .... Function which takes Boolean arguments a returns a Boolean result.

Command .... Line that begins with a right parenthesis.

Constant .... Object always associated with the same value, such as a number.

Count .... Number of items in an array.

Defined function .... Program used like a primitive function.

Defined operator .... Program used like a primitive operator.

Defined sequence .... Program used like a constant.

Definition mode .... State in which an expression entered becomes part of a program and is remembered for later evaluation.

Depth .... Degree of nesting of an array.

Derived function .... Function formed by the application of an operator to its operands.

Dyadic function .... Function applied to two arrays as arguments.

Dyadic operator .... Operator that applies to two operands.

Empty array .... Array that has zero items along at least one of its axes.

Explicit result .... Array produced by a function. It can be used as an argument of another function, assigned to a name, or displayed.

Expression .... Collection of symbols that can be evaluated to produce an array, a function, or an operator.

External name .... Operator, function, or array that can be used in an active workspace but which is defined outside the workspace.

Function .... Operation that applies to data and produces new data.

Global variable .... Variable whose value exists outside of any defined operation.

Immediate execution mode State in which an expression entered is immediately evaluated.

Interrupt .... Request for a program to stop executing immediately.

Library .... Collection of saved workspaces.

Local variable .... Variable defined only within some defined operation.

Mask .... Boolean vector used to control the application of a function.

Matrix .... Array with two dimensions.

Monadic function .... Function that in context is applied to one array as argument.

Monadic operator .... Operator that applies to one operand.

Nested array .... Array with at least one item which is not a simple scalar.

Nested scalar .... Array with no axes whose only item is not a simple scalar.

Nested vector .... Linear arrangement of data where at least one item is not a simple scalar.

Operand .... An array or function given to an operator as input.

Operator .... Operation that applies to functions and/or arrays and produces a new function as its result (called a derived function).

Primitive .... Function or operator defined as part of the APL2 language and always available—even in a clear workspace.

Program .... User-defined function, operator, or sequence.

Rank .... Number of axes of an array.

Relational function .... Function that performs comparisons.

Row-major order .... Listing of the items in an array that gives every item in row I before it gives any item in row $I+1$. **Ravel** lists items of an array in row-major order.

Scalar .... Array with zero axes.

Scalar function .... Function that applies independently to each simple scalar in its argument(s).

Selective assignment Assignment with a selection expression to the left of the left arrow.

Shadowed name .... Name of a global object which is hidden by a local object of the same name.

Simple array .... Array in which every item is a simple scalar.

Simple scalar .... Single number or single character of rank zero.

Simple vector .... Vector of simple scalars.

State indicator .... Place where the system keeps track of expressions and programs that have started execution but have not finished.

Variable .... Name with an array as its value.

Vector .... One-dimensional array.

Vector notation .... In the absence of functions or operators, two or more arrays written next to each other to form a vector of the values of the arrays.

Workspace .... Area of storage in main memory (active workspace) or in auxiliary storage (library workspace) that contains the definitions of variables and programs.

Bibliography

This bibliography contains selected titles on APL2 and works cited in the text. It does not contain historical references or references to other implementations of APL.

●

Brown, James A., "The Principles of APL2," IBM Santa Teresa Technical Report (TR 03.247) (March 1984).

Brown, James A., "Inside the APL2 workspace," APL *Quote Quad*, Vol. 15, No. 4 (1985).

Brown, James A., "A Development of APL2 Syntax," IBM *Journal of Research and Development*, Vol. 29, No. 1 (January 1985).

Brown, James A., "Why APL2: A discussion of Design Principles," APL *Quote Quad*, Vol. 17, No. 4 (1987)

Brown, James A. and Manuel Alfonseca, "Solutions to Logic Problems in APL2," APL *Quote Quad*, Vol. 17, No. 4 (1987)

Brown, James A., Edward V. Eusebi, Janice Cook,and Leo Groner, "Algorithms for Artificial Intelligence in APL2," IBM Santa Teresa Technical Report (TR 03.281) (May 1986).

Crowder, Harlan and James A. Brown, "Graphics Applications using Complex Numbers in APL2," IBM Santa Teresa Technical Report (TR 03.265) (March 1985).

Eusebi, Edward V., "Operators for Program Control." APL *Quote Quad*, Vol. 15, No. 4 (1985).

Eusebi, Edward V., "Operators for Recursion," APL *Quote Quad*, Vol. 15, No. 4 (1985).

Eusebi, Edward V. and James A. Brown, "APL2 and AI: A study of Search," APL *Quote Quad*, Vol. 16, No. 4 (1986).

Gamow, George, *One Two Three... INFINITY*, The New American Library, Mentor Books, New York (1947).

Graham, Alan, "Examples of Event Handling in APL2," APL Quote Quad, Vol. 13, No. 3, (1983)

Graham, Alan, "Idioms and Problem Solving Techniques in APL2," APL *Quote Quad*, Vol. 16, No. 4 (1986).

Groner, Leo. and Janice Cook, "Modelling the Arithmetic of Statistical Distributions," APL *Quote Quad, Vol. 16*, No. 4 (1986).

Haspel, Charles and Alphonse Thomas Vasquez, "N-dimensional Geometry Using APL2," APL *Quote Quad*, Vol. 15, No. 4 (1985).

Mayhew, Loren B., "Increasing Productivity with ISPF/APL2," APL *Quote Quad*, Vol. 16, No. 4 (1986).

Polivka, Raymond P., "The Impact of APL2 on Teaching APL," APL Quote Quad, Vol. 14, No. 4 (1984)

Polivka, Raymond P., "APL2—An Introduction (Concepts and Principles)" APL Quote Quad Vol. 16, No. 4, (1986)

Thomson, Norman, "APL2—A Mathematician's Delight," APL *Quote Quad*, Vol. 16, No. 4 (1986).

Thomson, Norman, "A Guide to Using APL2 Nested Arrays," *Vector: Journal of the British* APL *Society*, Vol. 2, No. 1 (July 1985).

Thomson, Norman, "A Guide to Using Operators in APL2." *Vector: Journal of the British* APL *Society*, Vol. 2, No. 3 (Jan. 1986).

Thomson, Norman, "APL2—A Very Superior Fortran," APL *Quote Quad*, Vol. 17, No. 4 (1987)

Vilenkin, N. Ya, "Combinatorics," Academic Press, 1971.

Answers to
Selected Problems

The answers presented here use parentheses to indicate nesting. It's alright if you use spacing to indicate nesting so your answers look like the results displayed by APL2 as long as you can unambiguously tell that you have the correct answer.

Because of the variety of functions in APL2, there is frequently more than one good solution to a problem. You may often come up with a different solution to a problem than the one shown here. If so, be sure that your solution is equivalent or better than the one shown.

Chapter 1: **Working with APL2**

Section 1.1 – Doing Ordinary Arithmetic

2.   a.   100
   b.   10
   c.   1
   d.   0.1
   e.   1400
   f. $-{}^-314159$

Section 1.2 – Arithmetic on Arrays

2.   a.   21
   b.   110   160

   You should be able to get this numerical answer even though the structure of the result has not been discussed.

   c.   315

4.   a. $X+Y$
   b. $X-Y$

Section 1.3 – Remembering Data

2.   a. X is 3
   b.   no change
   c. Y gets 4
   d.   no change
   e. Y gets 3

Section 1.4 – Evaluation of Expressions

2. a. 30
    b. 5
    c. ‾1
    d. 5 redundant
    e. 13
    f. 20
    g. 30
    h. 30 rightmost pair redundant
    i. 28
    j. 28
    k. 58 outer pair redundant

4. a. 10.1 10.2 10.5
    b. 10.1 20.2 30.5
    c. (10.1 20.1) 30.2 (40.5 50.5 60.5)
    d. (10.1 20.2) 30.5
    e. 10.1 (20.2 30.5)
    f. (10.1 20.1) (30.2 30.5)

6. a. (2 3) 4 ((1 5)(6 7))
    b. (3 4)(2 3)
    c. (2 3) 10
    d. (1 2) 9
    e. (2 3) 9
    f. 4 5 6
    g. 4 5 6
    h. ((1 5)(6 7)) 2 ((1 5)(6 7))
    i. (12 13) 14
    j. (4 6) 8

8. a. 1 2 3××/186281 365 24 60 60
    b. 1 2 3××/1.6 186281 365 24 60 60

10. 100×7 7.5 8.2×24

12. ×/.01 *STAX PRICE QTY*

14. (*A B*)←*B A*   or   (*B A*)←*A B*

Section 1.6 – Errors

2. a. three stars
    b. two stars
    c. empty
    d. empty

Chapter 2: Working with Vectors

Section 2.1 – Functions that Produce Vectors

2. a. 24 35
    b. 24 35
    c. 20 34 35
    d. 20 34 35
    e. 20 34 35
    f. 24 35
    g. 24 35
    h. 44 55
    i. 14 55

4. ‾1+2×ι10

6. *MONTHS←MONTHS*,65

Section 2.2 – Character Data

2. *'I''VE GOT IT!'*

4. All of these answers are one-item vectors:

    a. 2
    b. 7
    c. 2
    d. 2
    e. 7
    f. 2
    g. 2
    h. 8
    i. 7

Section 2.3 – Empty Vectors

2. P ι0

Section 2.4 – Functions that Manipulate Vectors

2. a. 2
   b. 1 4
   c. 2 3
   d. 3 1
   e. 3 2 1

4. a. *DE* 463
   b. 463
   c. 87
   d. *FGHI*
   e. *G*
   f. *ABC* 25
   g. *ABC*
   h. 25
   i. *FGHI* 87 12

6. `'TRIBUTARY'[4 5 6]`   or   `3↑3↓'TRIBUTARY'`

Section 2.5 – Scalar Functions

2. $-|V$

4. a. 3 2 (two-item vector)
   b. 12 (scalar)
   c. (empty vector)
   d. 10 20 (two-item vector)
   e. 10 (one-item vector)
   f. (empty vector)
   g. 10 (scalar)

6. a. `⌊80×5×7` ⟷ 57
   b. `⌊80×2×7` ⟷ 22
   c. `⌊5×(80−32)÷9` ⟷ 26

8. `2.5⌈×/.02 100 1.5`

10. a. `1500×(2+.09÷4)*2×4`
    b. `(5000×(1+12÷4)*3×4)−5000`

12. $AGE\lfloor 39$

14. a.   none
    b.   second −
    c.   second |
    d.   both
    e. $\lfloor$
    f.   − and second ×

16. a. $(\times/R1\ R2)\div+/R1\ R2$
    b. $(\times/R)\div+/R$

Chapter 3: Working with Programs

Section 3.1 – Operators Apply to Functions

2. a.   10
    b.   4 6 (a scalar)
    c.   3 7 (simple)
    d.   1 2 3 4
    e.   3 3 4
    f.   8 9 (scalar)

    4. ×/300000 365 24 60 60

Section 3.2 – Programs Remember Expressions

2.
```
        ∇ Z←PERDED DENTAL COST;PER;DED
   [1]    ⍝ compute dental cost
   [2]    (PER DED)←PERDED    ⍝ separate left arg
   [3]    Z←⌊PER×COST-DED     ⍝ part for insurance
   [4]    Z←(COST-Z)Z
        ∇
```

4.
```
        ∇ Z← MC CHARGE DIMEN;UC
   [1]    ⍝ compute shipping cost
   [2]    ⍝ MC is minimum charge and unit charge
   [3]    ⍝ DIMEN is three dimensions in inches
   [4]    (MC UC)←MC  ⍝ separate minimum and unit charges
   [5]    Z←MC⌈UC××/DIMEN÷12
   [6]    ∇
```

6.
```
        ∇ Z← PERCENT V
  [1]      ⍝ compute percentage distribution
  [2]      ⍝ V - vector of sets of answers to questions
  [3]      ⍝ Z - vector of question percentages
  [4]      Z←⌊100×V÷+/¨V
  [5]      ∇
```

8.
```
        ∇ Z←L PLUS R
  [1]      Z←L+R          ⍝ addition
  [2]   ∇
        ∇ Z←WHAT R
  [1]      Z←R            ⍝ do nothing
  [2]   ∇
        ∇ Z←IS R
  [1]      Z←R            ⍝ do nothing
  [2]   ∇
```

10. Assume three variables *AMT*, *YEARS*, and *RATE*.

$$AMT÷1+YEARS×RATE×.01$$

12. *XX* is a defined sequence with an explicit result, not a variable.

Chapter 4: Working in the APL2 Environment

Section 4.1 – Libraries

2.   1-i
     2-f
     3-p
     4-d
     5-n
     6-l
     7-h
     8-a
     9-m
     10-r
     11-g
     12-q
     13-j
     14-c
     15-e

Chapter 5: Working with Arrays

Section 5.1 – Properties of Arrays

2. a. simple, shape 3, depth 1
   b. simple, shape 2, depth 1
   c. simple, shape empty, depth 0
   d. simple, shape 4, depth 1
   e. nested, shape 2, depth 2
   f. nested, shape 2, depth 3
   g. nested, shape 2, depth 4

4. yes—a scalar that contains an empty array.

Section 5.2 – Building and Displaying Arrays

2. 5 0ρ0

4. a. R Cρ0
   b. $((\rho D),3)$ρ0

6. 2 3ρ (ι0)(ι0)

   Right argument can be any non-empty array containing only empty arrays.

Section 5.3 – Measuring Arrays

2. a. (ι0)ρ(ι0)(ι0)
      This is a scalar containing an empty vector.
   b. (ι0)(ι0)
   c. (ι0)(ι0)(ι0)
   d. (ι0)(ι0)
   e. (ι0)ρ(ι0)(ι0)
      This is a scalar containing an empty vector.
   f. (ι0)(ι0)(ι0)
   g. (ι0)(ι0)(ι0)(ι0)
   h. (1ρ3)(1ρ2)
   i. (1ρ3)(ι0)
   j. (1ρ2)(ι0)
   k. (1ρ2)(ι0)

4. Depth is 1. The rest of the result depends on the argument.

Section 5.4 – Unshaping and Nested Shaping of Arrays

2. a. shape 2, depth 2
    b. shape 3, depth 2
    c. shape empty, depth 3
    d. shape empty, depth 4
    e. shape empty, depth 3
    f. shape 2 3, depth 1
    g. shape 3 4, depth 1
    h. shape 3, depth 1
    i. shape 2 3 4, depth 1

4. 2 3ρ⊂'*RAY*'

6. $V[2]$←⊂M or (2⊃V)←M

Section 5.5 – Manipulating an Array along an Axis

2. a. shape N M, rank 2, depth 1
    b. shape M N, rank 2, depth 1
    c. *AXIS ERROR*
    d. *AXIS ERROR*
    e. *AXIS ERROR*
    f. shape L I M J N K, rank 6, depth 1
    g. shape M I L J N K, rank 6, depth 1

4. a. I J
    b. J K
    c. I J
    d. *AXIS ERROR*
    e. *AXIS ERROR*

6. A←'*AB*' '*CDE*'

8. a. ¯1↑[1]M
    b. 1↑[2]M
    c. ¯1↑[1]M
    d. ¯1 ¯1↑[1 2]M
    e. ¯1 ¯1 2↑[1 2 3]M or   ¯1 ¯1 2↑M

10. a. shape 3 3, value:

        11 12 13
        24 25 26
        37 38 39

b. shape 3 3, value:

```
11  22  33
14  25  36
17  28  39
```

c. *RANK ERROR*

d. shape 2 4 3, value:

```
 110   220   330
 410   520   630
 710   820   930
1010  1120  1230

1310  1420  1530
1610  1720  1830
1910  2020  2130
2210  2320  2430
```

e. shape 2 4 3, value:

```
 101   202   303
 404   505   606
 707   808   909
1010  1111  1212

1301  1402  1503
1604  1705  1806
1907  2008  2109
2210  2311  2412
```

f. shape 2 4 3, value:

```
 101   202   303
 404   505   606
 707   808   909
1010  1111  1212

1301  1402  1503
1604  1705  1806
1907  2008  2109
2210  2311  2412
```

12. ⊂[2]⊃[1] *D*   or   ⊂[1]⊃[2] *D*

14.

```
     ∇ Z←APPEND R;MAT;S;AXIS
[1]   ⍝ append scalar on each side of axis
[2]   (MAT S AXIS)←R          ⍝ unpack argument
[3]   Z←S,[AXIS]MAT,[AXIS]S   ⍝ append scalar
[4]  ∇
```

16. *M*×[1]*V*

18. *M*⌊[2]*V*

Section 5.6 – Other Functions on Higher-Rank Arrays

2. ↑ρ*M*

4. a. shape 4, depth 3
   b. shape 4, depth 1
   c. shape empty, depth 2
   d. shape 2 3, depth 1
   e. shape empty, depth 0
   f. shape empty, depth 0
   g. shape empty, depth 2
   h. *INDEX ERROR*
   i. shape empty, depth 0

6. a. 'APL2' (10 20 30)
   b. 6 'APL2' (10 20 30)

Section 5.7 – Other Primitive Operators

2. a. shape 3 4, depth 1, value:

   ```
   3  9  18  19
   8  10  14  18
   9  16  21  24
   ```

   b. shape 3 4, depth 1, value:

   ```
   3  ⁻3   6  5
   8   6  10  6
   9   2   7  4
   ```

   c. shape 3 4, depth 1, value:

   ```
    3   6   9  1
   11   8  13  5
   20  15  18  8
   ```

d.   shape 3 4, depth 1, value:

```
 ‾3   6    9   ‾1
 ‾5   4    5   ‾3
  4  11   10    0
```

4. a.   shape 1, depth 2, value:

```
22 44 66 88
11 33 55 77
99 22 44 66
88 11 33 55
```

b.   shape 2, depth 2, value:

```
 6 10 14      60 100 140
 4  8 12      40  80 120
11  6 10     110  60 100
 9  4  8      90  40  80
```

c.   shape 2, depth 2, value:

```
 3  7 11 15      30 70 110 150
10  5  9 13     100 50  90 130
17  3  7 11     170 30  70 110
```

d.   shape empty, depth 2, value:

```
0 0 0
0 0 0
0 0 0

0 0 0
0 0 0
0 0 0

0 0 0
0 0 0
0 0 0
```

e. shape empty, depth 2, value:

0 0 0
0 0 0
0 0 0

0 0 0
0 0 0
0 0 0

0 0 0
0 0 0
0 0 0

f. shape 2, depth 2, value:

6 15 24   ¯6 ¯15 ¯24
33 42 51   ¯33 ¯42 ¯51
60 69 78   ¯60 ¯69 ¯78

g. shape 2, depth 2, value:

30 33 36   ¯30 ¯33 ¯36
39 42 45   ¯39 ¯42 ¯45
48 51 54   ¯48 ¯51 ¯54

h. shape 2, depth 2, value:

12 15 18   ¯12 ¯15 ¯18
39 42 45   ¯39 ¯42 ¯45
66 69 72   ¯66 ¯69 ¯72

i. shape 2, depth 2, value:

3 5   ¯3 ¯5
9 11   ¯9 ¯11
15 17   ¯15 ¯17

21 23   ¯21 ¯23
27 29   ¯27 ¯29
33 35   ¯33 ¯35

39 41   ¯39 ¯41
45 47   ¯45 ¯47
51 53   ¯51 ¯53

j.   shape 2, depth 2, value:

```
11 13 15       ¯11 ¯13 ¯15
17 19 21       ¯17 ¯19 ¯21
23 25 27       ¯23 ¯25 ¯27

29 31 33       ¯29 ¯31 ¯33
35 37 39       ¯35 ¯37 ¯39
41 43 45       ¯41 ¯43 ¯45
```

k.   shape 2, depth 2, value:

```
 5  7  9        ¯5  ¯7  ¯9
11 13 15       ¯11 ¯13 ¯15

23 25 27       ¯23 ¯25 ¯27
29 31 33       ¯29 ¯31 ¯33

41 43 45       ¯41 ¯43 ¯45
47 49 51       ¯47 ¯49 ¯51
```

6.
```
      ∇Z←CHECK M
[1]   ⍝ 1 for row in ascending order
[2]   Z←∧/M=⌈\M
[3]   ∇
```

8. $N,/\iota S$

10.   63360 36 12 1 +.× 3 6 2 7

12. a.   shape 3 3, value:

```
 2    4     8
 5   25   125
10  100  1000
```

b.   shape 3 4, value:

```
1 2 3 4
2 2 3 4
3 3 3 4
```

c.   shape 4 3, value:

```
1 1 1
1 2 2
1 2 3
1 2 3
```

d. shape 3 2, value:
```
5   6   4
7   7   7
8   8   8
```

e. shape 2 3, value:
```
5 7   6 7   3 9
8 5   8 4   8 9
```

f. shape 3 2, value:
```
A     10
BC    30 40
AB    10 20
```

g. shape 3 2, value:
```
AX
BY
CZ
```

h. shape 3 2, value:
```
1 AB   1 CDE
2 AB   2 CDE
3 AB   3 CDE
```

i. shape 3 2, value:
```
1 AB      1 CDE
2 AB      2 CDE
3 AB      3 CDE
```

14. a. shape 3 3, value:
```
1 2 3
4 5 6
7 8 9
```

b. shape 3 3, value:
```
1 0 0 0   2 0 0 0   3 0 0 0
0 4 0 0   0 5 0 0   0 6 0 0
0 0 7 0   0 0 8 0   0 0 9 0
```

Chapter 6: Working with Data

Section 6.1 – Ways of Comparing

2. $A+2\times(A<0)\times A$

4. $+/RETAIL<10$

6. keeps only the first 1

8. a. shape 5, depth 1, value: 1 1 1 1 1
    b. shape 5, depth 1, value: 1 1 0 1 1
    c. *LENGTH ERROR* (scalar function)
    d. shape empty, depth 0, value: 1
    e. shape empty, depth 0, value: 0
    f. shape empty, depth 0, value: 0
    g. shape empty, depth 0, value: 1
    h. shape empty, depth 0, value: 0
    i. shape empty, depth 0, value: 1
    j. shape empty, depth 0, value: 0
    k. shape empty, depth 0, value: 1
    l. shape empty, depth 0, value: 0
    m. shape 2, depth 2, value: 1 1 0 1 1 1 1 1
    n. shape empty, depth 0, value: 0
    o. shape 2, depth 1, value: 0 1
    p. shape 2, depth 2, value: 1 0 1 0 0 1 0

10. $M+M=0$

Section 6.2 – Selecting Subsets of Arrays

2. $TM[1]$ is always a scalar. $\uparrow TM$ is, in general, an arbitrary array and, in particular, it is a 2 2 matrix.

4. $INVENTORY \sim INVENTORY \sim RLIST$

6. $((,M \neq N)/,N) \leftarrow'$ $'$

8. a. depth 1, value: *EE*
    b. depth 1, value: empty
    c. depth 1, value: *BYBY*
    d. depth 1, value: *BYEBYE*
    e. depth 2, value: *BYEBYE*
    f. depth 2, value: *CAB DAD*
    g. depth 2, value: *CB DAD*
    h. depth 2, value: *CAB DAD*
    i. depth 2, value: *C DD*

10. a. *A   PL*
     b. 10 0 0 20 30
     c. *A B C D E F*
     d. *AB C D*
         AB C D
         AB C D

     e. 1 2 3 4
         0 0 0 0
         0 0 0 0
         1 2 3 4
         0 0 0 0
         1 2 3 4

     f. *LENGTH ERROR*; length of right argument is not the sum of the left argument.
     g. 0
     h. 0 0; scalar containing two zeros
     i. (' ' 0)
     j. (0 ' ')
     k. *'ABC' '   ' (ι4) '   ' ('A' 4)*
     l. (ι4) (0 0 0 0) *'ABC'* (0 0 0 0) (*'A'* 4)
     m. (*'A'* 4) (' ' 0) (ι4) (' ' 0) *'ABC'*
     n. (4 *'A'*) (0 ' ') (ι4) (0 ' ') *'ABC'*

12. (,*M*)←12

Section 6.3 – Searching and Sorting

2. $(0\neq\epsilon,A)/,A$

4. $((\sim(,A)\epsilon\subset'N/A')/,A)\leftarrow100$

6.
```
      ∇ Z← I RECEIPT STOCK;T
[1]   ⍝ Z:  a matrix listing of names and prices
[2]   ⍝       matching I
[3]   ⍝ STOCK:  vector of vectors, each item consists of
[4]   ⍝  (inventory no.)(item name)(item price)
[5]   ⍝ Assume that values of I are always found in stock
[6]    T←↑¨STOCK
[7]    Z←⊃1↓¨ STOCK[T⍳I]
[8]   ∇
```

8. a. $\lozenge M$
    b. ϕM
    c. $\ominus M$

10. a. ϕA
    b. $\ominus A$
    c. $\phi\ominus A$
    d. $1\phi A$
    e. $2\phi A$
    f. $0\ 1\ 2\phi A$
    g. $1\ 0\ 3\phi A$
    h. $1\ 0\ 2\ 0\ominus A$

12. a. $(1\ 1\lozenge M)\leftarrow0$
    b. $(1\ 1\lozenge M)\leftarrow'Z'$
    c. $(1\ 1\lozenge M)\leftarrow Z'DIAG'$

14. $\wedge/,S=\lozenge S$

16. a. $(\subset[2]M)\epsilon\subset[2]N$
    b. $(\subset[2]N)\iota\subset[2]M$

18. $(\subset[2]M)\iota¨S$ or $1++/\wedge\backslash M\neq S$

20. a. 6 5 3 1 2 4
    b. 4 2 1 3 5 6
    c. 9 12 17 20 23 30
    d. 30 23 20 17 12 9
    e. 4 5 3 6 2 1

22. $(\rho A)\rho V\underline{\in},A$

Section 6.4 – Computation

2. a. $A\times.95\star5$

    (When you enter the sixth country, you have crossed five borders.)

    b. 90

4. $((\lceil 2\circledast N)\rho 2)\top N$

6. $'0123456789ABCDEF'[1+(8\rho 16)\top N]$

8. a. $\circ 2\times 45$
    b. $\circ(2\times 45+10)-2\times 45$ or $\circ 20$
    c. $\circ 20$

10. 0 24 60 60 $\top 800\times 800\times 8\times 6000\div 2.16E4$

12. a.
```
 _1    0    0  0
  ‾1   _1   0  0
   0   ‾1   1  0
   0    0  ‾1  1
```

    b.
```
 1  ‾1   _0   0
 0   1  ‾1   _0
 0   0   1  ‾1
 0   0   0   1
```

14. a. 2705
     b. 94
     c. 70
     d. 88
     e. 888
     f. 136
     g. 71
     h. 71
     i. 71
     j. 27
     k. 194
     l. 69 156 234
     m. 27 13
     n. 5445

Section 6.5 – Generating Random Numbers

2.   a.   ?6 6 6 6
      b.   5?52
      c.   2 3 5 7 11 13[?6]
      d.   (?10)ρ?25
      e.   ?3 4ρ99
      f.   .01×?99

Chapter 7: Working with Program Control

Section 7.1 – Control of Execution: Branching

2.   a.   →(*I*=1 2 3)/*L1 L2 L3*   (Falls through if *I* is incorrect.)
      b.   →(*L1 L2 L3*)[*I*]   (Fails if *I* is incorrect.)

4.   a.   *A* simple
      b.   *N* integer
      c.   first three characters of *ANS* are '*END*'
      d.   *C* is 5
      e.   *C* is not 5
      f.   *WORD* contains a vowel
      g.   Three-way branch for negative, zero, or positive (assuming three names are labels)
      h.   *ANS* is empty

Section 7.2 – Debugging Your Program

2.   experimentation only

Section 7.3 – Prompting for Input

2.   ⍾̈⊂[2]*M*

4.   ⍾(∈*N*),'←⍾̈*N*'

6.   a.   ⊃⍕̈⊂[2]*M*
      b.   none— shorter row would be padded

Section 7.4 – Output with Quad and Quote-Quad

2. $\square\leftarrow AVER\leftarrow(+/X)\div\rho X\leftarrow\square$

Section 7.5 – Controlling Output

2.
```
     ∇ Z←NUMBER A;R
[1]    R←↑ρA
[2]    Z←⊃[2]'[',¨(⊂[2]⍕(R,1)ριR),¨']',¨⊂[2]A
[3] ∇
```

4.   (**Note:** "~" indicates where blanks appear in the result, to assist you in seeing the spacing.)

For: $W\leftarrow 93.725 \quad {}^-27.8 \quad {}^-192.83 \quad 6754$

a.   shape 40:
```
      '-5,551.55 '⍕W
   93.73    -27.8    -192.83  6,754
~~~      ~~~~     ~~~~      ~~  ~~~~
```

b.   shape 48:
```
      '$5,551.50CR '⍕W
   93.73       $27.80CR   $192.83CR  6,754.00
~~~~    ~~~~~~~       ~~~        ~~         ~~~
```

c.   shape 52:
```
       '$_5,553.10CR '⍕W
  $ 93.73       $ 27.80CR   $ 192.83CR $ 6,754.00
~~~ ~      ~~~~~~~        ~~~ ~       ~ ~       ~~~
```

d.   shape 48:
```
       '$ -5,551.55 '⍕W
 $       93.73 $     -27.8 $     -192.83 $  6,754
    ~~~~~~     ~ ~~~~     ~~ ~~~      ~ ~~      ~~~~
```

e.   shape 48:
```
       '$_-5,551.55 '⍕W
   93.73      $ -27.8      $ -192.83      6,754
~~~~~~     ~~~~~ ~       ~~~~ ~       ~~~~      ~~~~
```

f.   shape 56:
```
       '$_5,554.10_CR '⍕W
 $     93.73     $     27.80 CR $    192.83 CR $ 6,754.00
   ~~~~      ~~~~~ ~~~~       ~ ~~~      ~ ~ ~         ~~~~
```

g.   error:
```
      '5,555.55 '⍕W
DOMAIN ERROR   (no provision for negative sign)
```

Section 7.6 – Control of Execution: Iteration

2.

```
     ∇ Z←INTERVAL N;I
[1]   ⍝ loop simulating monadic iota
[2]    Z←⍳0
[3]    I←1
[4]  L1:→(I>N)/0
[5]    Z←Z,I
[6]    I←I+1
[7]    →L1
[8] ∇
```

Section 7.7 – Control of Execution: Recursion

2.   a.

```
     ∇ Z←ADDREC R
[1]   ⍝ recursive routine to add up numbers
[2]    Z←R
[3]    →(2>⍴R)/0
[4]    Z←ADDREC(R[1]+R[2]),2↓R
[5] ∇
```

b.

```
     ∇ Z←ADDLOOP R;I
[1]   ⍝ looping routine to add up numbers
[2]    I←Z←0
[3]  L1:I←I+1
[4]    →(I>⍴R)/0
[5]    Z←Z+R[I]
[6]    →L1
[7] ∇
```

(It is ge᠁   y more efficient to use indexing rather than to use ↑R a᠁   ⍵R.)

c.   +/R

4.

```
     ∇ Z←INTERVALR N;I
[1]   ⍝ recursive routine simulating monadic iota
[2]    Z←⍳0
[3]    →(N≤0)/0
[4]    Z←(INTERVAL N−1),N
[5] ∇
```

6. ρ*MDEPTH* ρ*MDEPTH A*

8.

```
      ∇ Z←(F MDEPTH1 N)R
[1]   ⍝ apply F to each array of depth N
[2]   →(N<≡R)/L1        ⍝ branch not requested depth
[3]   Z←F R             ⍝ F of simple
[4]   →0                ⍝ exit
[5]   L1:Z←(F MDEPTH1 N)¨R    ⍝ recur
[6]   ∇
```

10.

```
      ∇ Z←L(F DDEPTHB)R
[1]   ⍝ apply F to each simple array in R
[2]   →(1<≡R)/L1        ⍝ branch not simple
[3]   Z←L F R           ⍝ F of simple
[4]   →0                ⍝ exit
[5]   L1:Z←(⊂L)(F DDEPTHB)¨R    ⍝ recur
[6]   ∇
```

Chapter 8: Working with Applications

Section 8.1 – A Magazine Collection

2.

```
      ∇ Z←SORTUPBY R;N
[1]   ⍝ R is the field to sort on, matrix
[2]   (N Z)←R
[3]   Z←Z[⍋Z[;N];]
[4]   ∇
```

4.

```
      ∇ADD R;IN
[1]   ⍝ R is the new issue number
[2]   L1:'enter values for issue number ' R
[3]   '     ' 'Vol' 'No' 'Year' 'Mon' 'Price' 'Value' 'Own'
[4]   IN←⍞               ⍝ read input
[5]   →((,7)≡ρIN)/OK      ⍝ must be 7 items
[6]   'error – enter 7 items'
[7]   →L1
[8]   OK:MAG←MAG,[1]R,IN    ⍝ add new row
[9]   ∇
```

Section 8.2 – Simulation of a Vector Computer

2.

```
      ∇ LOADS R;V;A;S
[1]    (V A)←R
[2]   ⍝ load scalar register V from address in A
[3]    SR[V]←MM[A]
[4]   ∇
```

```
      ∇ STORES R;V;A
[1]    (V A)←R
[2]   ⍝ store scalar register V in address A
[3]    MM[A]←SR[V]
[4]   ∇
```

4.

```
      ∇ VPROBLEM4
[1]    26 SETMEMORY 10 9 87 6 5 4 3
[2]    3 SETMEMORY 26
[3]    4 SETMEMORY 7
[4]    1 SETMEMORY 0
[5]    LOADS 2 1
[6]   LOOP:LOADVCT 4
[7]    →(0=VCT)/0
[8]    LOADV 4 3 1
[9]    PLUSREDUCE 4 2
[10]   →LOOP
[11]  ∇
```

Section 8.3 – A Puzzle-Solving Program

2.

```
       ∇ Z←STRT(MOVE SEARCH1CHK)G;B;M;NEWP;CNT
[1]    ⍝ find path from start to goal
[2]    ⍝ STRT ←→ starting position
[3]    ⍝ I ←→ count of loops
[4]    ⍝ G ←→ goal position
[5]    ⍝ MOVE ←→ program to compute next positions
[6]    M←,⊂,⊂STRT            ⍝ initial path is STRT
[7]    Z←⍳0                  ⍝ return empty on failure
[8]    I←0                   ⍝ initial count
[9]    LOOP:→(0=⍴M)/0        ⍝ quit no more paths
[10]   →(G≡B←↑↑M)/DONE       ⍝ done if goal
[11]   NEWP←MOVE B           ⍝ compute new positions
[12]   NEWP←(~NEWP∊↑,/M)/NEWP ⍝ keep new positions
[13]   M←(1↓M),(⊂¨NEWP),¨M[1] ⍝ add to paths
[14]   I←I+1                 ⍝ increment loop count
[15]   →(0≠20|I)/LOOP        ⍝ continue if not 20 loops
[16]   ⎕←I 'LOOPS - CONTINUE? (Y/N)'
[17]   →('Y'∊⎕)/LOOP         ⍝ back for next path
[18]   →0                    ⍝ exit early
[19]   DONE:Z←⌽↑M            ⍝ return with path
[20]∇
```

4.

```
       ∇ Z←MOVE8 M;IB;MI;IN
[1]    ⍝ move generator for 8 puzzle
[2]    IB←(,M∊' ')/,MI←(⍳3)∘.,⍳3
[3]    IN←(IN∊MI)/IN←,(0 1)(0 ¯1)(1 0)(¯1 0)∘.+IB
[4]    Z←IN RMOVE8¨⊂M
[5]    Z←Z (Z≡¨⊂3 3⍴'1238 4765')
[6]    ∇
```

```
      ∇Z←RMOVE8 M
[1]    ⍝ recursive replacer, subfunction of MOVE8
[2]    (IB⊃Z)←(⊂I)⊃Z←M
[3]    ((⊂I)⊃Z)←' '
[4]    ∇
```

6.

```
      ∇Z←EST1 P
[1]    ⍝ number out of position est for 8 puzzle
[2]    Z←+/,P≠3 3⍴'1238 4765'
[3]    ∇
```

Index

A

abort (→) 272
absolute value 70
active workspace 106, 110, 115
   adding to 113
   changing name of 110
   contents of 115
   name of 110
   removing objects from 115
   replacing contents of 113
add a set of numbers 8
addition (+) 2, 8
addition of exponents 241
addition-reduction (+/) 8
alphabet

   for names 12
and (∧) 193
APL keyboard 1, 392
APL2
   active workspace 110
   data 30
   function 2, 31
   libraries 107
   operator 8, 32
APL2 operator 9
arccos 257
arccosh 257
arc cosine 257
arc cosine hyperbolic 257
arcsine 257
arc sine hyperbolic 257
arcsinh 257
arctan 257

arc tangent   257
arc tangent hyperbolic   257
arctanh   257
arguments of a function   31
   conformability with scalar
    functions   62
   placement of for dyadic
    functions   31
   placement of for monadic
    functions   32
arithmetic   2
arithmetic progression   36
array processing
   feature of APL2   18
arrays
   applying a function to   7
   applying scalar functions to   62,
   173
   axes of   120, 125, 147
   classes of   121
   columns of   120
   count   120, 135
   defined   1, 30, 120
   depth of   121, 136
   display of   124
   index of   199
   intersection of   212
   items   120
   manipulating along an axis   147
   matrix   120
   nested   30, 65, 121
   prototype of   171
   rank   135
   rank of   120
   rows of   120
   scalar   120
   search for items using index
    of   220
   selecting a subset   198
   shape of   121
   simple   30, 121
   sorting items in   225
   unshaping with enlist   142
   unshaping with ravel   140
   vector   17, 120
arrow
   assignment   10, 19, 303

to clear errors   26
assignment   10, 19, 303
   of data to a variable   10
   selective   58
assignment arrow (←)   10
associated processors   373
asterisk (*)
   in state indicator   116
   not used for multiplication   3
   power   66, 241
attention   277
auxiliary processors   373
average, program for   91
axes of an array   120
axis
   adding   156
   default   148
   fractional   153
   length   121
   manipulation of array along   147
   names of   125
   of an array   120
axis specification
   empty with ravel   156
   fractional with catenate   153
   with catenate   152
   with disclose   160
   with drop   149
   with enclose   158
   with n-wise reduction   179
   with ravel   155
   with reduction   157
   with scalar functions   163
   with scan   177
   with take   149

B

bar chart   204
binomial (!)   253
blank character
   representation of   41
blanks
   as padding   52
   character   41

in numbers 5
redundant 17
removing from a character
  vector 212
separate names 11
to indicate grouping 8
body
of a program 88
Boolean functions 193
with reduction 194
bottom-up programming 338
brackets
for axis specification 148
for indexing 55, 199
branch (→)
conditional 274
escape 272
for looping 276
niladic 272
out of range 272
to an empty vector 271
unconditional 274
without an argument 272
breadth-first search 366

C

caret (∧)
in error report 27
catenate (,) 37
compared to vector notation 38
to an empty vector 47
catenate with axis (, []) 152
ceiling (⌈) 68
character data 41
as argument to a function 44
converted to numbers 221
converted to numeric 299
in a vector with numeric
  data 43
input 295
with equal 190
with not equal 190
character input after output
character input (⎕) 295

character set 392
character string 41, 294
character vectors 41, 295
effect of parentheses on 42
circle (○) 256
classes of arrays 121
)CLEAR 110
CLEAR WS 110
closed formula 321
columns of an array 120
comma (,) 5
not used to separate groups of
  digits 5
symbol for catenate 37
symbol for ravel 140
command 377
)CLEAR 110
)COPY 113
)DROP 108
)EDITOR 377
)ERASE 115
)FNS 115
)IN 114
)LIB 107
)LOAD 108
)NMS 115
)OFF 107
)OPS 115
)PCOPY 114
)SAVE 107, 111
)SIS 116
)VARS 115
)WSID 110
comments (⍝) 89, 98, 100
common logarithm (⍟) 245, 246
comparison tolerance 191
complex conjugate 257
complex number
conjugate of 257
imaginary part 257
phase 257
real part 257
representation of 243
complex numbers 372
compress (/)
See replicate
conditional branch 274

conformability of scalar function
   dyadic 62
   monadic 63
conjugate of a complex number 257
CONTINUE
   to save work and quit APL2 25
CONTINUE workspace 106
   dangers of using 109
   features of 109
control structures 313
converting characters to
 numbers 299
)*COPY* 113
   protected 114
cosh 257
cosine 257
cosine hyperbolic 257
count of an array 120, 135
cube roots 243

D

data
   character 41
   collected in an array 30
   grouping of for computation 8
   item of 30
   selecting from an array
      with drop (↓) 54
      with first (↑) 51
      with index ([]) 55
      with pick (⊃) 50
      with take (↑) 52
   selecting repeatedly 56
   terms for 30
deal (?) 266
debugging your program 285
decimal point 3
decode (⊥) 248
default
   axis 148
   order of execution 15
defined function 87, 89
defined operator 89
defined sequence 87, 90

definition mode 92, 99
del (∇) 89, 377
depth (≡)
   increased by enclose 143
   of an array 121, 136
   of a nested array 121
   of a simple array 121
   of a simple scalar 121
derived functions 32
   names of 80
direction (×) 70
   relationship to magnitude (|) 71
disclose (⊃) 144
   relationship to enclose (⊂) 144
disclose with axis (⊃[]) 160
display
   of arrays 124
   of numbers 3
DISPLAY function 21, 132
   summary 132
division (÷) 3
   alternate symbols not allowed 3
DOMAIN ERROR 27
domino 259
)*DROP* 108
drop (↓) 54
drop with axis (↓[]) 149
dyadic function 31

E

e 244
each (¨) 83
   as iterative process 313
editing
   del to initiate 89
   del to leave 89
   selection of editor 377
   with full-screen editor 378
   with line editor 381
)*EDITOR* 377
empty vector
   branch to 271
   character 46
   creating with reshape 128

defined   46
how created   46
need for   47
numeric   46
reduction of   82
enclose (⊂)   143
  relationship to disclose (⊃)   144
enclose with axis (⊂[])   158
encode (⊤)   251
endless loop   276
enlist (∊)   142
  relationship to ravel (,)   142
E notation   3, 308
enter key
  to signal end of input   2
environment   106
equal (=)   189
)ERASE   115
error checking   99
error reports
  DOMAIN ERROR   27
  INDEX ERROR   203
  LENGTH ERROR   27
  purpose of caret (∧)   27
  SYNTAX ERROR   26
  types of   26
  VALUE ERROR   26
errors
  clearing with →   28
  clearing with)RESET   28
  during function execution   99
  types of   27
error trapping   372
escape branch (→)   272
evaluated input (□)   292
evaluation
  how different from
    arithmetic   15
  of expressions   14
  of expression with
    parentheses   16
  order of   14
  right-to-left rule   15
event handling   372
exclusive or (≠)   193
execute (⍎)   297
execution

default order of   15
interrupting   278
of an expression   15
of expression with
  parentheses   16
restarting   289
termination of   272
exit APL2
  with)CONTINUE   25
expand (\)   209
expand (⍀)   211
explicit result
  of a defined function   89
  of a function   31
exponential (*)   241
exponential notation   308
expressions
  as items of a vector   17
  evaluation of   14
  several functions in one   14
external names   373

F

factorial (!)   253
Fibonacci numbers   319
find (⍷)   224
first (↑)   51, 170
  compared to take (1↑)   53
  of an empty   51
  on empty   170
  relationship to pick (⊃)   51
floor (⌊)   68
)FNS   115
format by specification   307
format (⍕)
  by example   309
  by specification   306
formula, closed   321
function   2
  applied to character data   44
  Boolean   193
  compared to operator   79
  comparison of dyadic and
    monadic   32

defined   31, 87
defined operator   87
derived   32, 79
dyadic   31
dyadic used with reduction   79
inverse   258
monadic   32
name of derived   80
primitive   31
relational   189
scalar   61, 173
several in an expression   14
functions
system   372
fuzz   191

G

global names   96
shadowed by local names   96
grade down (⍒)   225
grade up (⍋)   225
graphs   204
greater than (>)   189
greater than or equal (≥)   189
groups
copying   114

H

header
of a defined function   89
of a defined operator   89
of a defined sequence   90
of a program   88
parts of   88
to access APL2 editor   378
header syntax   93
histogram   204
hyperbolic arc cosine   257
hyperbolic arc sine   257
hyperbolic arc tangent   257

hyperbolic cosine   257
hyperbolic functions   256
hyperbolic sine   257
hyperbolic tangent   257
hyperplanes   125

I

identity element
using reduction to determine   82
identity matrix   259
imaginary part of a complex
number   257
immediate execution mode   92, 116,
292
implication   198
)IN   114
indexed assignment   198, 213
indexed specification   198, 213
INDEX ERROR   203
indexing
scatter   396
indexing ([])   199
inverse of index of   222
of arrays   199
of vectors   55
rank of   199, 202
shape of   202
values selected by   203
indexing (⌷)   395
index of (⍳)   220
infinite loop   276, 279, 326
infinite recursion   326
inner product (.)   181, 248
input   292
after output   305
APL2 prompt for   2
character (⍞)   295
evaluated (⎕)   292
quad (⎕)   292
quad-prime (⍞)   295
integers
identify public libraries   109
producing consecutive   36
producing even   36

representation of   3
round to the nearest   68
interrupt   278
interruption execution   278
intersection of two arrays   212
interval (ι)   36
interval-each (ι⁝)   83
inverse   258
inverse of a matrix   258
items   120
    in a vector   17
iteration
    defined   313
    not always needed in APL2   6

line zero
    alternative name for header of a
        program   88
)*LOAD*   108
local names   94, 96, 101
    shadowing global names   96
logarithm (⊛)   245
    common   246
    natural   247
loop   281
    implicit   281
    infinite   276, 279
    termination of   272
    tracing   291

K

keyboard   1, 392

L

labels   96, 273
laminate (,[ ])   153
least squares fit   260, 261
length
    of an empty vector   46
    of a vector   35
    of axis   121
LENGTH ERROR   27
less than (<)   189
less than or equal (≤)   189
letters
    used in names   12
)*LIB*   107, 109
libraries
    adding workspaces to   107
    numbers of   109
    private   107
    public   109
    removing workspaces from   108
    retrieving a workspace from   108
library workspace   107

M

magnitude (|)   70
    relationship to direction (×)   71
mask   206
match (≡)   191
matrix   120
    adding a column to   153
    adding a row to   152
    from vectors using catenate with
        fractional axis   153
    from vectors using laminate   153
    name of rank-2 array   120
    rank of   120
    reshape to create   123
    turning a vector into a one
        column matrix   156
matrix inverse   259
matrix product   183, 259
maximum (⌈)   67
maximum-reduction (⌈/)   80
membership (∈)   222
minimum (⌊)   67
minimum-reduction (⌊/)   80
    of empty vector   82
minus sign   4
modulus   72
monadic function   32
monadic operator   80
moving-window reduction   177

multiplication (×) 3
  alternate symbols not allowed 3
  relationship to logarithm 245
  relationship to power 66, 241
multiplication-reduction
  of empty vector 82

N

names
  assignment of 10
  changing the name of the active
   workspace 110
  external 373
  global 96, 101
  local 94, 101
  local to a program 96
  of active workspace 110
  rules for constructing 12
  shadowed 96
  shared 373
  variables for data 10
nand (⍲) 193
Napier
  and logarithms 245
natural logarithm (⍟) 247
negation (−) 2
negative number 4
negative sign (‾) 4
  differs from minus sign (−) 4
nested array 30, 65, 121
nested scalar
  created by reduction 81
  created with enclose 143
nested vector 30
nested versus simple array 30
niladic branch (→) 272
niladic function 87
)*NMS* 115
nor (⍱) 193
not (~) 193
not equal (≠) 189
numbers
  complex 243, 372
  consecutive 36

conventions not recognized in
 APL2 5
counting digits in 247
determine number of digits
 in 246
display of 3
entering 3
Fibonacci 319
formatting 306
fractional 3
from character data 221
generating random 266
mixed base 249
negative 4
random 266
representation of 3
roots of 242
rounding 3, 68
used in names 12
very large or very small 3
number sequence
  decreasing 37
  increasing 36
numeric data
  from character data 299
  in a vector with character
   data 43
n-wise reduction (/) 177

O

)*OFF* 107
one
  as truth value 189
operands of an operator 32, 80
operation 31
operator 9
  compared to function 79
  defined 32, 87
  deriving functions 32
  dyadic 93
  inner product 181
  monadic 80, 93
  n-wise reduction 177
  outer product 180

primitive 32
reduction 8
scan 176
use of 79
)*OPS* 115
or (∨) 193
outer product (∘.) 180
output 131, 303
before input 305
quad 303
quad-prime 303

P

parentheses
evaluating an expression
with 16
in assignment 213
in header 89
redundant 16, 18
to group items in a vector 17
parity check
expression for 194
partition (⊂) 398
)*PCOPY* 114
period (.)
not used to separate groups of
digits 5
phase of a complex number 257
pick (⊃) 50, 171
on a matrix 171
relationship to first (↑) 51
relationship to indexing 57
pick-each ⊃ 84
pi-times 256
plus-reduction (+/) 8
of empty vector 82
to add up the first 100
integers 36
power (*) 66, 241
to find square root 242
with negative exponents 242
primitive functions 31
primitive operator 32
private libraries 107

processors
associated 373
programming
bottom-up 338
prompting for input 292
structured 313
top-down 338
programs
body 88
branch control in 271
debugging 285
header 88
labels 273
list of 13, 115
looping 276
restarting 289
stopping 288
structure of 88
tracing 291
types of 90
prompting for input 292
protected copy 114
prototype 171
pythagoriean functions 256

Q

quad input (⎕) 292
quad output (⎕) 303
quad-prime input after output
quad-prime input (⍞) 295
quad-prime output (⍞) 304
quad-quote output (⍞) 303
quit APL2
with)*CONTINUE* 25
with)*OFF* 107
quotation mark (⊤)
as a character 42
to delimit character data 41
quote-quad input after output
quote-quad output (⍞) 303, 304

R

random numbers 266
rank 120, 135
ravel (,) 140
    relationship to enlist (ε) 142
    relationship to reshape (ρ) 141
ravel with axis (,[]) 155
real numbers 242
real part of a complex number 257
reciprocal (÷) 72
recursion 318, 326
recursive function 318
reduction
    with inner product 181
reduction (/)
    as iterative process 313
    domain of 79
    of an empty vector 82
    on vectors 79
    to add a set of numbers 8
    to find the largest or smallest
      in 80
    with Boolean functions 194
    with catenate 80
    with nested arguments 81
reduction with axis (/[]) 157
relational functions 189
    effect of machine arithmetic 190
relational structures 330
remainder 72
replacement of values 213
replicate (/) 205
replicate with axis (/[]) 207
)RESET 28
reshape (ρ) 123
    relationship to ravel (,) 141
    relationship to shape (ρ) 134
residue (|) 72
restarting your program 289
result
    displayed at left margin of the
      next line. 2
result, explicit
    of a function 31
resuming execution 289

return key
    to signal end of input 2
reverse (φ) 229
reverse with axis (φ[]) 230
reversing a selection with not 194
right arrow (→)
    to clear error 28
    to clear state indicator 116
    to terminate program
      execution 272
right-to-left rule 15
roll (?) 266
roots 242, 243
rotate (φ) 231
rotate with axis (φ[]) 232
rounding 3, 68, 308
row-major order 124, 142
rows of an array 120
rules
    for evaluation of expressions 15
    for names 12

S

SΔ
    See stop facility
)SAVE 107, 111
saving workspace
    with)CONTINUE 25, 106
    with)SAVE 107
scalar 120
    created with enclose 143
    from a vector 79
    name of rank-0 array 120
    nested 81, 143
    produced by reduction 81
    rank of 120
    simple 30, 120, 121
scalar extension 63, 64, 173
scalar functions 61, 173
    Boolean 193
    conformability of arguments
      with 62
    each has no effect on 85

extension for conformability   63
maximum (⌈)   67
minimum (⌊)   67
power (⋆)   66
properties of   61
relational   189
 with nested arguments   173
scalar functions with axis   163
scan (\\)   176
 with Boolean functions   195
scatter indexing   396
scientific notation   308
search for items in an array   220
selecting unique items from a
 vector   222
selection of data in an array
 with drop (↓)   54
 with drop with axis (↓[])   149
 with first (↑)   51
 with index ([])   55
 with pick (⊃)   50
 with take (↑)   52
 with take with axis (↑[])   149
selective assignment   58, 198, 213
shadowed names   96
shape (ρ)   35
 of an array   134
 of an empty array   134
 relationship to reshape (ρ)   134
 symbol ρ   134
 to determine rank of an
  array   135
shape of an array   121
shared names   373
shared variables   373
signum (×)   70
 relationship to magnitude (|)   71
simple array   121
simple scalar   30, 120
 depth of   121
simple vector   30
simple versus nested array   30
sine   257
sine hyperbolic   257
singular matrix   260
sinh   257
)SIS   28, 116

slash (/)
 not used for division   3
sort items in an array   225
spaces
 not used to separate groups of
  digits   5
 redundant   17
 used in display to indicate data
  grouping   8
 used to separate items in an
  array   6
square root   242
state indicator   116
 command for   28, 116
 in debugging   278
 interrupted function in   117
 right arrow (→) to clear   116
state indicator with statements
)SIS   28
stop APL2
 with)CONTINUE   25
stop facility   288
stopping execution   288
stopping your program   276, 288
structured programming   313
subtraction (−)   2
summation   8
symbol ,   37, 41, 140, 189, 193
symbol .   181
symbol <   189
symbol +   2
symbol +/   8
symbol ⋆   66
symbol /   8, 177, 205
symbol /[]   157, 207
symbol >   189
symbol ?   266
symbol ∧   27, 193
symbol ¨   83
symbol ∈   224
symbol ∨   193
symbol =   189
symbol ~   193, 212
symbol ↑   51, 52, 170
symbol ↑[]   149
symbol ↓   54
symbol ↓[]   149

symbol ≤   189
symbol ⌈   67, 68
symbol ⌈/   80
symbol ⌊   67, 68
symbol ⌊/   80
symbol →   271
symbol ⊃   50, 144, 171
symbol ⊃̈   84
symbol ⊃[]   160
symbol ⊂   143, 398
symbol ⊂[]   158
symbol ○   256
symbol ←   10
symbol ‾
    meaning of   4
symbol ⊥   248
symbol []   55, 152, 155, 199
symbol ≥   189
symbol ∘.   180
symbol ∈   142, 222
symbol ι   36, 220
symbol ϊ   83
symbol ρ   35, 123
symbol ×   3, 70, 241
symbol ×/   79
symbol \   176, 209
symbol ÷   3, 72
symbol ∇   89, 377
symbol ⊤   251
symbol | 70, 72
symbol ⋏   193
symbol ⋎   193
symbol ⍤   395
symbol φ   229, 231
symbol φ[]   230
symbol ⍉   233
symbol !)   253
symbol ⍒   225
symbol ⍋   225
symbol ⍝   89, 98, 100
symbol ≡   121, 136, 191
symbols
    used in names   12
symbol *S*Δ   288
symbol *T*Δ   291
symbol ⍀   177, 211
symbol ⊖   230, 232

symbol ⊛   245, 247
symbol ⍖   297
syntax
    of headers   93
SYNTAX ERROR   26
system command
)*CLEAR*   110
)*CONTINUE*   25
)*COPY*   113
)*DROP*   108
)*EDITOR*   377
)*ERASE*   115
)*FNS*   115
)*IN*   114
)*LIB*   107
)*LOAD*   108
)*NMS*   13, 92, 115
)*OFF*   107
)*OPS*   115
)*PCOPY*   114
)*RESET*   28
)*SAVE*   107, 111
)*SIS*   28, 116
)*VARS*   115
)*WSID*   110
system functions   372
system variables   372

T

*T*Δ
    See trace facility
table   120
take (↑)   52
take with axis (↑[])   149
tangent   257
tangent hyperbolic   257
tanh   257
termination of execution   272
times-reduction (×/)   80
    to calculate count of an
        array   135
top-down programming   338
tower of Hanoi   321

trace facility 291
tracing execution 291
transfer file 114
transpose (⍉) 233
trapping of errors 372
trigonometric function 256
   arc cosine 257
   arc sine 257
   arc tangent 257
   cosine 257
   hyperbolic arc cosine 257
   hyperbolic arc sine 257
   hyperbolic arc tangent 257
   hyperbolic cosine 257
   hyperbolic sine 257
   hyperbolic tangent 257
   sine 257
   tangent 257
truth values 189

U

unconditional branch 274
unique items
   selecting from a vector 222

V

VALUE ERROR 26, 91
variables
   adding data to with catenate 37
   as items in a vector 18
   assigning value to 10
   changing the value of 11
   defined 10
   how used 10
   rules for constructing names 12
   shared 373
   system 372
   to display value of 10
)*VARS* 115
vector notation 17, 20

cannot create one-item
   vector 123
compared to catenate 38
vectors 120, 141
   as items in a vector 19
   assignment 19
   character 41
   created with enlist 142
   created with ravel 140
   creating empty vector with
    reshape 128
   creating one-item vector 128
   defined 17, 30
   empty 46, 128, 171
   joining with catenate 37
   length of 35
   mixture of character and numeric
    data 43
   name of rank-1 array 120
   nested 30
   replacing items in 58
   shape of 35
   simple 30
   to initialize 47
   using ravel to create one-item
    vector 141

W

without (~) 212
workspace 107
   active 110
   adding to 113
   CONTINUE 109
)*WSID* 110

X

XEDIT   377

Z

zero
    as exponent   241
    as padding   52
    as truth value   189
    in format specification   308